THE PICTURE OF DORIAN GRAY

A GRAPHIC NOVEL

OSCAR WILDE'S

THE PICTURE OF
DORIAN GRAY

A GRAPHIC NOVEL

ILLUSTRATED BY
I.N.J. CULBARD
ADAPTED BY
IAN EDGINTON

SELF MADE HERO

First published 2008
by SelfMadeHero
A division of Metro Media Ltd
5 Upper Wimpole Street
London W1G 6BP
www.selfmadehero.com

Illustrator: I. N. J. Culbard
Adaptor: Ian Edginton
Cover Designer: Jeff Willis
Designer: Andy Huckle
Wilde biography/introduction: Dan Lockwood
Editorial Assistance: Jane Laporte
Publishing Director: Emma Hayley

With thanks to Doug Wallace and Jane Goodsir

Dedications
To the trio of lovely ladies in my life: my wife, Jane, and daughters,
Constance and Corinthia – Ian Edginton

For Katy and for Joseph.
With thanks to Emma, Ian and Matt – I. N. J. Culbard

A CIP record for this book is available from the British Library

ISBN: 978-0-9558169-3-2

10 9 8 7 6 5 4 3 2 1

Printed and bound in Slovenia

With its chilling portrayal of double lives, secret vices, and the depths to which one man can sink, *The Picture of Dorian Gray* has captured readers' imaginations for over a hundred years.

The novel's enduring popularity can be attributed to its masterful balance of tone: Dorian's journey from malleable naïf to voracious predator is a tale both sinister and entertaining, as horrible as it is amusing. While we wince at Dorian's ghastly situation, we also laugh when his friend, Lord Henry, unleashes his scathing, pointed barbs. (Wilde knew when he had an audience-pleaser on his hands: many of the most memorable lines in *Dorian Gray* ended up getting recycled in Wilde's plays.) Even those who haven't read the novel before may find that they recognize some of its sharpest dialogue.

The controversy that surrounded *The Picture of Dorian Gray* upon its original publication may seem surprising to us now, but we should remember that, for a late Victorian audience, the novel contained – or at least hinted at – many things that were considered highly shocking and distasteful. The indulgent, decadent lifestyles portrayed in the book were widely viewed as a reflection of Wilde's own lifestyle, and the author was eventually forced to defend both himself and his work in court. He died in disgrace in 1900. Like Dorian Gray, however, he left a beautiful, enduring work of art behind.

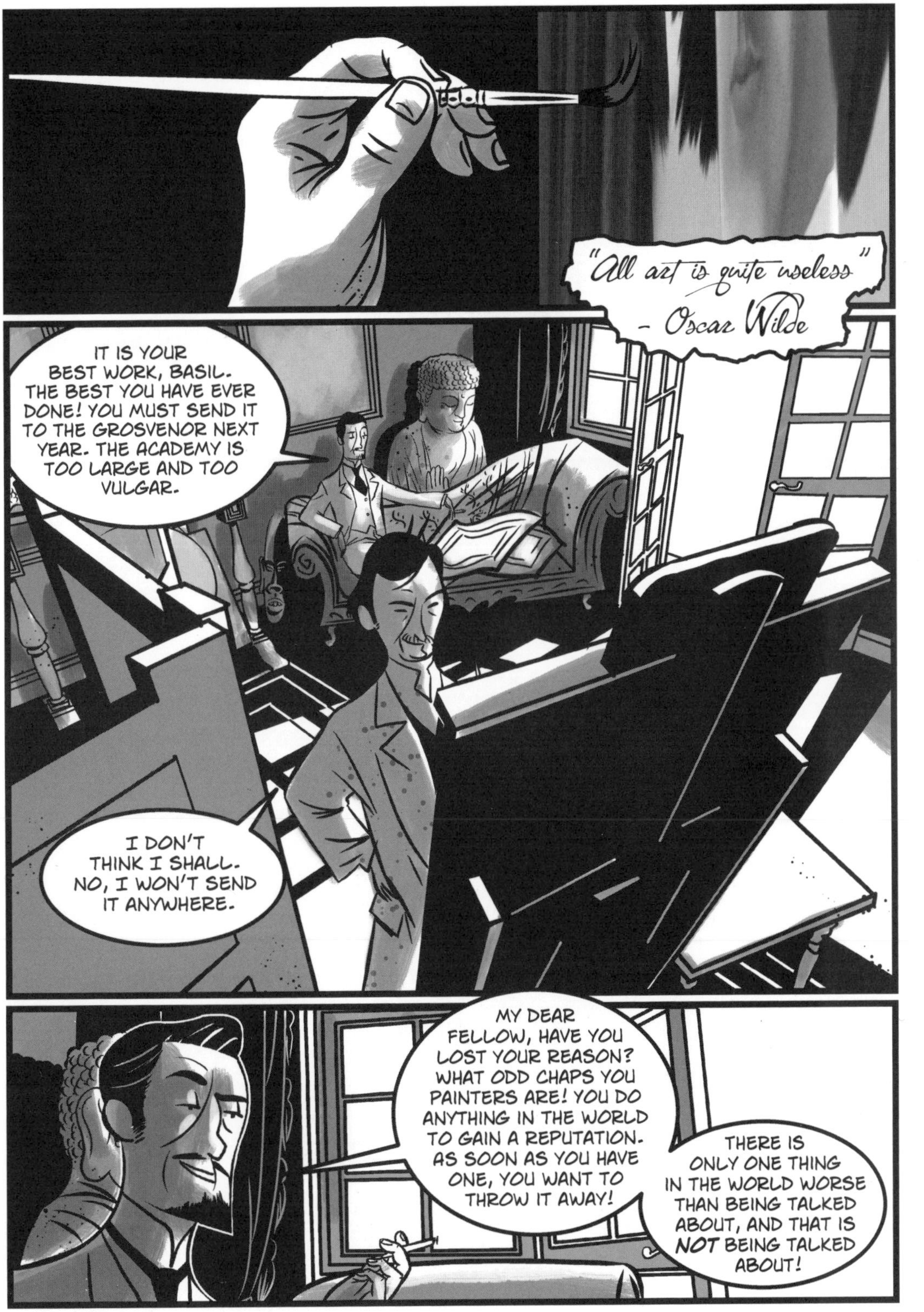
"All art is quite useless"
- Oscar Wilde
IT IS YOUR BEST WORK, BASIL. THE BEST YOU HAVE EVER DONE! YOU MUST SEND IT TO THE GROSVENOR NEXT YEAR. THE ACADEMY IS TOO LARGE AND TOO VULGAR.
I DON'T THINK I SHALL. NO, I WON'T SEND IT ANYWHERE.
MY DEAR FELLOW, HAVE YOU LOST YOUR REASON? WHAT ODD CHAPS YOU PAINTERS ARE! YOU DO ANYTHING IN THE WORLD TO GAIN A REPUTATION. AS SOON AS YOU HAVE ONE, YOU WANT TO THROW IT AWAY!
THERE IS ONLY ONE THING IN THE WORLD WORSE THAN BEING TALKED ABOUT, AND THAT IS NOT BEING TALKED ABOUT!

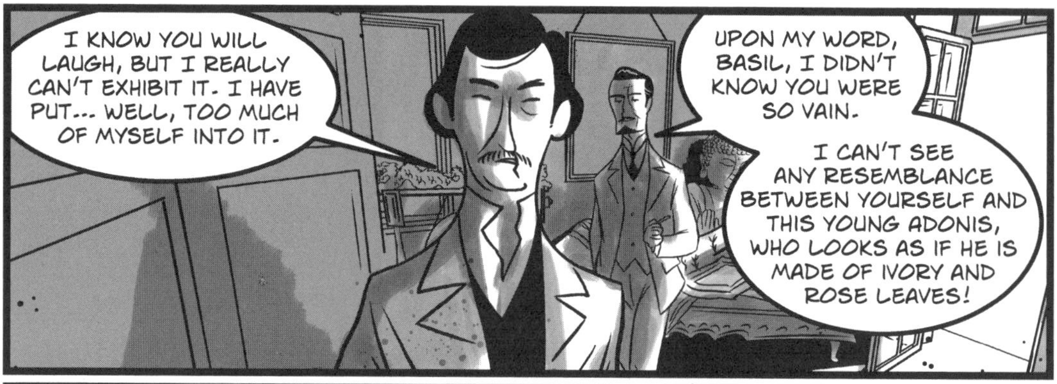
I KNOW YOU WILL LAUGH, BUT I REALLY CAN'T EXHIBIT IT. I HAVE PUT... WELL, TOO MUCH OF MYSELF INTO IT.
UPON MY WORD, BASIL, I DIDN'T KNOW YOU WERE SO VAIN.
I CAN'T SEE ANY RESEMBLANCE BETWEEN YOURSELF AND THIS YOUNG ADONIS, WHO LOOKS AS IF HE IS MADE OF IVORY AND ROSE LEAVES!

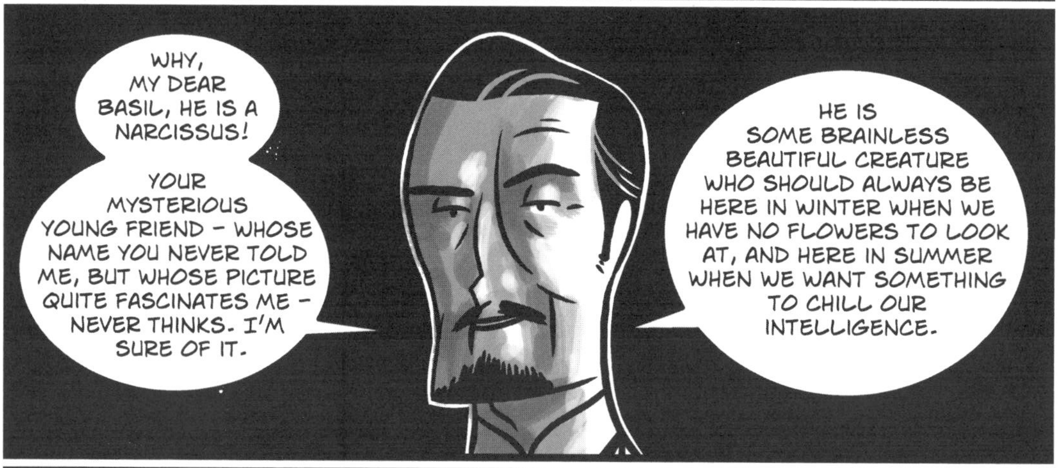
WHY, MY DEAR BASIL, HE IS A NARCISSUS!
YOUR MYSTERIOUS YOUNG FRIEND – WHOSE NAME YOU NEVER TOLD ME, BUT WHOSE PICTURE QUITE FASCINATES ME – NEVER THINKS. I'M SURE OF IT.
HE IS SOME BRAINLESS BEAUTIFUL CREATURE WHO SHOULD ALWAYS BE HERE IN WINTER WHEN WE HAVE NO FLOWERS TO LOOK AT, AND HERE IN SUMMER WHEN WE WANT SOMETHING TO CHILL OUR INTELLIGENCE.

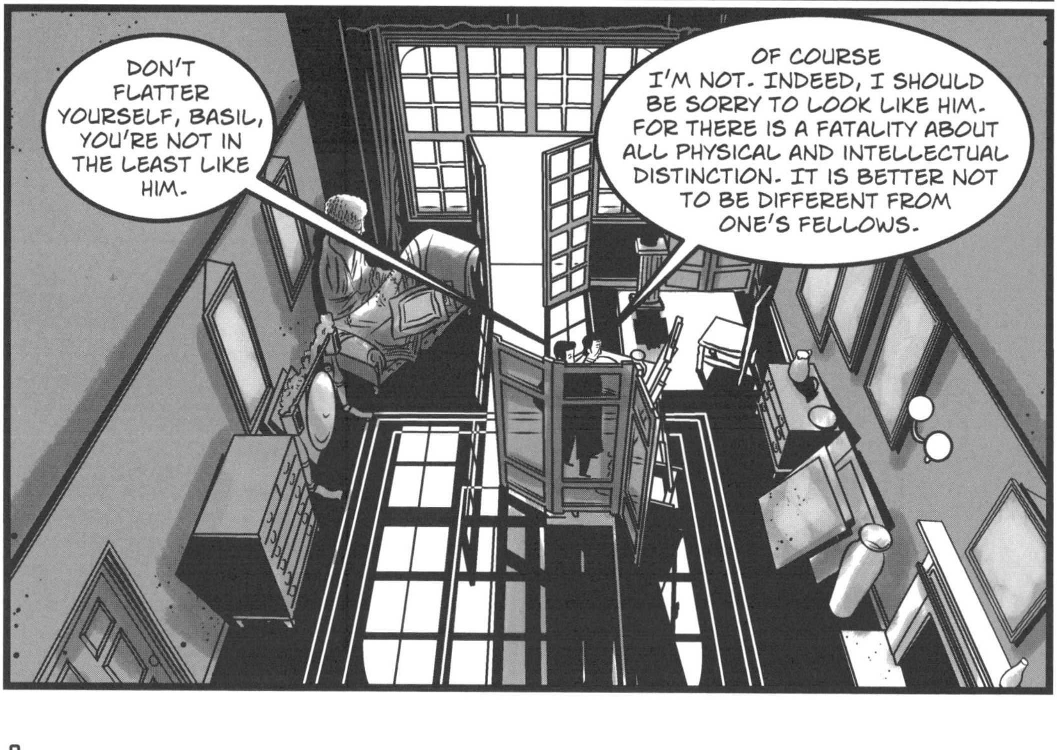
DON'T FLATTER YOURSELF, BASIL, YOU'RE NOT IN THE LEAST LIKE HIM.
OF COURSE I'M NOT. INDEED, I SHOULD BE SORRY TO LOOK LIKE HIM. FOR THERE IS A FATALITY ABOUT ALL PHYSICAL AND INTELLECTUAL DISTINCTION. IT IS BETTER NOT TO BE DIFFERENT FROM ONE'S FELLOWS.

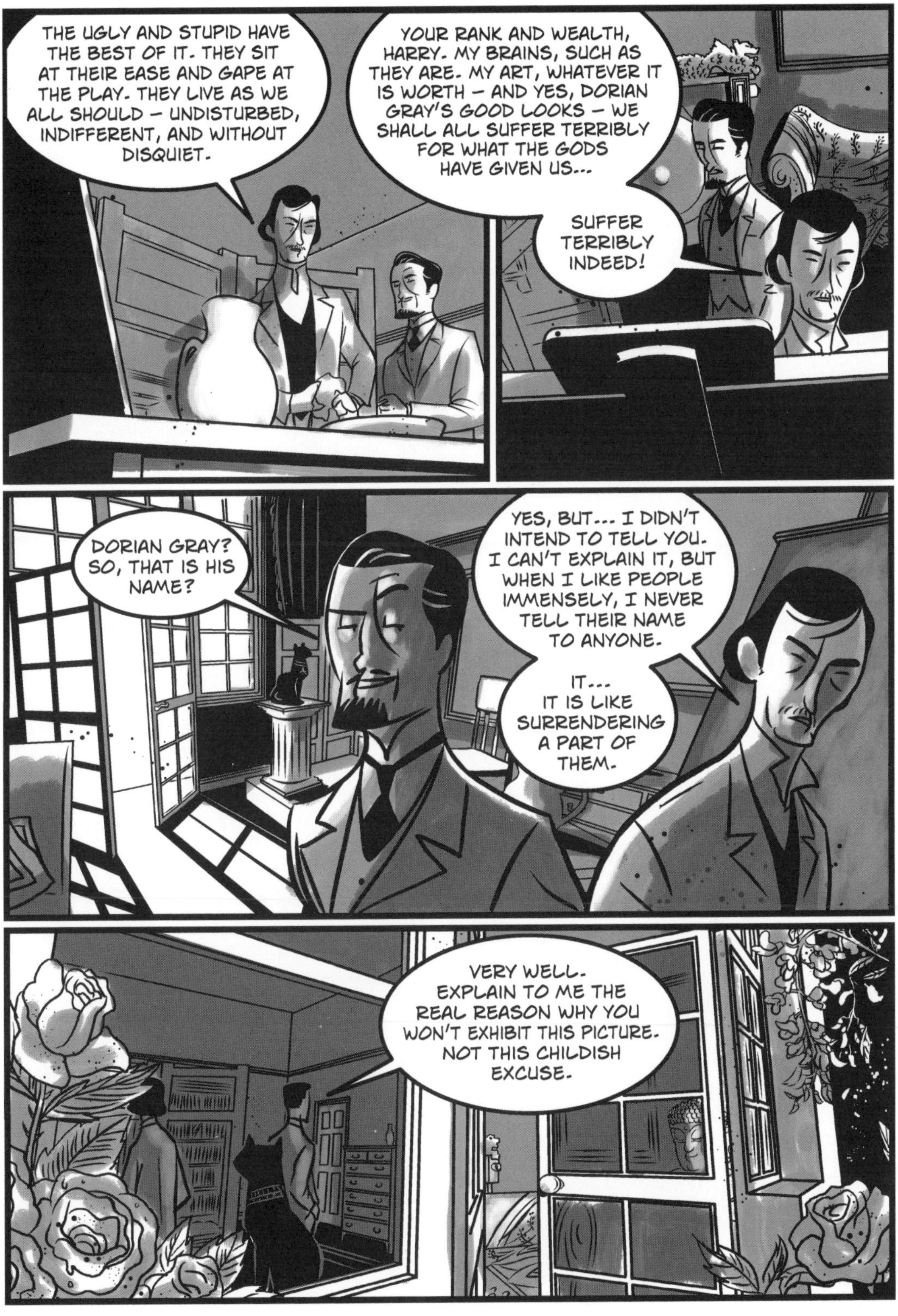
THE UGLY AND STUPID HAVE THE BEST OF IT. THEY SIT AT THEIR EASE AND GAPE AT THE PLAY. THEY LIVE AS WE ALL SHOULD – UNDISTURBED, INDIFFERENT, AND WITHOUT DISQUIET.
YOUR RANK AND WEALTH, HARRY. MY BRAINS, SUCH AS THEY ARE. MY ART, WHATEVER IT IS WORTH – AND YES, DORIAN GRAY'S GOOD LOOKS – WE SHALL ALL SUFFER TERRIBLY FOR WHAT THE GODS HAVE GIVEN US...
SUFFER TERRIBLY INDEED!
DORIAN GRAY? SO, THAT IS HIS NAME?
YES, BUT... I DIDN'T INTEND TO TELL YOU. I CAN'T EXPLAIN IT, BUT WHEN I LIKE PEOPLE IMMENSELY, I NEVER TELL THEIR NAME TO ANYONE.
IT... IT IS LIKE SURRENDERING A PART OF THEM.
VERY WELL. EXPLAIN TO ME THE REAL REASON WHY YOU WON'T EXHIBIT THIS PICTURE. NOT THIS CHILDISH EXCUSE.

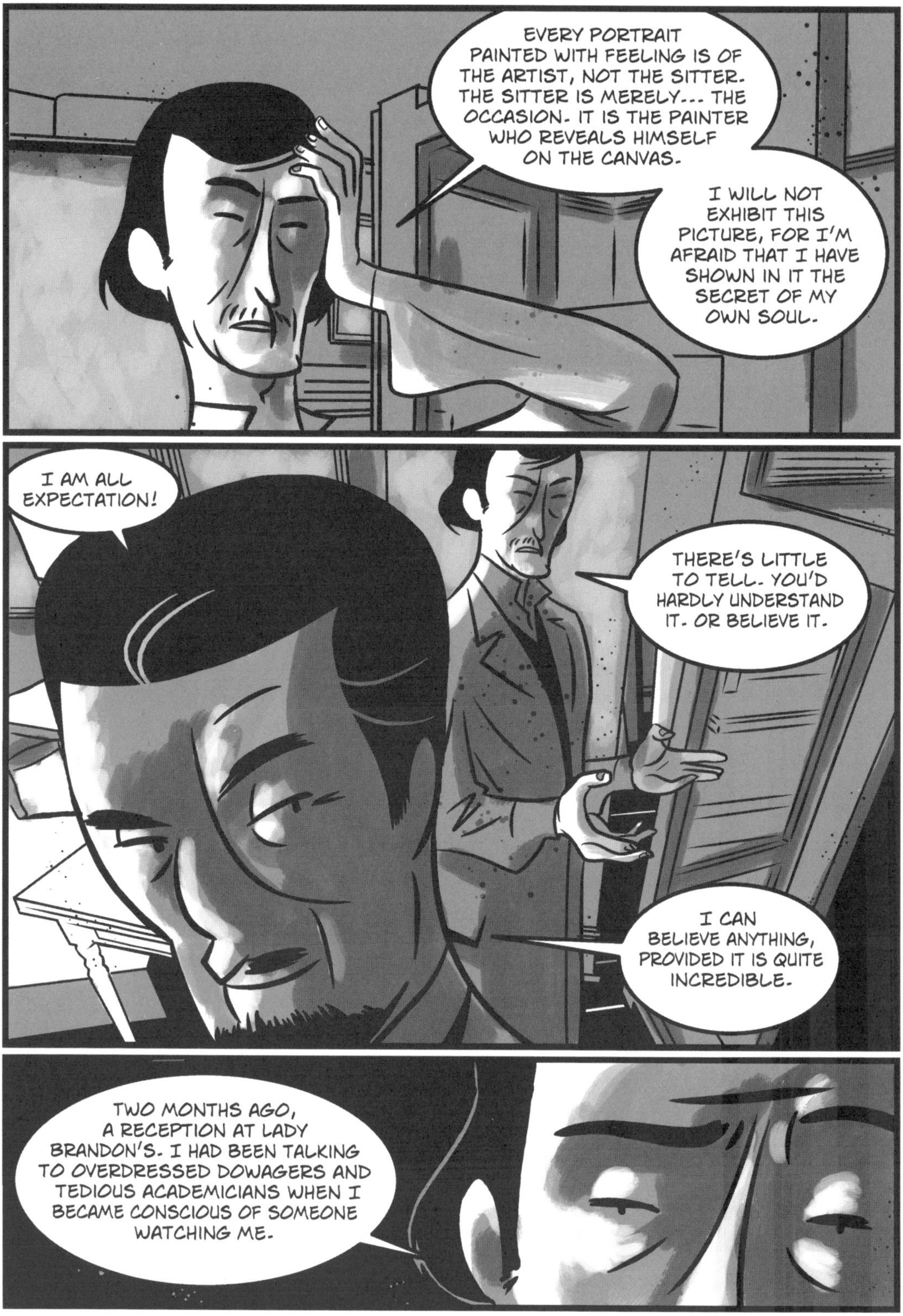
EVERY PORTRAIT PAINTED WITH FEELING IS OF THE ARTIST, NOT THE SITTER. THE SITTER IS MERELY... THE OCCASION. IT IS THE PAINTER WHO REVEALS HIMSELF ON THE CANVAS.
I WILL NOT EXHIBIT THIS PICTURE, FOR I'M AFRAID THAT I HAVE SHOWN IN IT THE SECRET OF MY OWN SOUL.
I AM ALL EXPECTATION!
THERE'S LITTLE TO TELL. YOU'D HARDLY UNDERSTAND IT. OR BELIEVE IT.
I CAN BELIEVE ANYTHING, PROVIDED IT IS QUITE INCREDIBLE.
TWO MONTHS AGO, A RECEPTION AT LADY BRANDON'S. I HAD BEEN TALKING TO OVERDRESSED DOWAGERS AND TEDIOUS ACADEMICIANS WHEN I BECAME CONSCIOUS OF SOMEONE WATCHING ME.

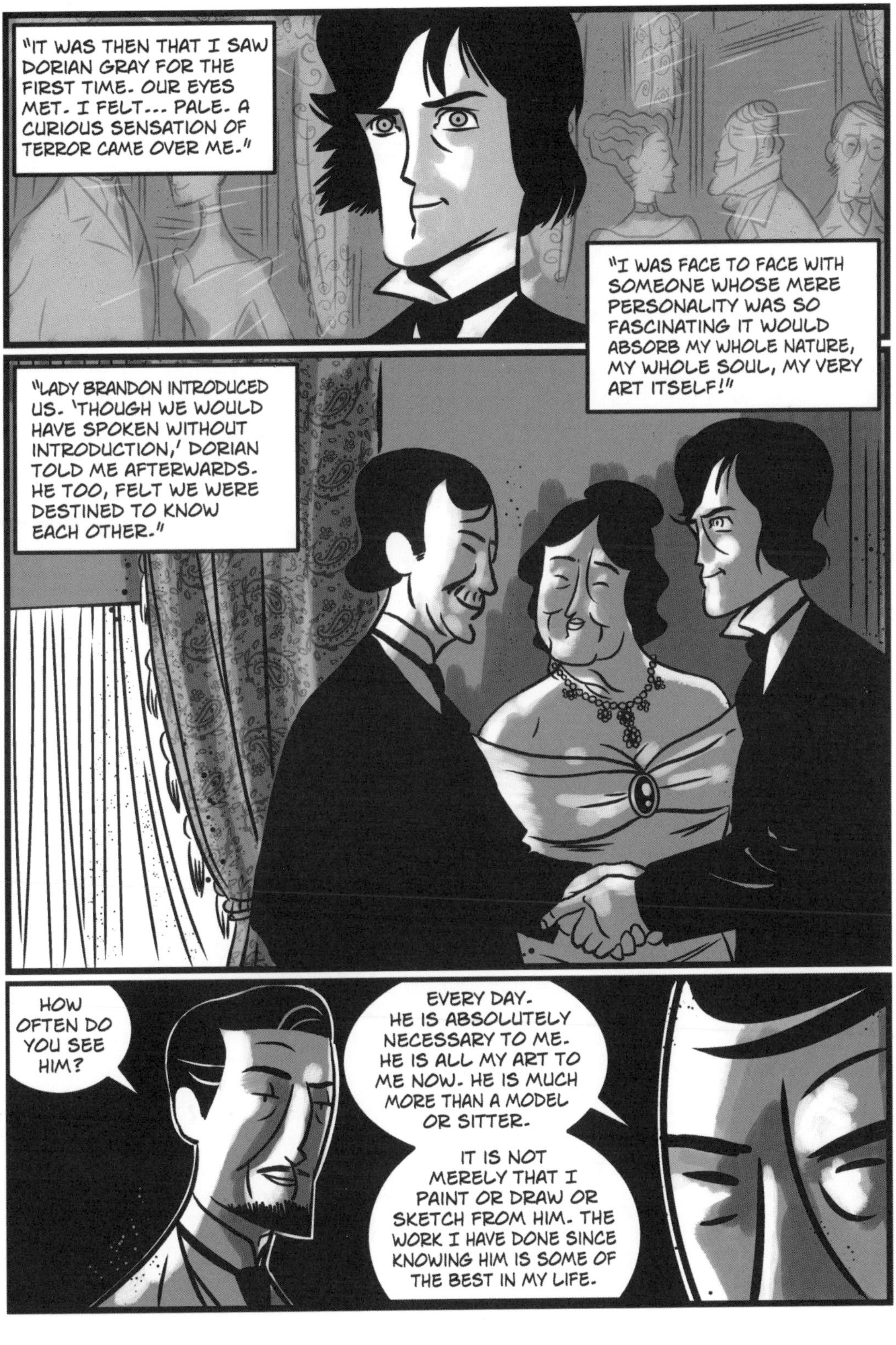
"IT WAS THEN THAT I SAW DORIAN GRAY FOR THE FIRST TIME. OUR EYES MET. I FELT... PALE. A CURIOUS SENSATION OF TERROR CAME OVER ME."
"I WAS FACE TO FACE WITH SOMEONE WHOSE MERE PERSONALITY WAS SO FASCINATING IT WOULD ABSORB MY WHOLE NATURE, MY WHOLE SOUL, MY VERY ART ITSELF!"
"LADY BRANDON INTRODUCED US. 'THOUGH WE WOULD HAVE SPOKEN WITHOUT INTRODUCTION,' DORIAN TOLD ME AFTERWARDS. HE TOO, FELT WE WERE DESTINED TO KNOW EACH OTHER."
HOW OFTEN DO YOU SEE HIM?
EVERY DAY. HE IS ABSOLUTELY NECESSARY TO ME. HE IS ALL MY ART TO ME NOW. HE IS MUCH MORE THAN A MODEL OR SITTER.
IT IS NOT MERELY THAT I PAINT OR DRAW OR SKETCH FROM HIM. THE WORK I HAVE DONE SINCE KNOWING HIM IS SOME OF THE BEST IN MY LIFE.

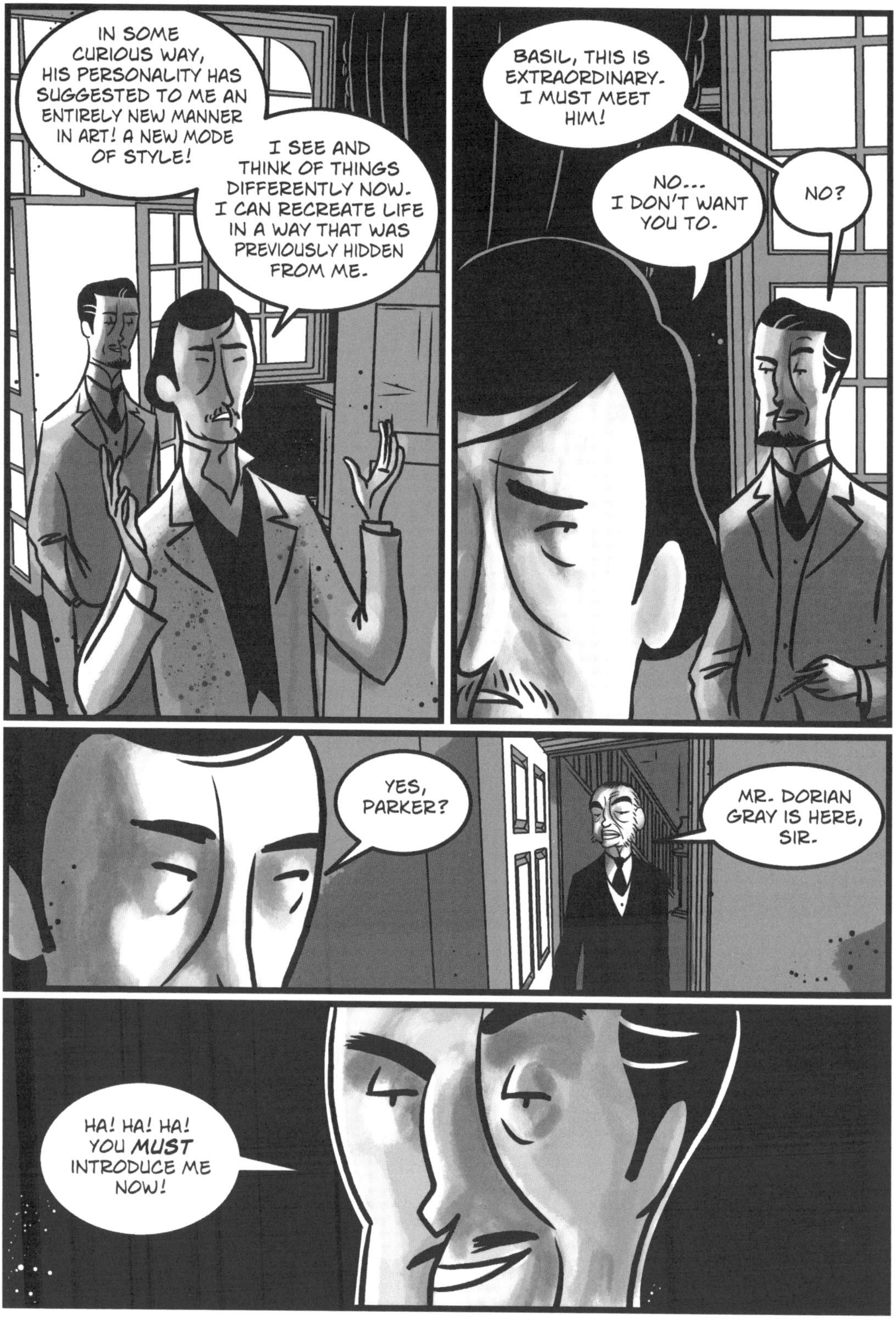
IN SOME CURIOUS WAY, HIS PERSONALITY HAS SUGGESTED TO ME AN ENTIRELY NEW MANNER IN ART! A NEW MODE OF STYLE!
I SEE AND THINK OF THINGS DIFFERENTLY NOW. I CAN RECREATE LIFE IN A WAY THAT WAS PREVIOUSLY HIDDEN FROM ME.
BASIL, THIS IS EXTRAORDINARY. I MUST MEET HIM!
NO... I DON'T WANT YOU TO.
NO?
YES, PARKER?
MR. DORIAN GRAY IS HERE, SIR.
HA! HA! HA! YOU *MUST* INTRODUCE ME NOW!

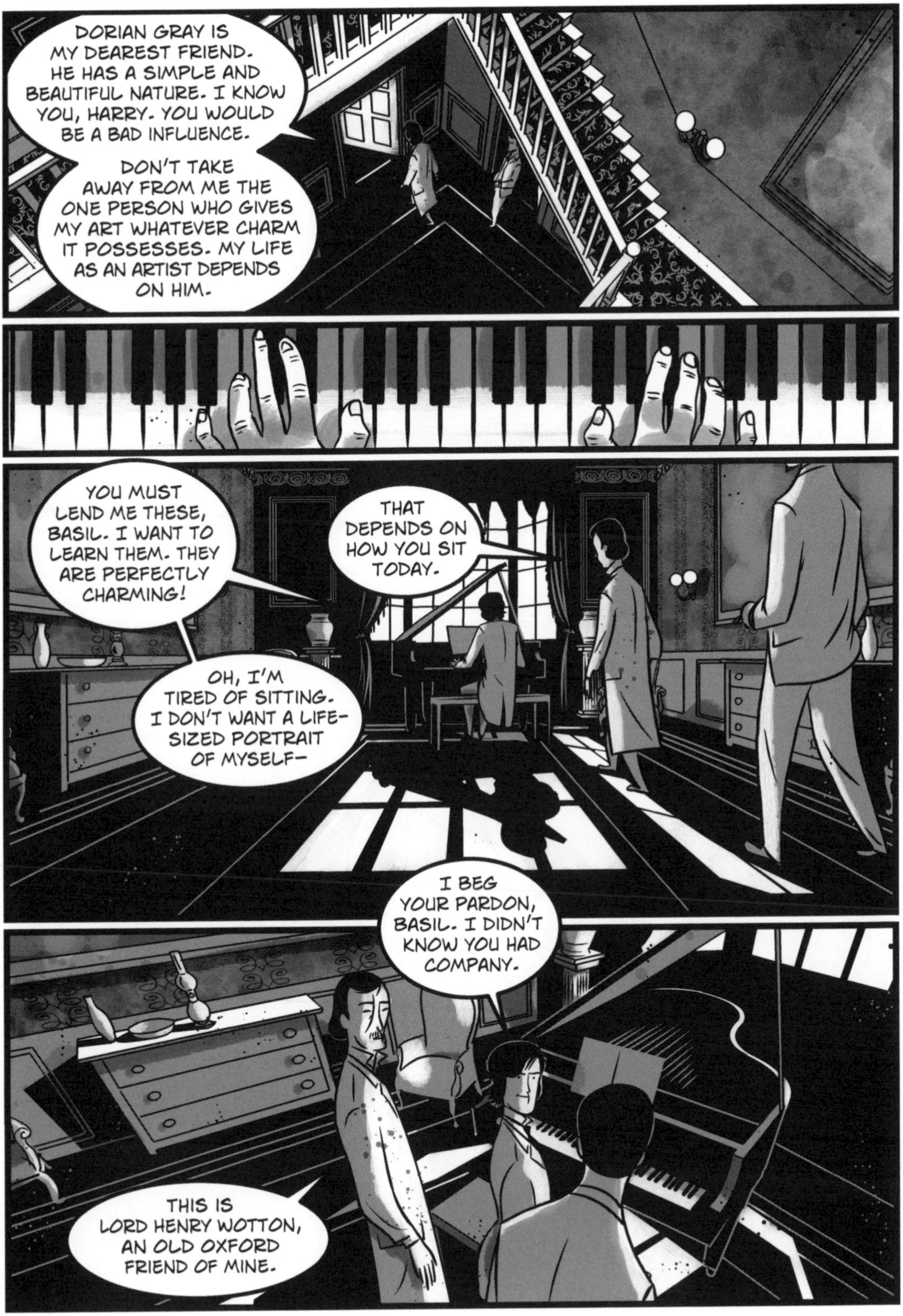
DORIAN GRAY IS MY DEAREST FRIEND. HE HAS A SIMPLE AND BEAUTIFUL NATURE. I KNOW YOU, HARRY. YOU WOULD BE A BAD INFLUENCE.
DON'T TAKE AWAY FROM ME THE ONE PERSON WHO GIVES MY ART WHATEVER CHARM IT POSSESSES. MY LIFE AS AN ARTIST DEPENDS ON HIM.
YOU MUST LEND ME THESE, BASIL. I WANT TO LEARN THEM. THEY ARE PERFECTLY CHARMING!
THAT DEPENDS ON HOW YOU SIT TODAY.
OH, I'M TIRED OF SITTING. I DON'T WANT A LIFE-SIZED PORTRAIT OF MYSELF—
I BEG YOUR PARDON, BASIL. I DIDN'T KNOW YOU HAD COMPANY.
THIS IS LORD HENRY WOTTON, AN OLD OXFORD FRIEND OF MINE.

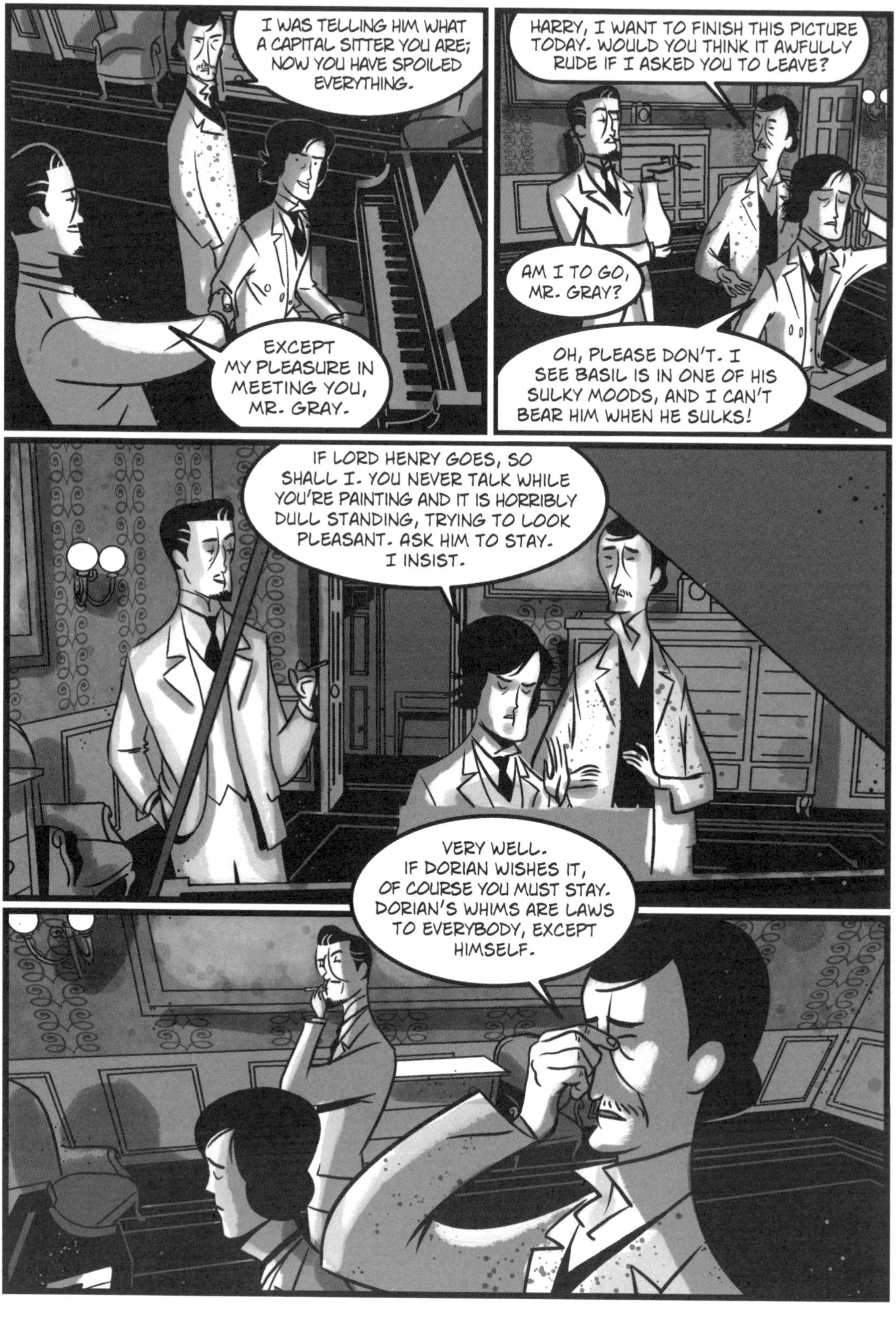
I WAS TELLING HIM WHAT A CAPITAL SITTER YOU ARE; NOW YOU HAVE SPOILED EVERYTHING.
EXCEPT MY PLEASURE IN MEETING YOU, MR. GRAY.
HARRY, I WANT TO FINISH THIS PICTURE TODAY. WOULD YOU THINK IT AWFULLY RUDE IF I ASKED YOU TO LEAVE?
AM I TO GO, MR. GRAY?
OH, PLEASE DON'T. I SEE BASIL IS IN ONE OF HIS SULKY MOODS, AND I CAN'T BEAR HIM WHEN HE SULKS!
IF LORD HENRY GOES, SO SHALL I. YOU NEVER TALK WHILE YOU'RE PAINTING AND IT IS HORRIBLY DULL STANDING, TRYING TO LOOK PLEASANT. ASK HIM TO STAY. I INSIST.
VERY WELL. IF DORIAN WISHES IT, OF COURSE YOU MUST STAY. DORIAN'S WHIMS ARE LAWS TO EVERYBODY, EXCEPT HIMSELF.

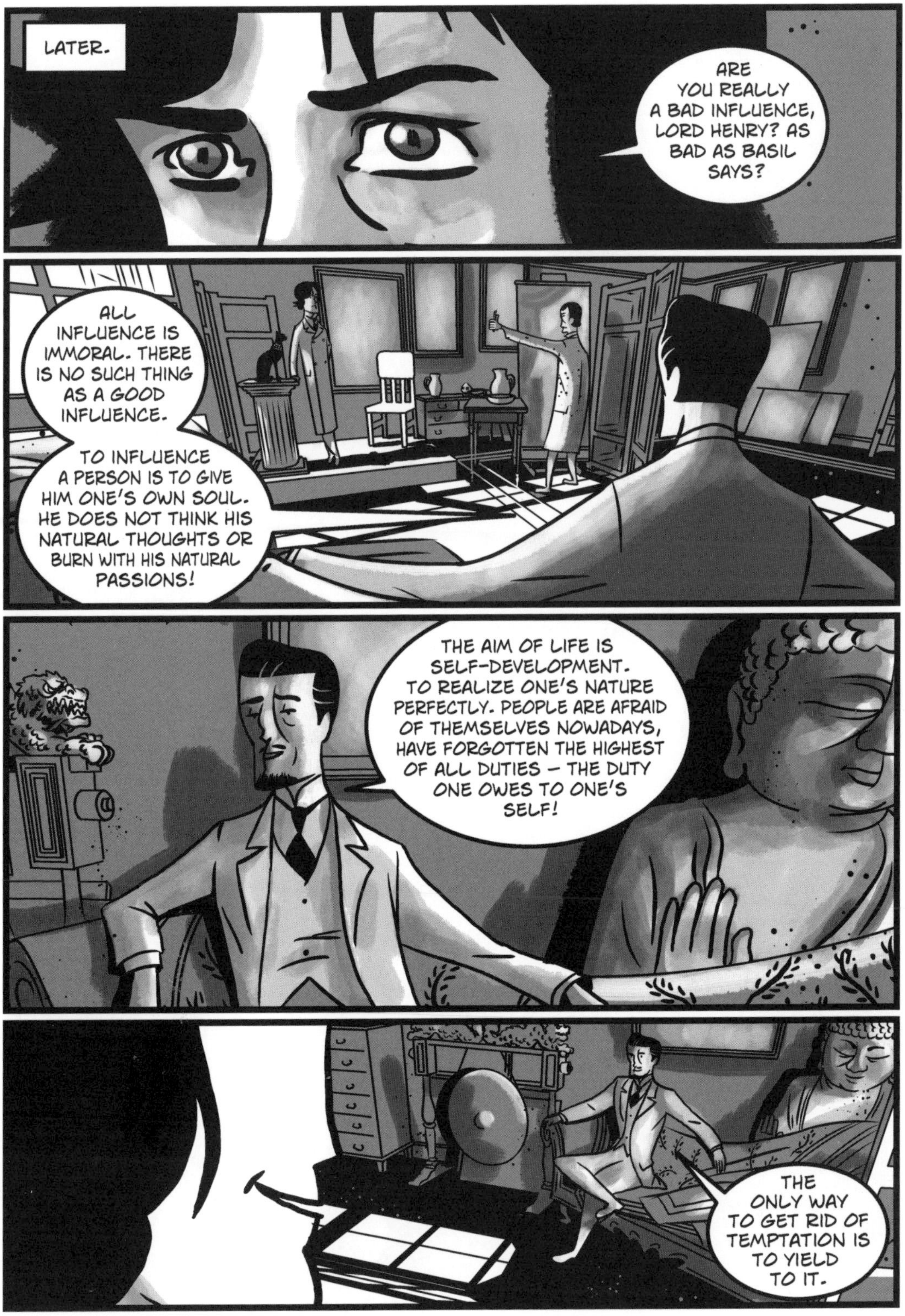
LATER.
ARE YOU REALLY A BAD INFLUENCE, LORD HENRY? AS BAD AS BASIL SAYS?
ALL INFLUENCE IS IMMORAL. THERE IS NO SUCH THING AS A GOOD INFLUENCE.
TO INFLUENCE A PERSON IS TO GIVE HIM ONE'S OWN SOUL. HE DOES NOT THINK HIS NATURAL THOUGHTS OR BURN WITH HIS NATURAL PASSIONS!
THE AIM OF LIFE IS SELF-DEVELOPMENT. TO REALIZE ONE'S NATURE PERFECTLY. PEOPLE ARE AFRAID OF THEMSELVES NOWADAYS, HAVE FORGOTTEN THE HIGHEST OF ALL DUTIES – THE DUTY ONE OWES TO ONE'S SELF!
THE ONLY WAY TO GET RID OF TEMPTATION IS TO YIELD TO IT.

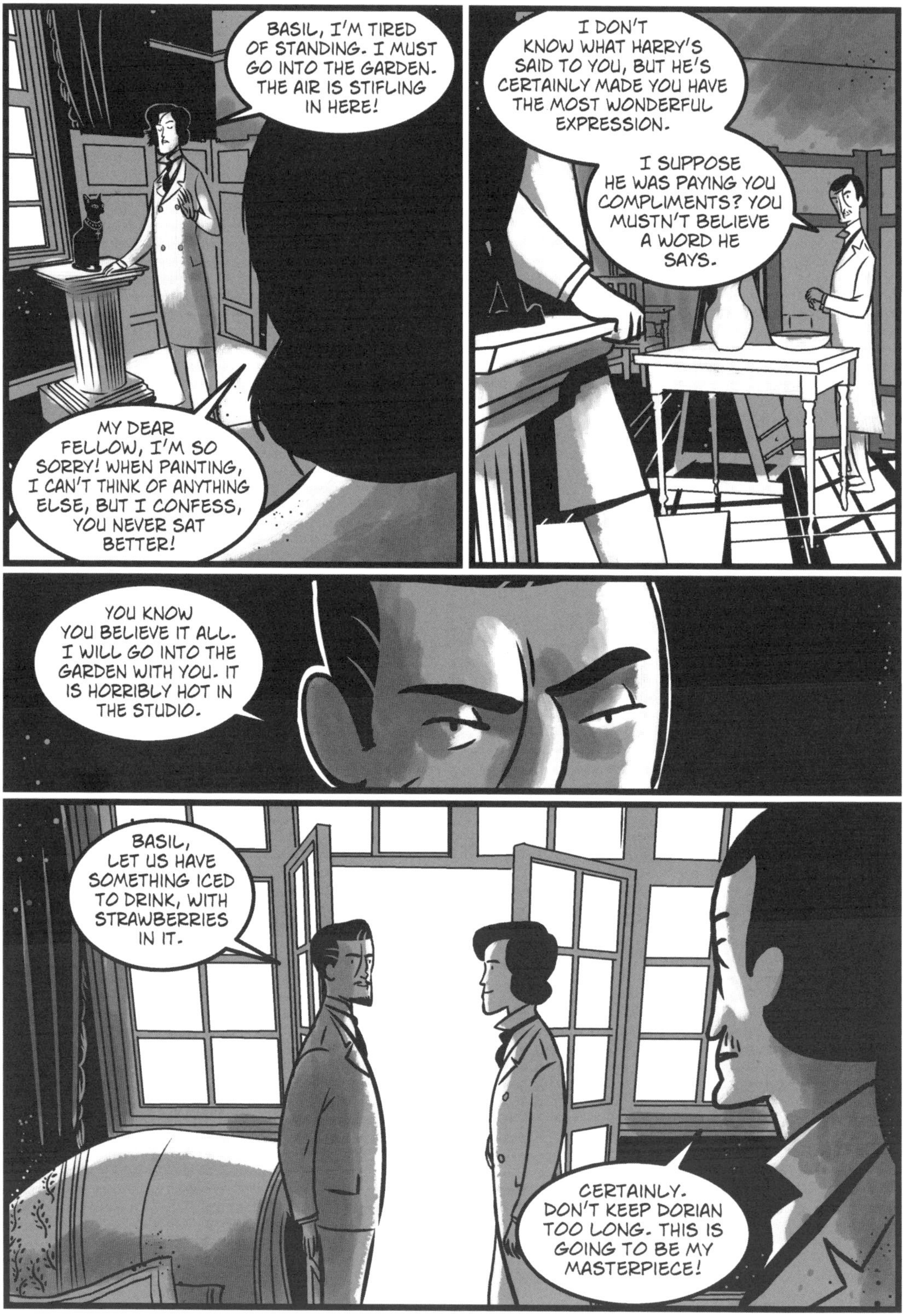
BASIL, I'M TIRED OF STANDING. I MUST GO INTO THE GARDEN. THE AIR IS STIFLING IN HERE!
MY DEAR FELLOW, I'M SO SORRY! WHEN PAINTING, I CAN'T THINK OF ANYTHING ELSE, BUT I CONFESS, YOU NEVER SAT BETTER!
I DON'T KNOW WHAT HARRY'S SAID TO YOU, BUT HE'S CERTAINLY MADE YOU HAVE THE MOST WONDERFUL EXPRESSION.
I SUPPOSE HE WAS PAYING YOU COMPLIMENTS? YOU MUSTN'T BELIEVE A WORD HE SAYS.
YOU KNOW YOU BELIEVE IT ALL. I WILL GO INTO THE GARDEN WITH YOU. IT IS HORRIBLY HOT IN THE STUDIO.
BASIL, LET US HAVE SOMETHING ICED TO DRINK, WITH STRAWBERRIES IN IT.
CERTAINLY. DON'T KEEP DORIAN TOO LONG. THIS IS GOING TO BE MY MASTERPIECE!

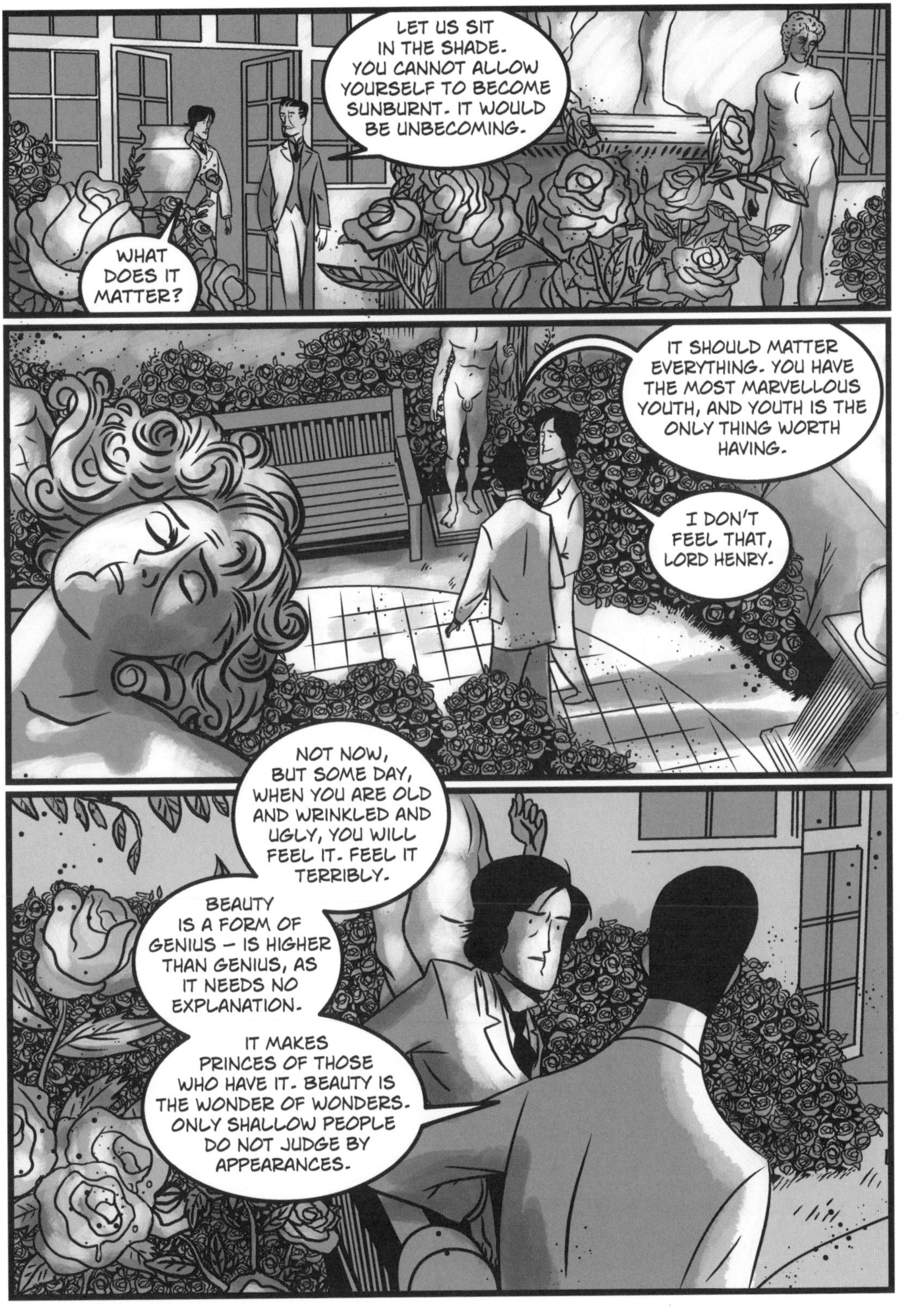
LET US SIT IN THE SHADE. YOU CANNOT ALLOW YOURSELF TO BECOME SUNBURNT. IT WOULD BE UNBECOMING.
WHAT DOES IT MATTER?
IT SHOULD MATTER EVERYTHING. YOU HAVE THE MOST MARVELLOUS YOUTH, AND YOUTH IS THE ONLY THING WORTH HAVING.
I DON'T FEEL THAT, LORD HENRY.
NOT NOW, BUT SOME DAY, WHEN YOU ARE OLD AND WRINKLED AND UGLY, YOU WILL FEEL IT. FEEL IT TERRIBLY.
BEAUTY IS A FORM OF GENIUS – IS HIGHER THAN GENIUS, AS IT NEEDS NO EXPLANATION.
IT MAKES PRINCES OF THOSE WHO HAVE IT. BEAUTY IS THE WONDER OF WONDERS. ONLY SHALLOW PEOPLE DO NOT JUDGE BY APPEARANCES.

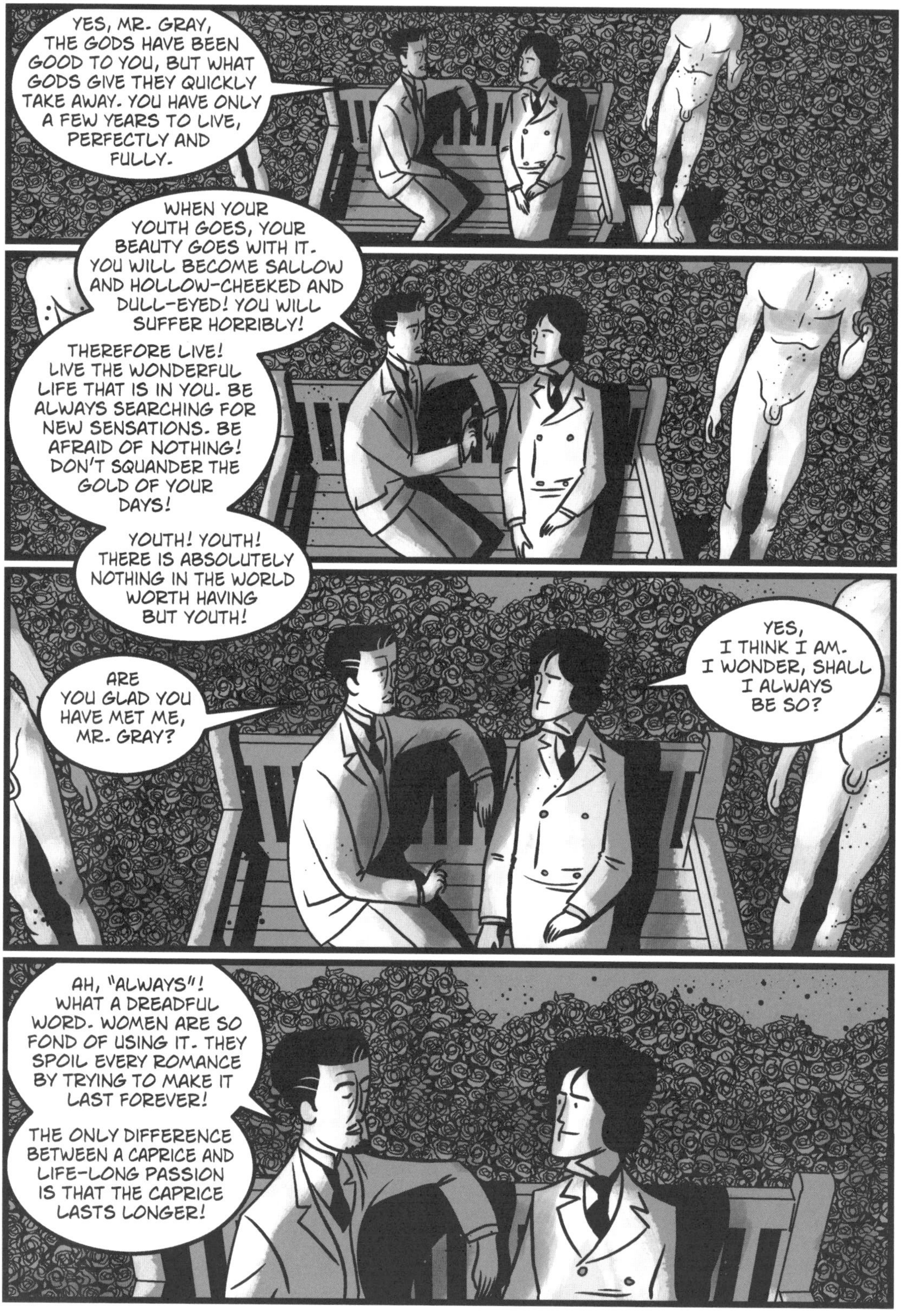
YES, MR. GRAY, THE GODS HAVE BEEN GOOD TO YOU, BUT WHAT GODS GIVE THEY QUICKLY TAKE AWAY. YOU HAVE ONLY A FEW YEARS TO LIVE, PERFECTLY AND FULLY.
WHEN YOUR YOUTH GOES, YOUR BEAUTY GOES WITH IT. YOU WILL BECOME SALLOW AND HOLLOW-CHEEKED AND DULL-EYED! YOU WILL SUFFER HORRIBLY!
THEREFORE LIVE! LIVE THE WONDERFUL LIFE THAT IS IN YOU. BE ALWAYS SEARCHING FOR NEW SENSATIONS. BE AFRAID OF NOTHING! DON'T SQUANDER THE GOLD OF YOUR DAYS!
YOUTH! YOUTH! THERE IS ABSOLUTELY NOTHING IN THE WORLD WORTH HAVING BUT YOUTH!
ARE YOU GLAD YOU HAVE MET ME, MR. GRAY?
YES, I THINK I AM. I WONDER, SHALL I ALWAYS BE SO?
AH, "ALWAYS"! WHAT A DREADFUL WORD. WOMEN ARE SO FOND OF USING IT. THEY SPOIL EVERY ROMANCE BY TRYING TO MAKE IT LAST FOREVER!
THE ONLY DIFFERENCE BETWEEN A CAPRICE AND LIFE-LONG PASSION IS THAT THE CAPRICE LASTS LONGER!

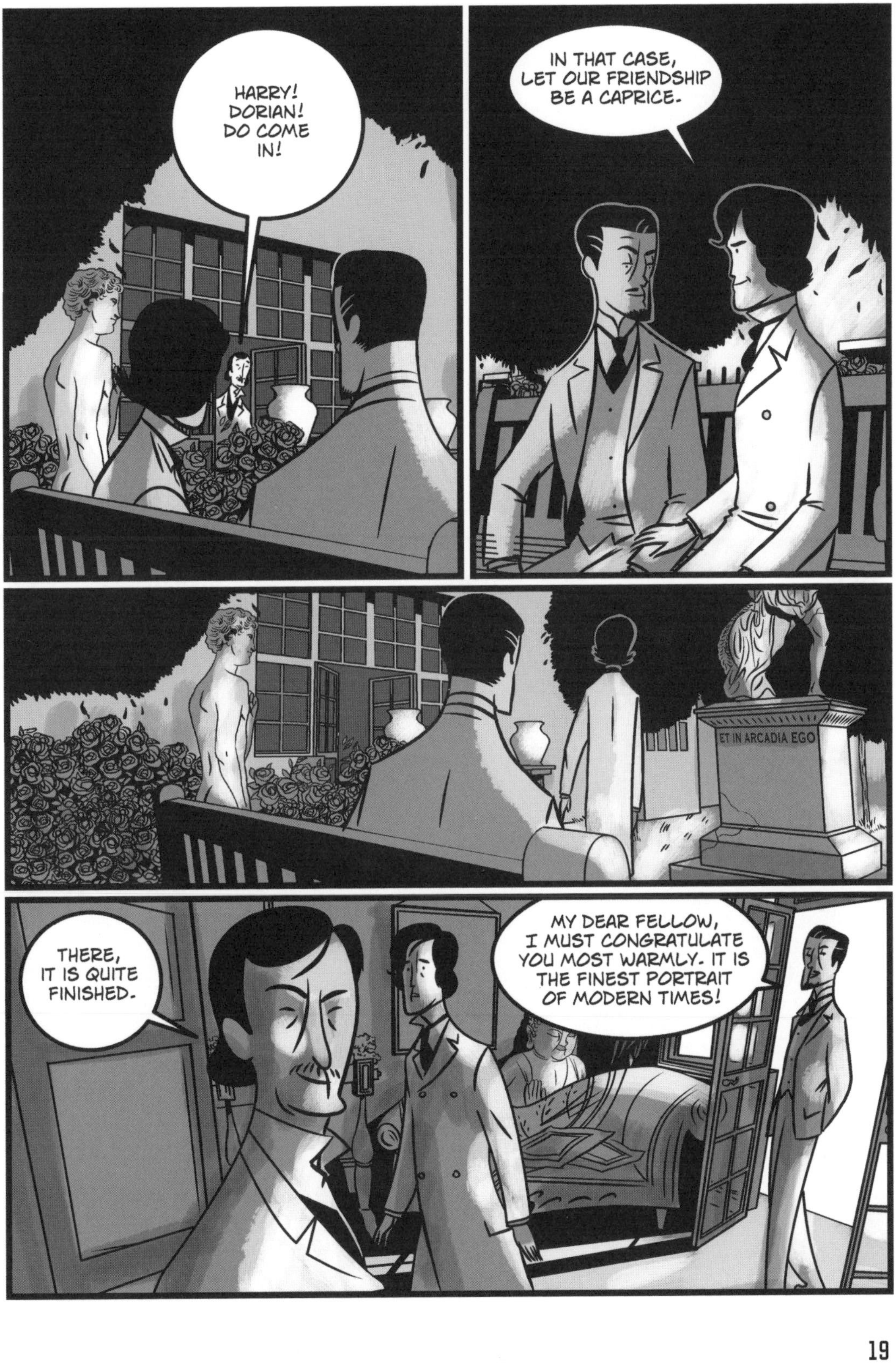
HARRY! DORIAN! DO COME IN!
IN THAT CASE, LET OUR FRIENDSHIP BE A CAPRICE.
ET IN ARCADIA EGO
THERE, IT IS QUITE FINISHED.
MY DEAR FELLOW, I MUST CONGRATULATE YOU MOST WARMLY. IT IS THE FINEST PORTRAIT OF MODERN TIMES!

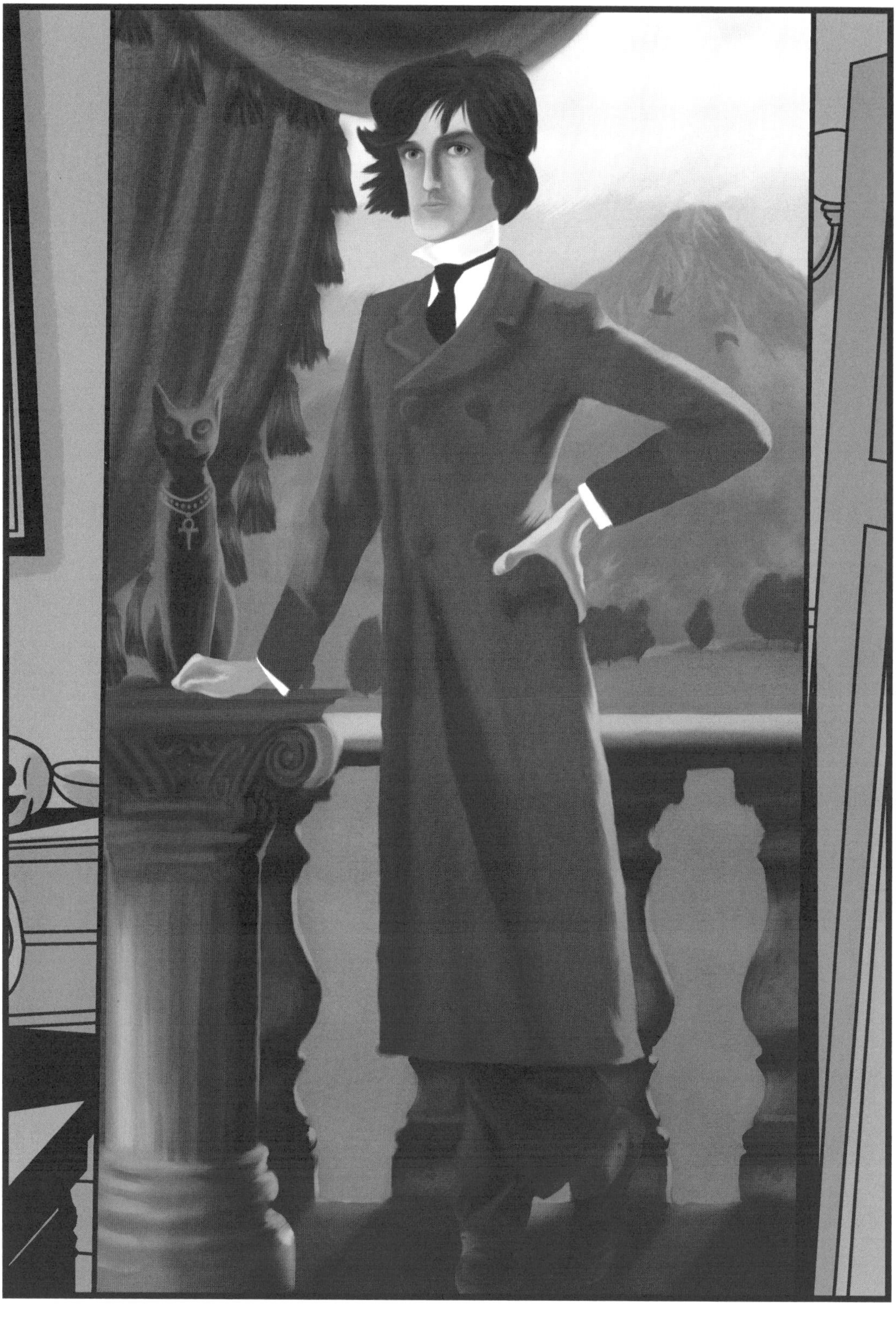

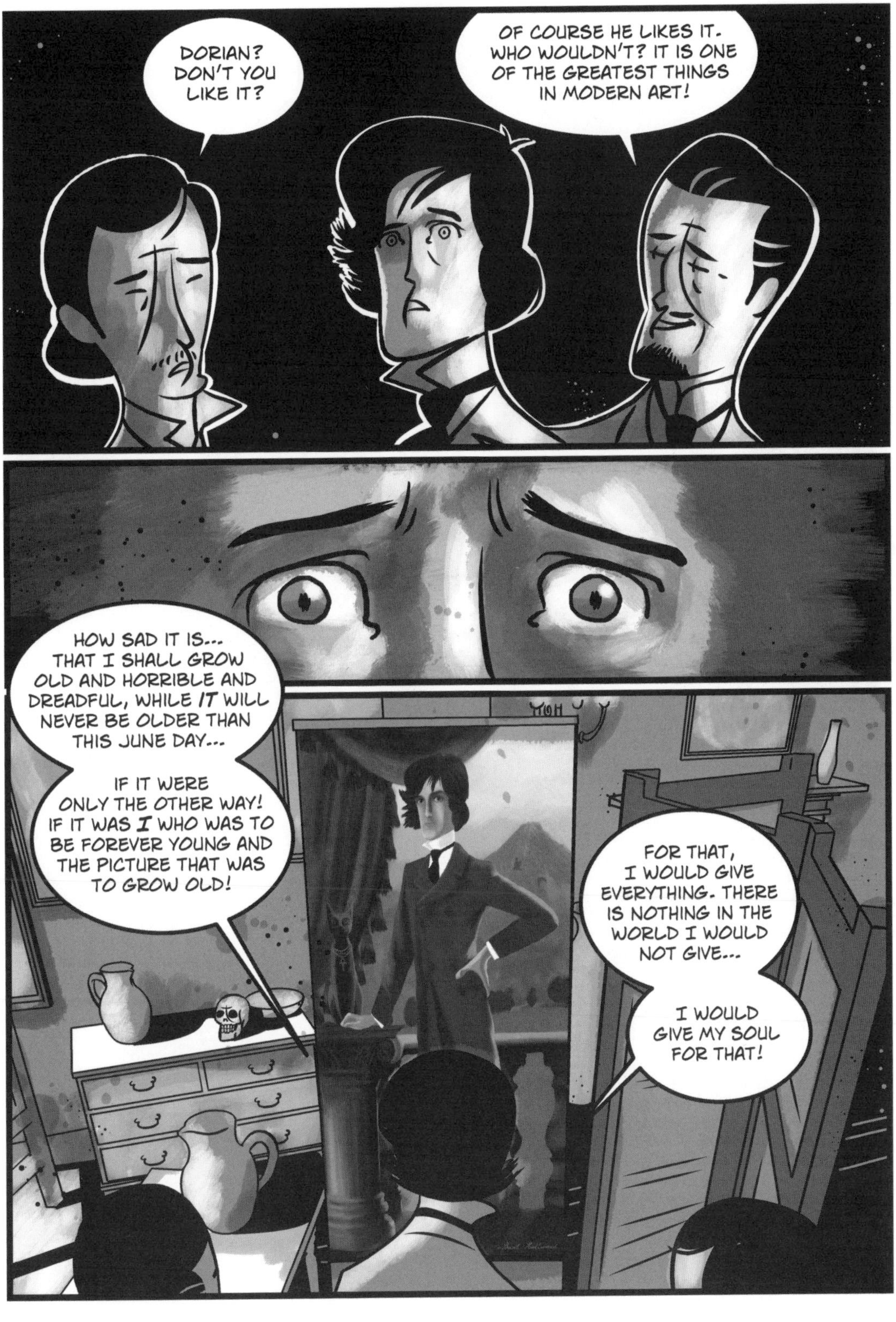
DORIAN? DON'T YOU LIKE IT?
OF COURSE HE LIKES IT. WHO WOULDN'T? IT IS ONE OF THE GREATEST THINGS IN MODERN ART!
HOW SAD IT IS... THAT I SHALL GROW OLD AND HORRIBLE AND DREADFUL, WHILE *IT* WILL NEVER BE OLDER THAN THIS JUNE DAY...
IF IT WERE ONLY THE OTHER WAY! IF IT WAS *I* WHO WAS TO BE FOREVER YOUNG AND THE PICTURE THAT WAS TO GROW OLD!
FOR THAT, I WOULD GIVE EVERYTHING. THERE IS NOTHING IN THE WORLD I WOULD NOT GIVE...
I WOULD GIVE MY SOUL FOR THAT!

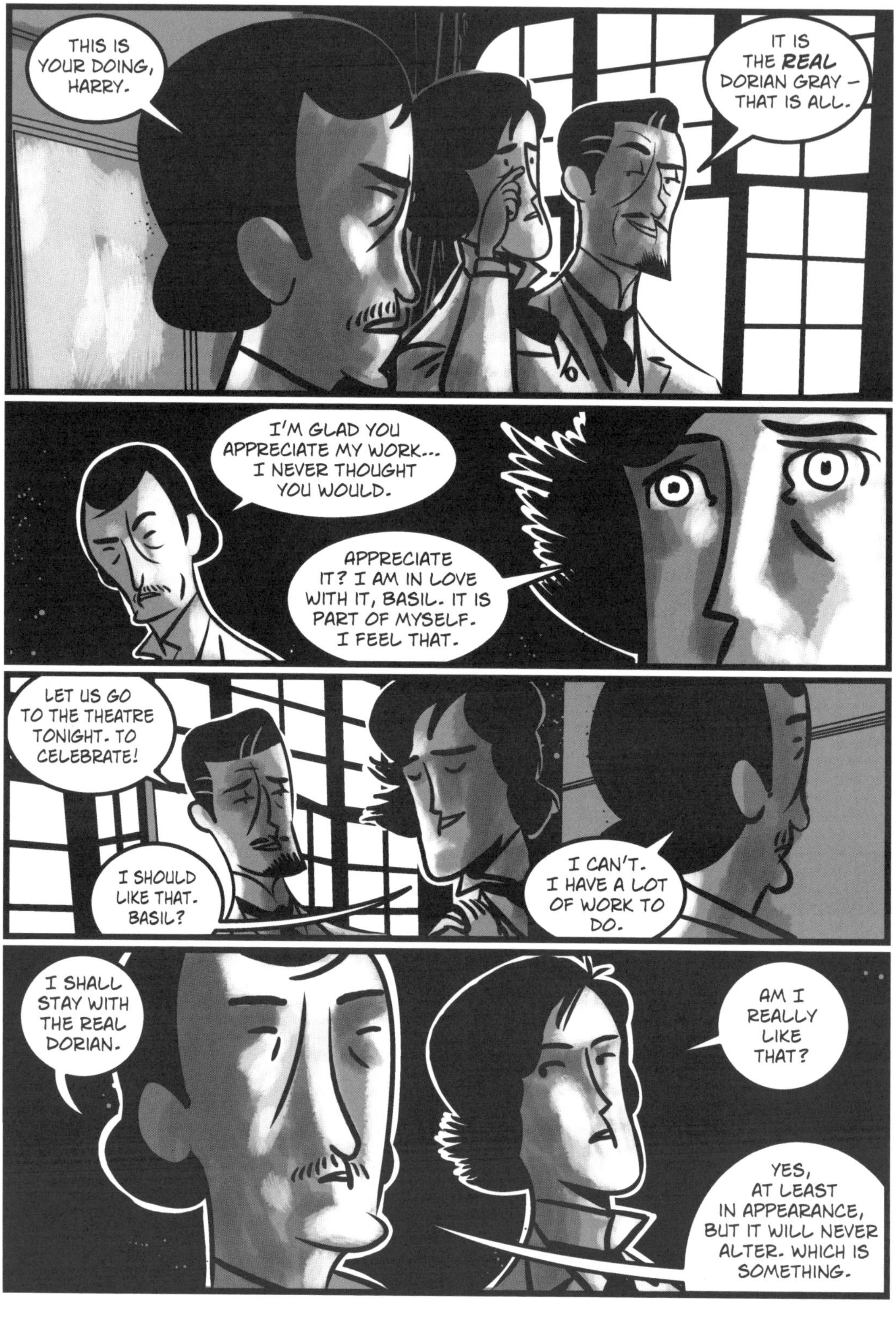
THIS IS YOUR DOING, HARRY.
IT IS THE **REAL** DORIAN GRAY – THAT IS ALL.
I'M GLAD YOU APPRECIATE MY WORK... I NEVER THOUGHT YOU WOULD.
APPRECIATE IT? I AM IN LOVE WITH IT, BASIL. IT IS PART OF MYSELF. I FEEL THAT.
LET US GO TO THE THEATRE TONIGHT. TO CELEBRATE!
I SHOULD LIKE THAT. BASIL?
I CAN'T. I HAVE A LOT OF WORK TO DO.
I SHALL STAY WITH THE REAL DORIAN.
AM I REALLY LIKE THAT?
YES, AT LEAST IN APPEARANCE, BUT IT WILL NEVER ALTER. WHICH IS SOMETHING.

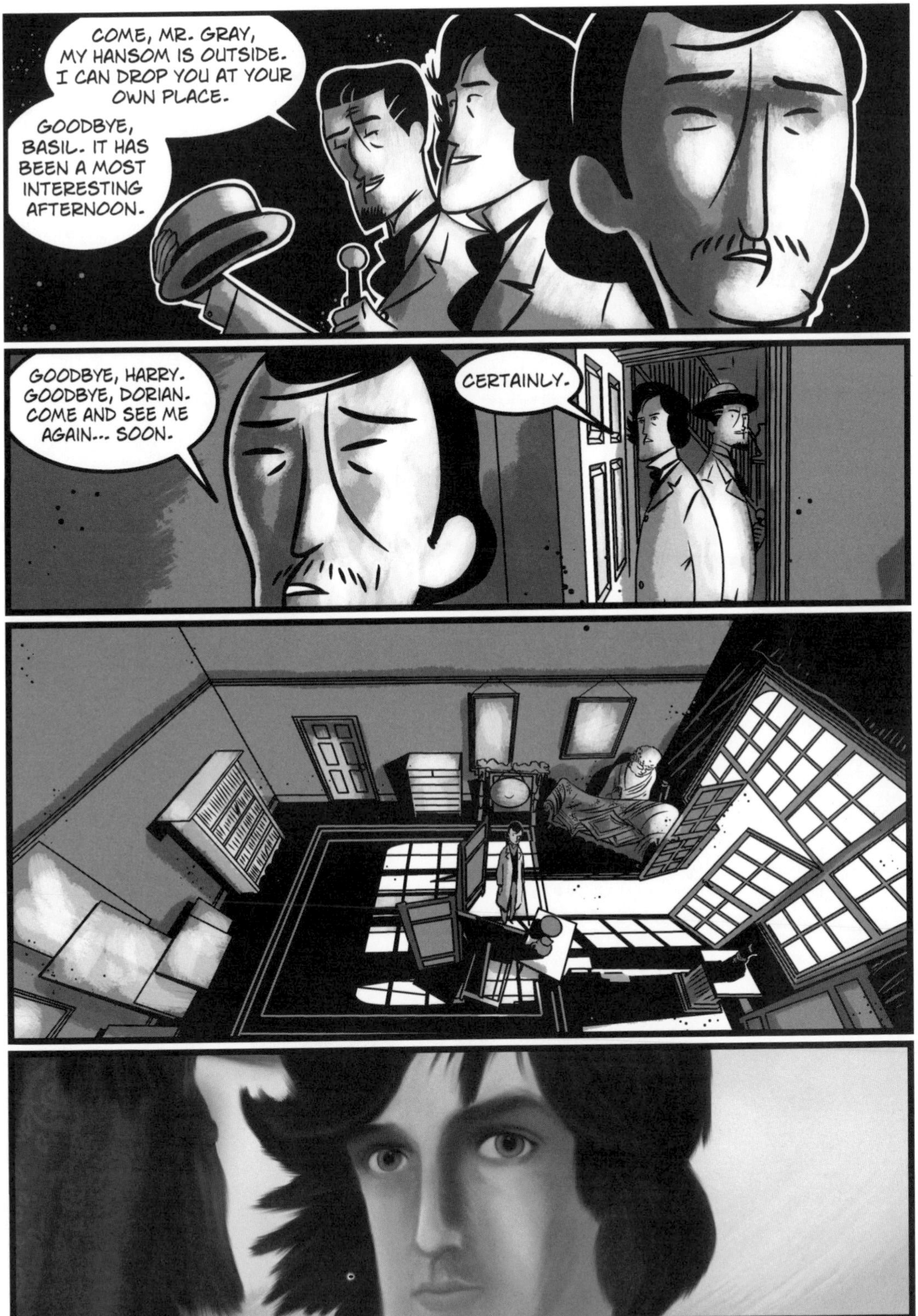
COME, MR. GRAY, MY HANSOM IS OUTSIDE. I CAN DROP YOU AT YOUR OWN PLACE.
GOODBYE, BASIL. IT HAS BEEN A MOST INTERESTING AFTERNOON.
GOODBYE, HARRY. GOODBYE, DORIAN. COME AND SEE ME AGAIN... SOON.
CERTAINLY.

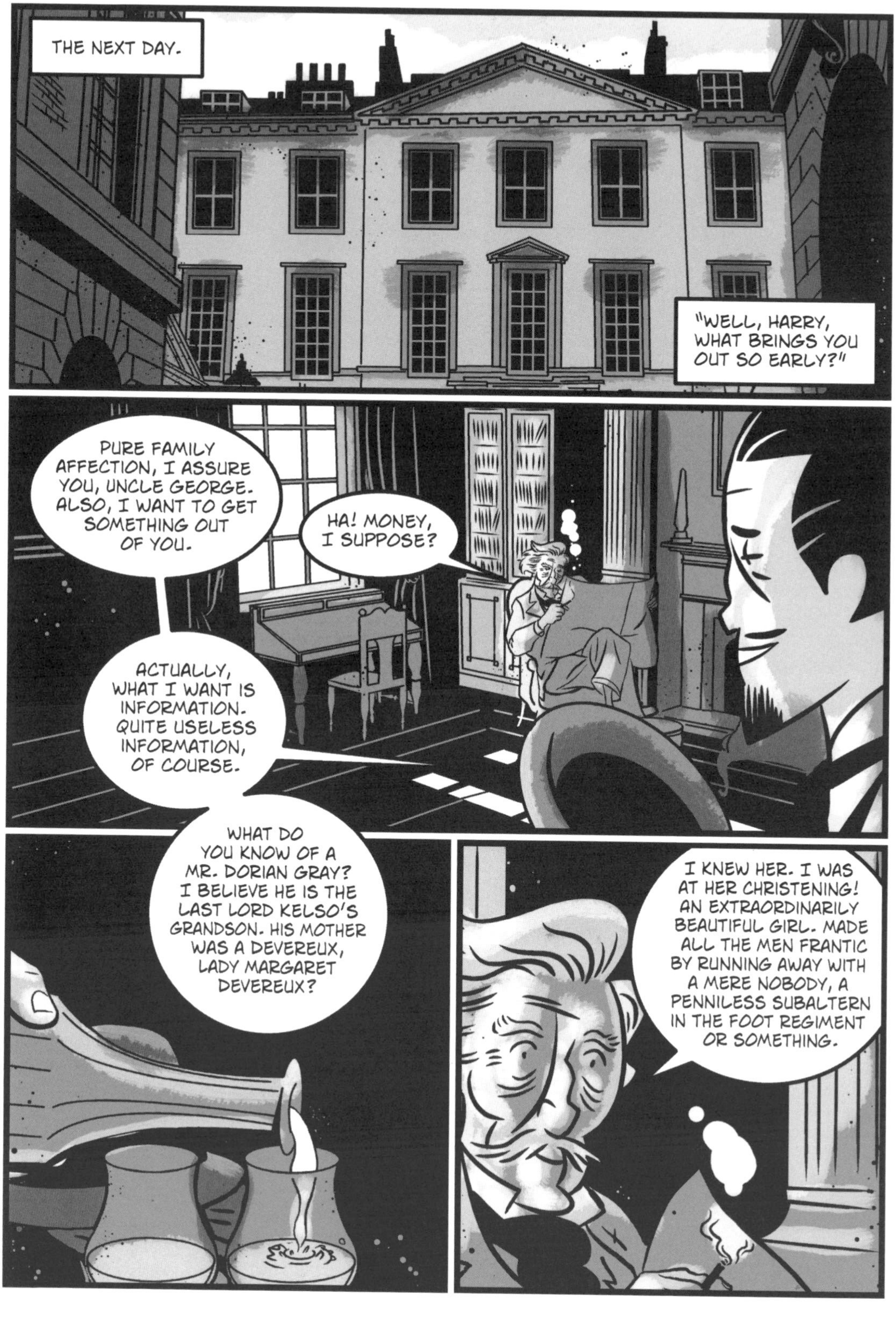
THE NEXT DAY.
"WELL, HARRY, WHAT BRINGS YOU OUT SO EARLY?"
PURE FAMILY AFFECTION, I ASSURE YOU, UNCLE GEORGE. ALSO, I WANT TO GET SOMETHING OUT OF YOU.
HA! MONEY, I SUPPOSE?
ACTUALLY, WHAT I WANT IS INFORMATION. QUITE USELESS INFORMATION, OF COURSE.
WHAT DO YOU KNOW OF A MR. DORIAN GRAY? I BELIEVE HE IS THE LAST LORD KELSO'S GRANDSON. HIS MOTHER WAS A DEVEREUX, LADY MARGARET DEVEREUX?
I KNEW HER. I WAS AT HER CHRISTENING! AN EXTRAORDINARILY BEAUTIFUL GIRL. MADE ALL THE MEN FRANTIC BY RUNNING AWAY WITH A MERE NOBODY, A PENNILESS SUBALTERN IN THE FOOT REGIMENT OR SOMETHING.

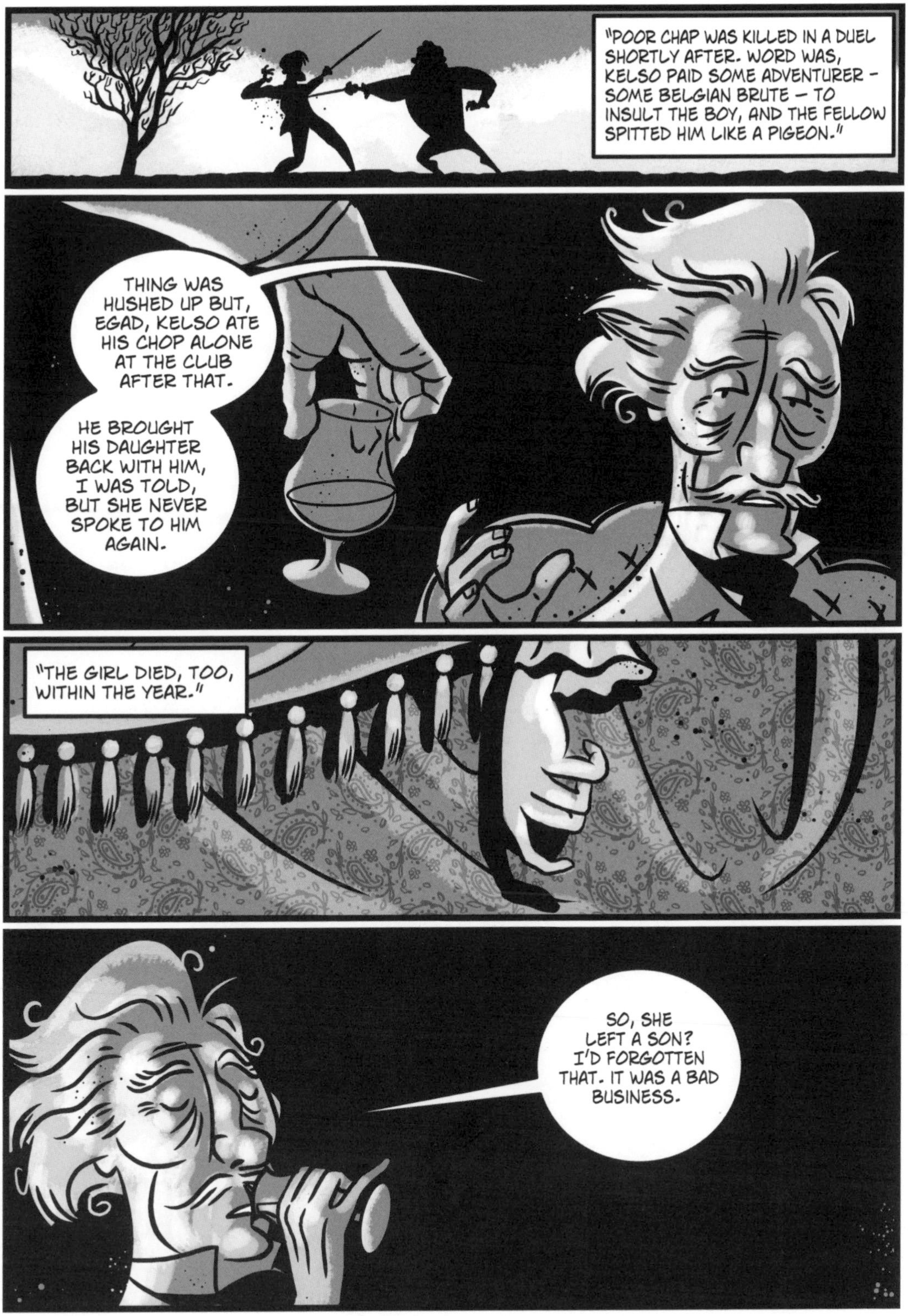
"POOR CHAP WAS KILLED IN A DUEL SHORTLY AFTER. WORD WAS, KELSO PAID SOME ADVENTURER - SOME BELGIAN BRUTE — TO INSULT THE BOY, AND THE FELLOW SPITTED HIM LIKE A PIGEON."
THING WAS HUSHED UP BUT, EGAD, KELSO ATE HIS CHOP ALONE AT THE CLUB AFTER THAT.
HE BROUGHT HIS DAUGHTER BACK WITH HIM, I WAS TOLD, BUT SHE NEVER SPOKE TO HIM AGAIN.
"THE GIRL DIED, TOO, WITHIN THE YEAR."
SO, SHE LEFT A SON? I'D FORGOTTEN THAT. IT WAS A BAD BUSINESS.

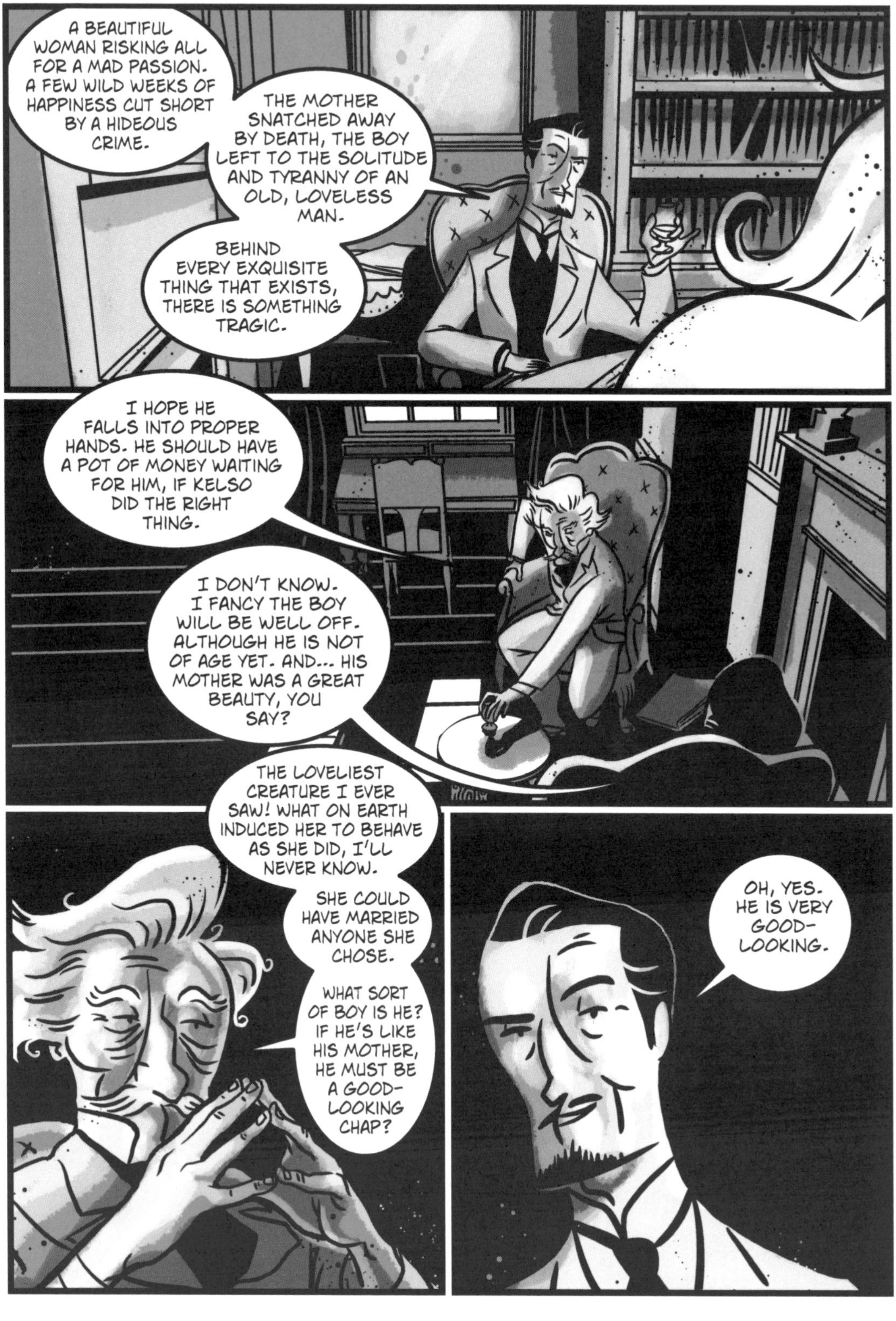
A BEAUTIFUL WOMAN RISKING ALL FOR A MAD PASSION. A FEW WILD WEEKS OF HAPPINESS CUT SHORT BY A HIDEOUS CRIME.
THE MOTHER SNATCHED AWAY BY DEATH, THE BOY LEFT TO THE SOLITUDE AND TYRANNY OF AN OLD, LOVELESS MAN.
BEHIND EVERY EXQUISITE THING THAT EXISTS, THERE IS SOMETHING TRAGIC.
I HOPE HE FALLS INTO PROPER HANDS. HE SHOULD HAVE A POT OF MONEY WAITING FOR HIM, IF KELSO DID THE RIGHT THING.
I DON'T KNOW. I FANCY THE BOY WILL BE WELL OFF. ALTHOUGH HE IS NOT OF AGE YET. AND... HIS MOTHER WAS A GREAT BEAUTY, YOU SAY?
THE LOVELIEST CREATURE I EVER SAW! WHAT ON EARTH INDUCED HER TO BEHAVE AS SHE DID, I'LL NEVER KNOW.
SHE COULD HAVE MARRIED ANYONE SHE CHOSE.
WHAT SORT OF BOY IS HE? IF HE'S LIKE HIS MOTHER, HE MUST BE A GOOD-LOOKING CHAP?
OH, YES. HE IS VERY GOOD-LOOKING.

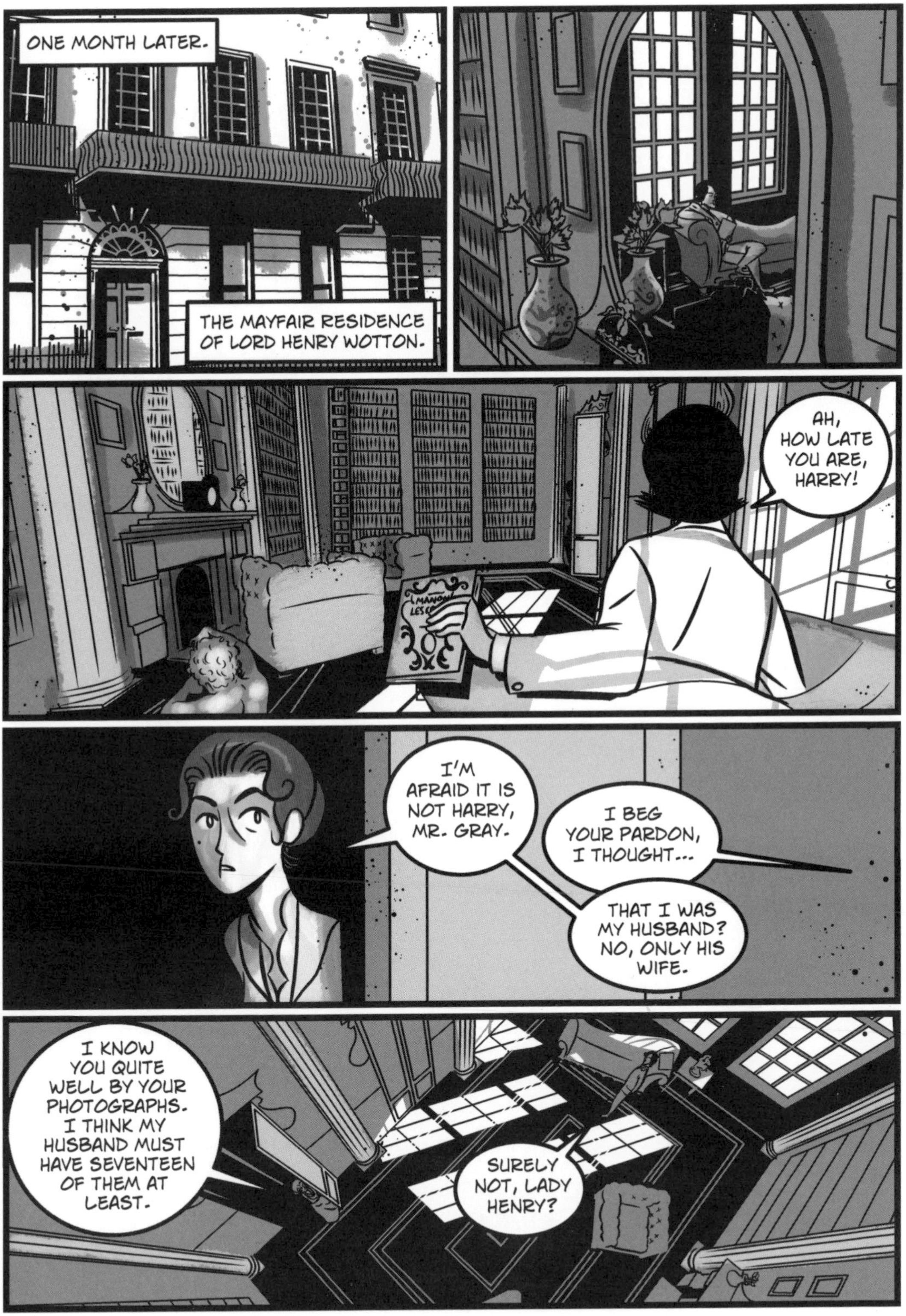
ONE MONTH LATER.
THE MAYFAIR RESIDENCE OF LORD HENRY WOTTON.
AH, HOW LATE YOU ARE, HARRY!
I'M AFRAID IT IS NOT HARRY, MR. GRAY.
I BEG YOUR PARDON, I THOUGHT...
THAT I WAS MY HUSBAND? NO, ONLY HIS WIFE.
I KNOW YOU QUITE WELL BY YOUR PHOTOGRAPHS. I THINK MY HUSBAND MUST HAVE SEVENTEEN OF THEM AT LEAST.
SURELY NOT, LADY HENRY?

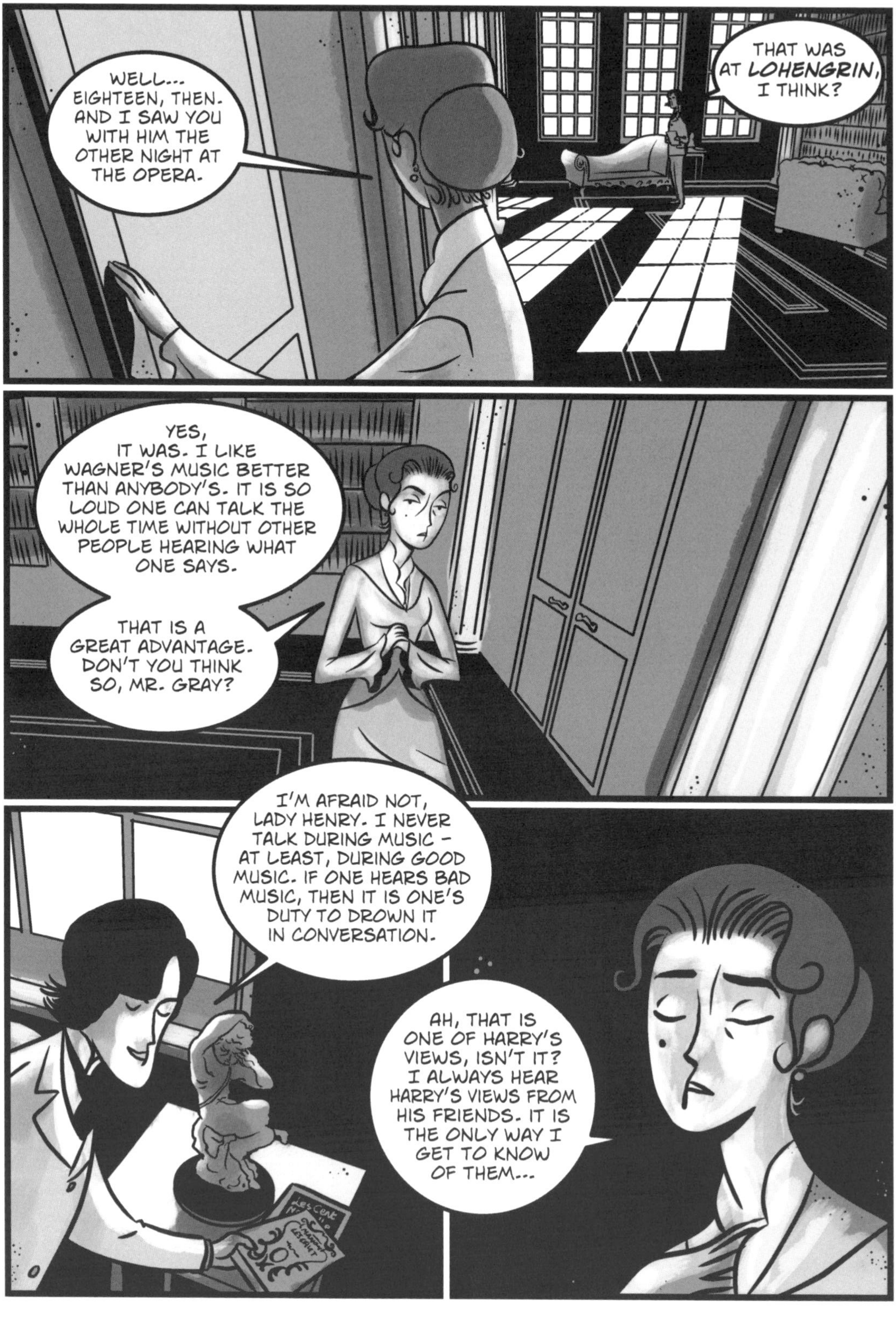
WELL... EIGHTEEN, THEN. AND I SAW YOU WITH HIM THE OTHER NIGHT AT THE OPERA.
THAT WAS AT **LOHENGRIN**, I THINK?
YES, IT WAS. I LIKE WAGNER'S MUSIC BETTER THAN ANYBODY'S. IT IS SO LOUD ONE CAN TALK THE WHOLE TIME WITHOUT OTHER PEOPLE HEARING WHAT ONE SAYS.
THAT IS A GREAT ADVANTAGE. DON'T YOU THINK SO, MR. GRAY?
I'M AFRAID NOT, LADY HENRY. I NEVER TALK DURING MUSIC – AT LEAST, DURING GOOD MUSIC. IF ONE HEARS BAD MUSIC, THEN IT IS ONE'S DUTY TO DROWN IT IN CONVERSATION.
AH, THAT IS ONE OF HARRY'S VIEWS, ISN'T IT? I ALWAYS HEAR HARRY'S VIEWS FROM HIS FRIENDS. IT IS THE ONLY WAY I GET TO KNOW OF THEM...

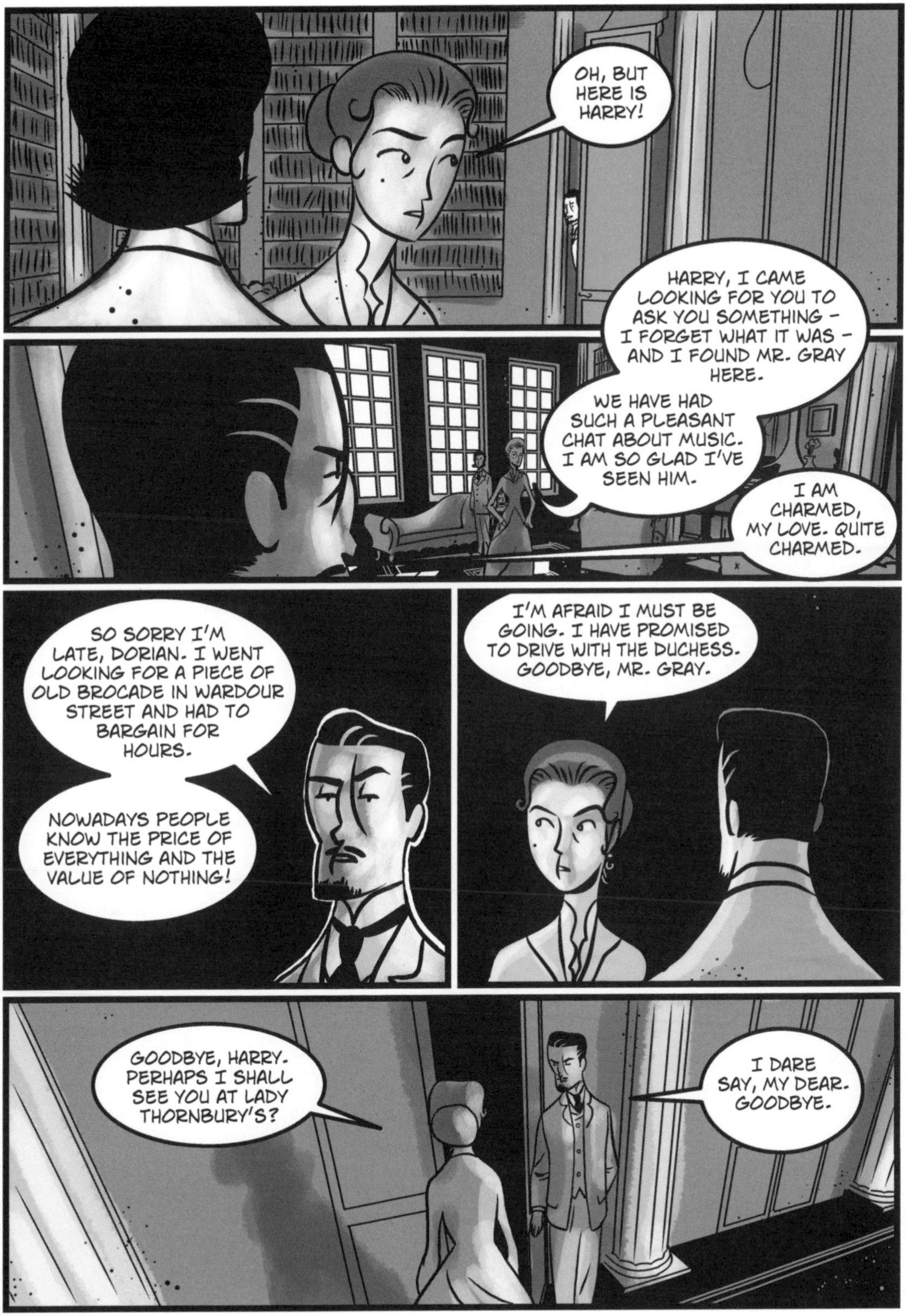
OH, BUT HERE IS HARRY!
HARRY, I CAME LOOKING FOR YOU TO ASK YOU SOMETHING – I FORGET WHAT IT WAS – AND I FOUND MR. GRAY HERE.
WE HAVE HAD SUCH A PLEASANT CHAT ABOUT MUSIC. I AM SO GLAD I'VE SEEN HIM.
I AM CHARMED, MY LOVE. QUITE CHARMED.
SO SORRY I'M LATE, DORIAN. I WENT LOOKING FOR A PIECE OF OLD BROCADE IN WARDOUR STREET AND HAD TO BARGAIN FOR HOURS.
NOWADAYS PEOPLE KNOW THE PRICE OF EVERYTHING AND THE VALUE OF NOTHING!
I'M AFRAID I MUST BE GOING. I HAVE PROMISED TO DRIVE WITH THE DUCHESS. GOODBYE, MR. GRAY.
GOODBYE, HARRY. PERHAPS I SHALL SEE YOU AT LADY THORNBURY'S?
I DARE SAY, MY DEAR. GOODBYE.

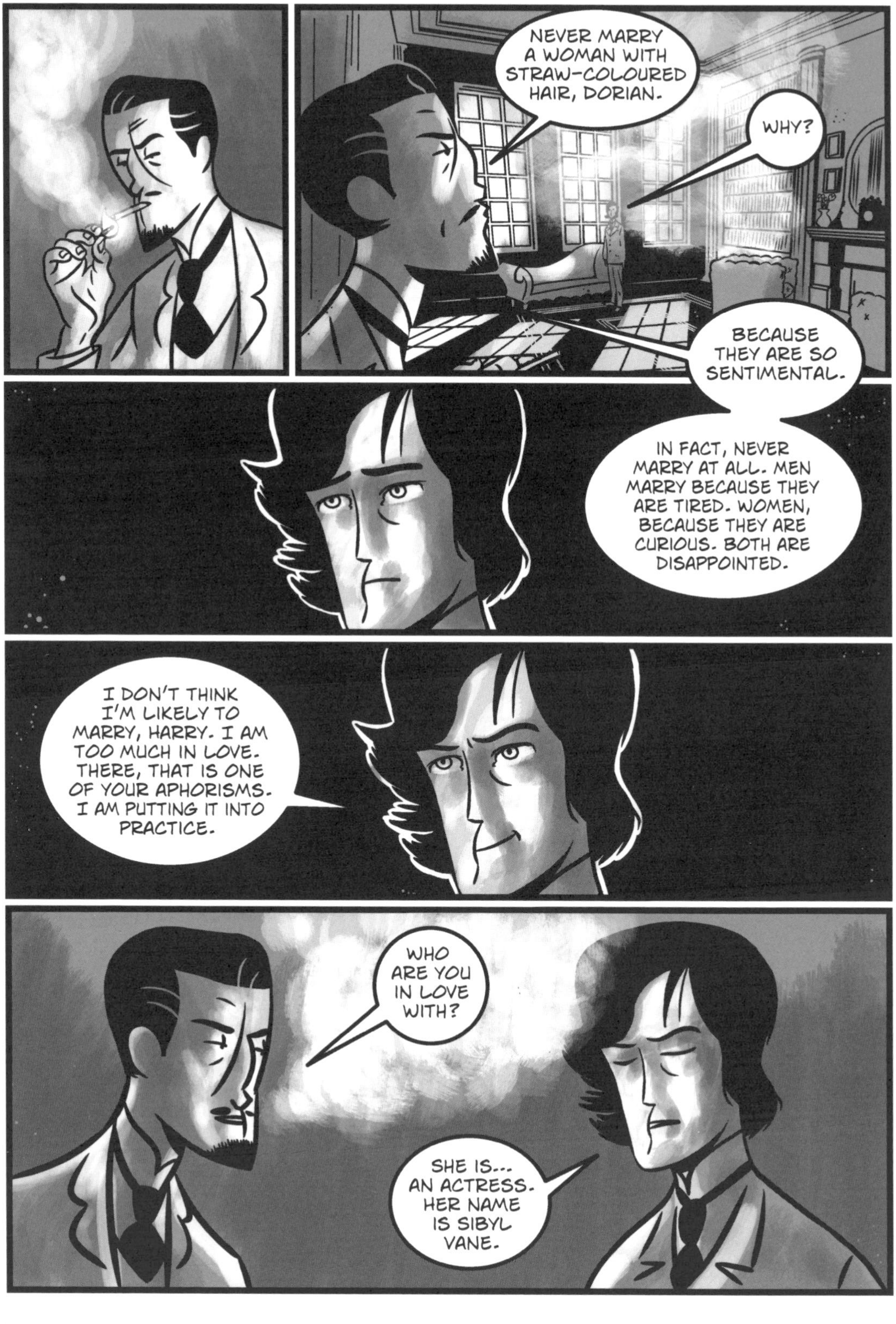
NEVER MARRY A WOMAN WITH STRAW-COLOURED HAIR, DORIAN.
WHY?
BECAUSE THEY ARE SO SENTIMENTAL.
IN FACT, NEVER MARRY AT ALL. MEN MARRY BECAUSE THEY ARE TIRED. WOMEN, BECAUSE THEY ARE CURIOUS. BOTH ARE DISAPPOINTED.
I DON'T THINK I'M LIKELY TO MARRY, HARRY. I AM TOO MUCH IN LOVE. THERE, THAT IS ONE OF YOUR APHORISMS. I AM PUTTING IT INTO PRACTICE.
WHO ARE YOU IN LOVE WITH?
SHE IS... AN ACTRESS. HER NAME IS SIBYL VANE.

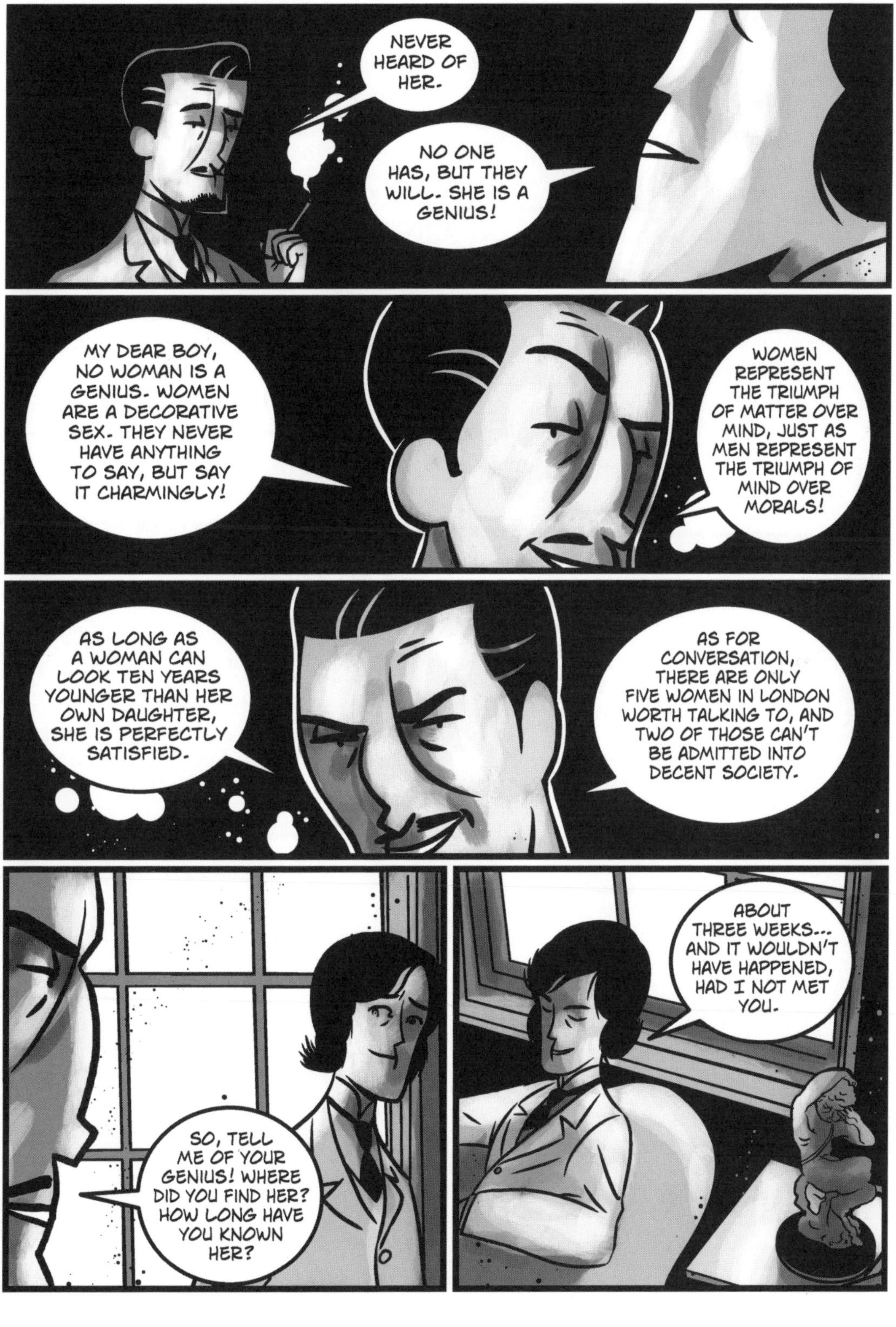
NEVER HEARD OF HER.
NO ONE HAS, BUT THEY WILL. SHE IS A GENIUS!
MY DEAR BOY, NO WOMAN IS A GENIUS. WOMEN ARE A DECORATIVE SEX. THEY NEVER HAVE ANYTHING TO SAY, BUT SAY IT CHARMINGLY!
WOMEN REPRESENT THE TRIUMPH OF MATTER OVER MIND, JUST AS MEN REPRESENT THE TRIUMPH OF MIND OVER MORALS!
AS LONG AS A WOMAN CAN LOOK TEN YEARS YOUNGER THAN HER OWN DAUGHTER, SHE IS PERFECTLY SATISFIED.
AS FOR CONVERSATION, THERE ARE ONLY FIVE WOMEN IN LONDON WORTH TALKING TO, AND TWO OF THOSE CAN'T BE ADMITTED INTO DECENT SOCIETY.
SO, TELL ME OF YOUR GENIUS! WHERE DID YOU FIND HER? HOW LONG HAVE YOU KNOWN HER?
ABOUT THREE WEEKS... AND IT WOULDN'T HAVE HAPPENED, HAD I NOT MET YOU.

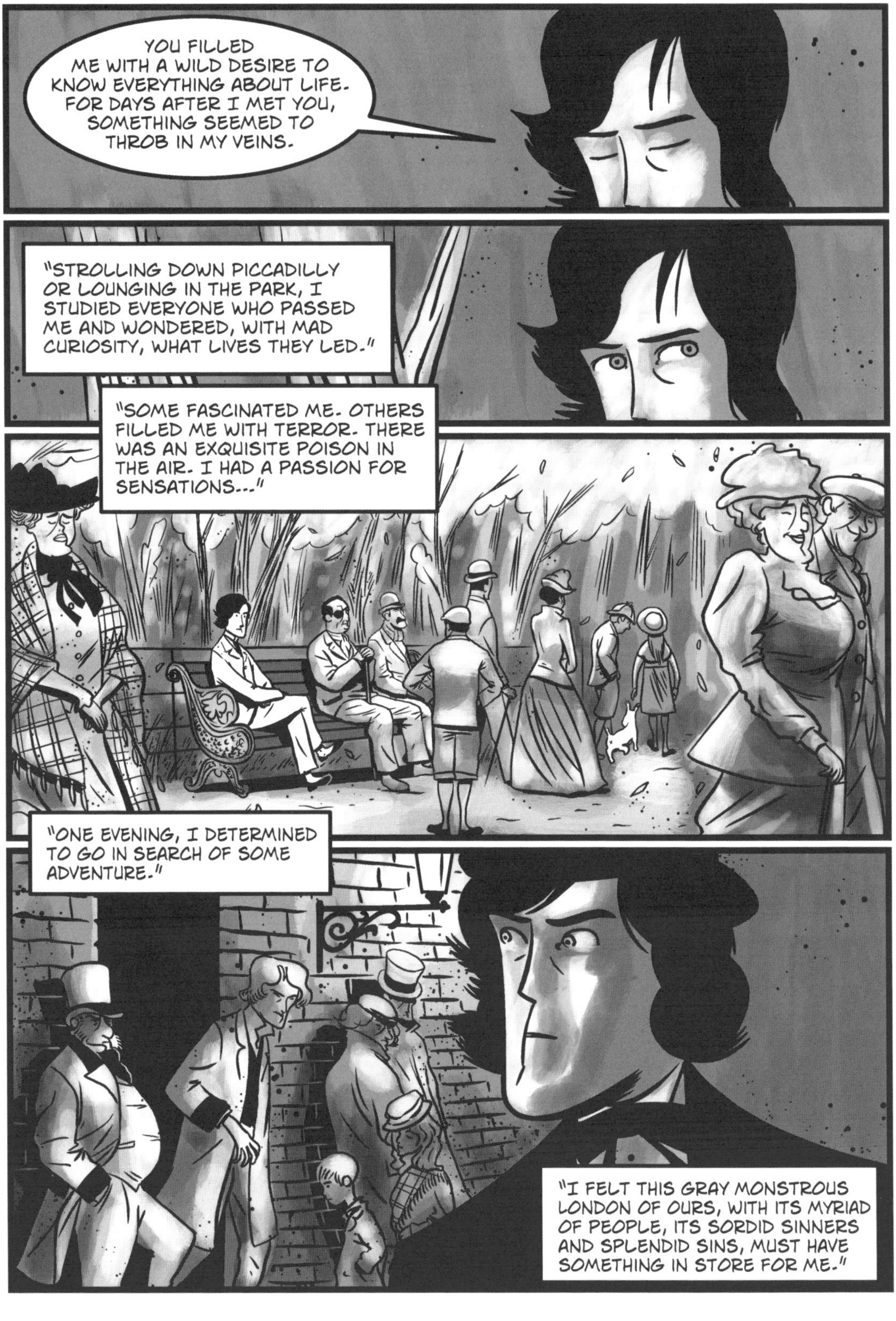
YOU FILLED ME WITH A WILD DESIRE TO KNOW EVERYTHING ABOUT LIFE. FOR DAYS AFTER I MET YOU, SOMETHING SEEMED TO THROB IN MY VEINS.
"STROLLING DOWN PICCADILLY OR LOUNGING IN THE PARK, I STUDIED EVERYONE WHO PASSED ME AND WONDERED, WITH MAD CURIOSITY, WHAT LIVES THEY LED."
"SOME FASCINATED ME. OTHERS FILLED ME WITH TERROR. THERE WAS AN EXQUISITE POISON IN THE AIR. I HAD A PASSION FOR SENSATIONS..."
"ONE EVENING, I DETERMINED TO GO IN SEARCH OF SOME ADVENTURE."
"I FELT THIS GRAY MONSTROUS LONDON OF OURS, WITH ITS MYRIAD OF PEOPLE, ITS SORDID SINNERS AND SPLENDID SINS, MUST HAVE SOMETHING IN STORE FOR ME."

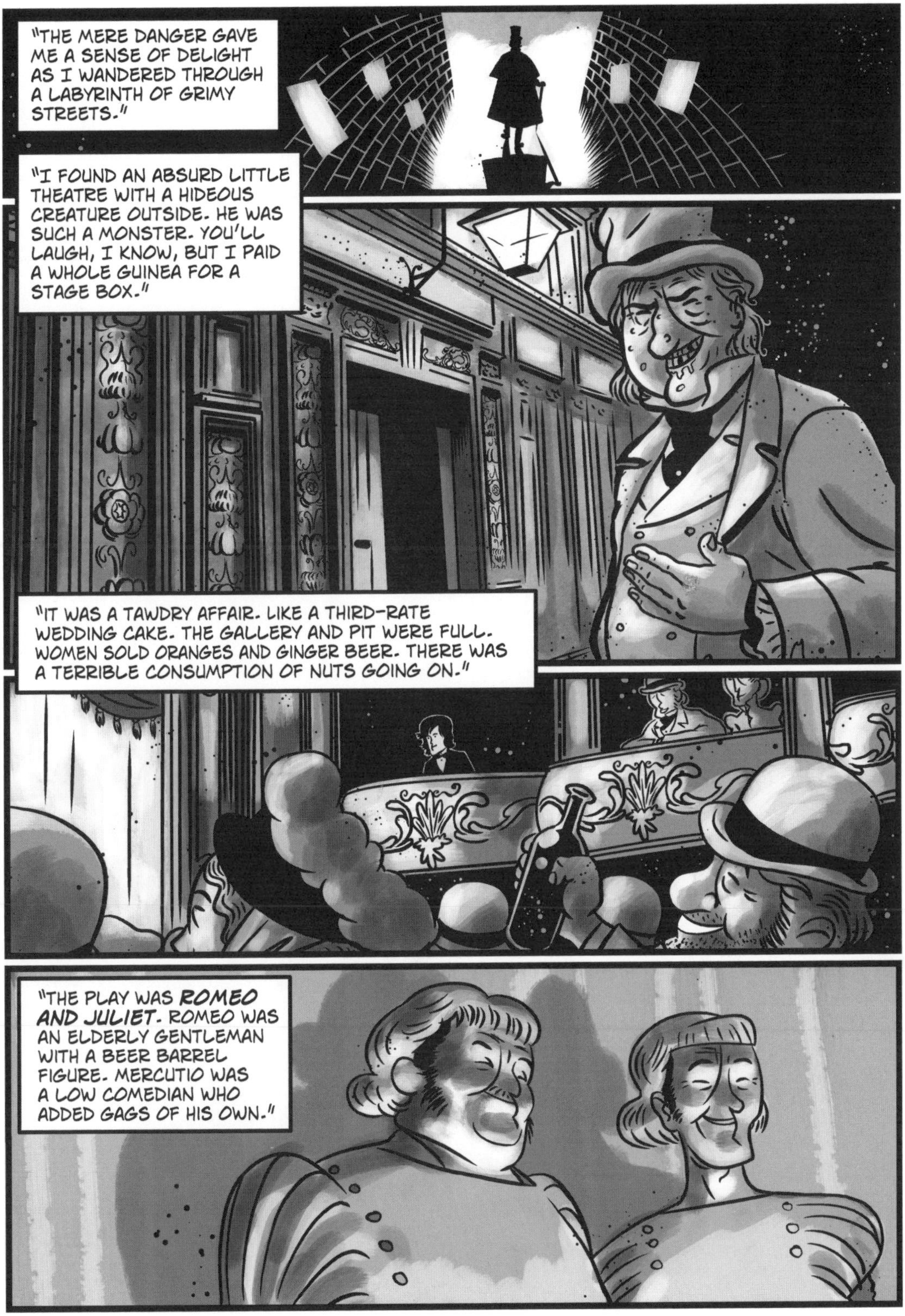
"THE MERE DANGER GAVE ME A SENSE OF DELIGHT AS I WANDERED THROUGH A LABYRINTH OF GRIMY STREETS."
"I FOUND AN ABSURD LITTLE THEATRE WITH A HIDEOUS CREATURE OUTSIDE. HE WAS SUCH A MONSTER. YOU'LL LAUGH, I KNOW, BUT I PAID A WHOLE GUINEA FOR A STAGE BOX."
"IT WAS A TAWDRY AFFAIR. LIKE A THIRD-RATE WEDDING CAKE. THE GALLERY AND PIT WERE FULL. WOMEN SOLD ORANGES AND GINGER BEER. THERE WAS A TERRIBLE CONSUMPTION OF NUTS GOING ON."
"THE PLAY WAS ***ROMEO AND JULIET***. ROMEO WAS AN ELDERLY GENTLEMAN WITH A BEER BARREL FIGURE. MERCUTIO WAS A LOW COMEDIAN WHO ADDED GAGS OF HIS OWN."

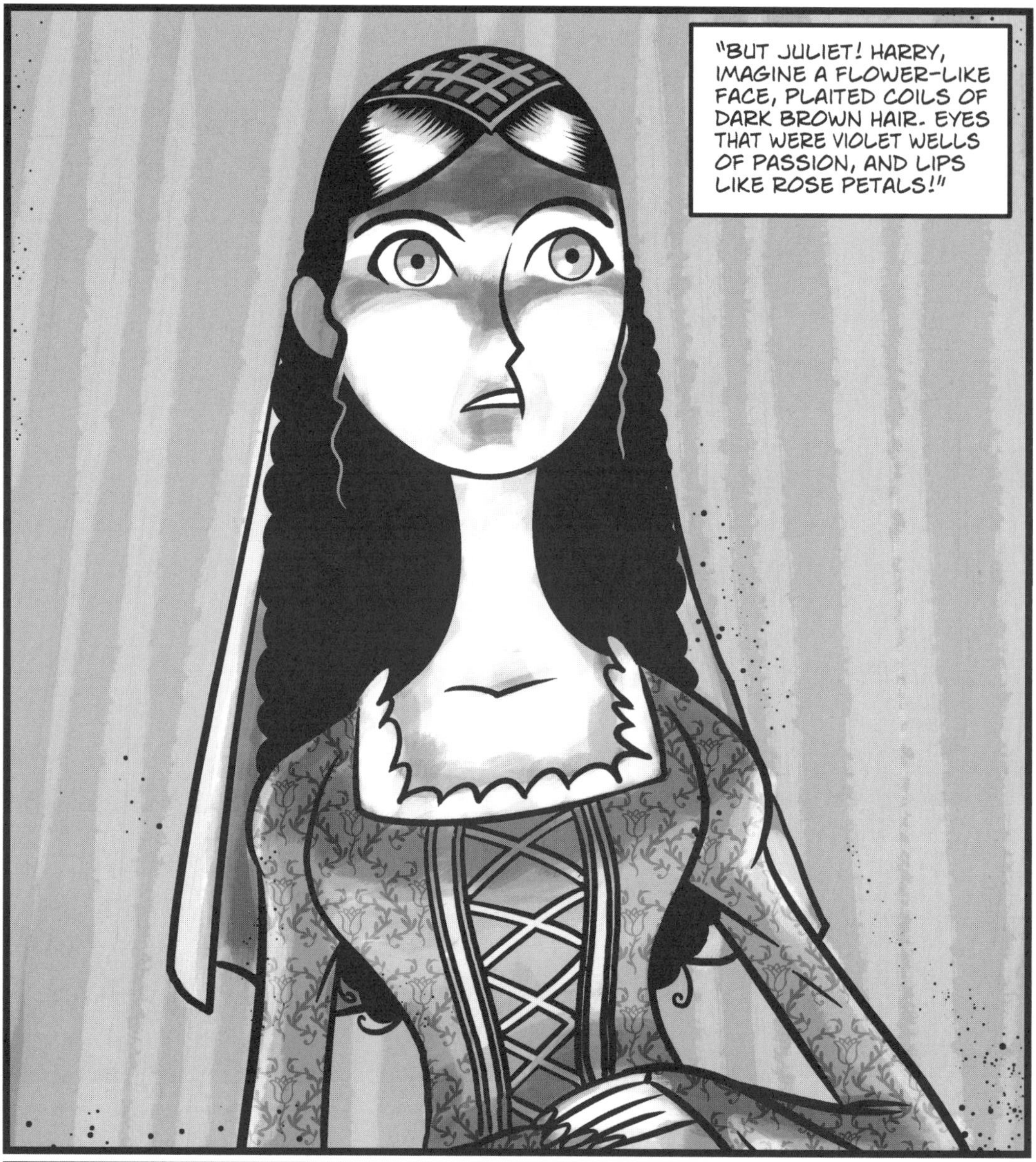
"BUT JULIET! HARRY, IMAGINE A FLOWER-LIKE FACE, PLAITED COILS OF DARK BROWN HAIR. EYES THAT WERE VIOLET WELLS OF PASSION, AND LIPS LIKE ROSE PETALS!"

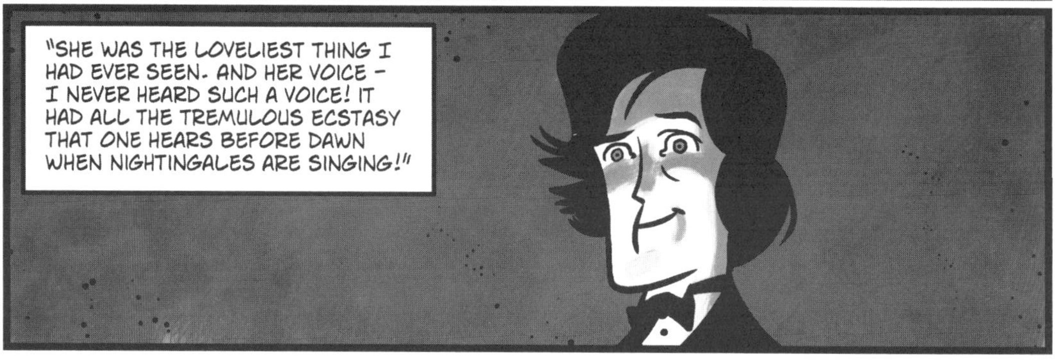
"SHE WAS THE LOVELIEST THING I HAD EVER SEEN. AND HER VOICE - I NEVER HEARD SUCH A VOICE! IT HAD ALL THE TREMULOUS ECSTASY THAT ONE HEARS BEFORE DAWN WHEN NIGHTINGALES ARE SINGING!"

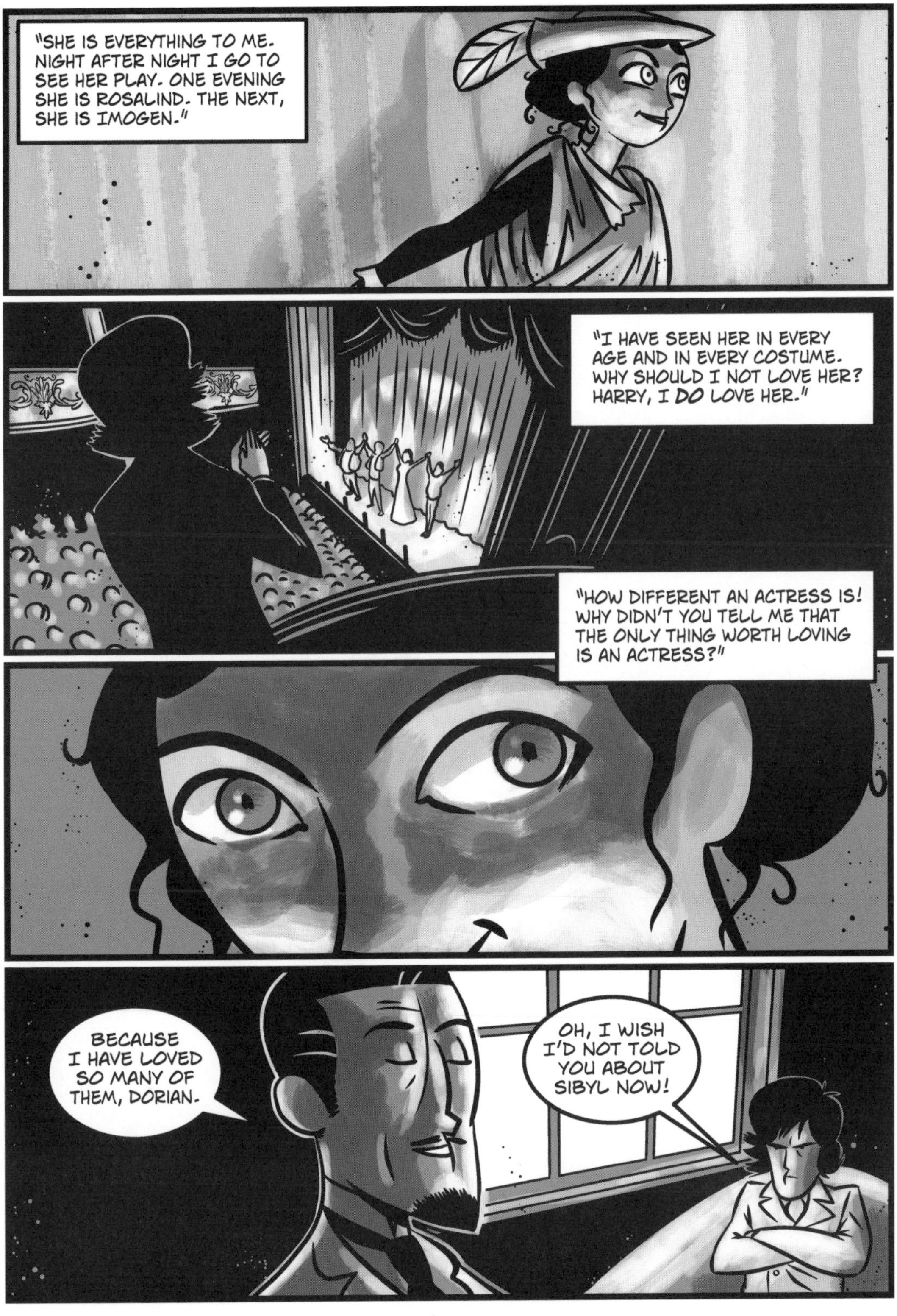
"SHE IS EVERYTHING TO ME. NIGHT AFTER NIGHT I GO TO SEE HER PLAY. ONE EVENING SHE IS ROSALIND. THE NEXT, SHE IS IMOGEN."
"I HAVE SEEN HER IN EVERY AGE AND IN EVERY COSTUME. WHY SHOULD I NOT LOVE HER? HARRY, I *DO* LOVE HER."
"HOW DIFFERENT AN ACTRESS IS! WHY DIDN'T YOU TELL ME THAT THE ONLY THING WORTH LOVING IS AN ACTRESS?"
BECAUSE I HAVE LOVED SO MANY OF THEM, DORIAN.
OH, I WISH I'D NOT TOLD YOU ABOUT SIBYL NOW!

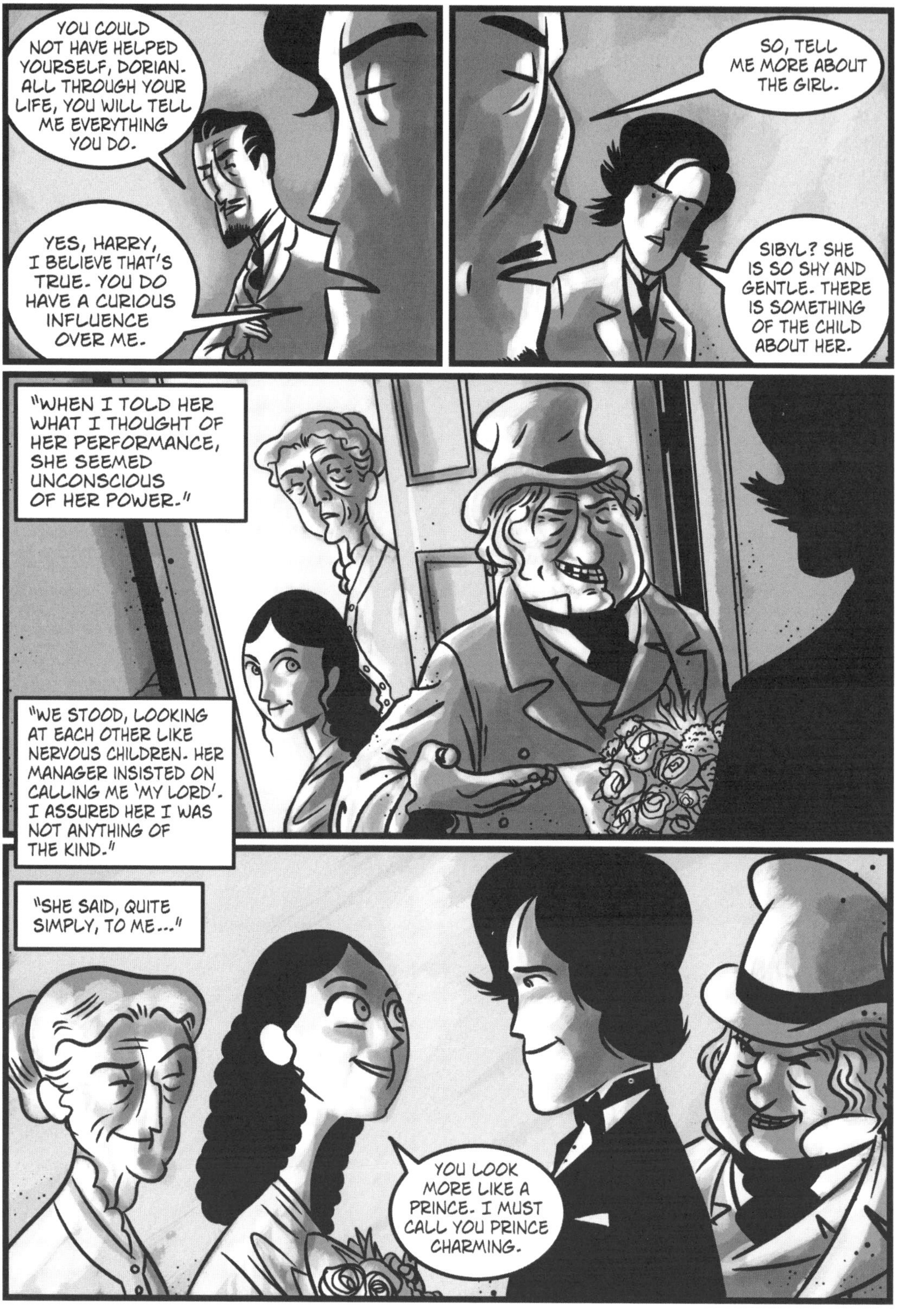
YOU COULD NOT HAVE HELPED YOURSELF, DORIAN. ALL THROUGH YOUR LIFE, YOU WILL TELL ME EVERYTHING YOU DO.
YES, HARRY, I BELIEVE THAT'S TRUE. YOU DO HAVE A CURIOUS INFLUENCE OVER ME.
SO, TELL ME MORE ABOUT THE GIRL.
SIBYL? SHE IS SO SHY AND GENTLE. THERE IS SOMETHING OF THE CHILD ABOUT HER.
"WHEN I TOLD HER WHAT I THOUGHT OF HER PERFORMANCE, SHE SEEMED UNCONSCIOUS OF HER POWER."
"WE STOOD, LOOKING AT EACH OTHER LIKE NERVOUS CHILDREN. HER MANAGER INSISTED ON CALLING ME 'MY LORD'. I ASSURED HER I WAS NOT ANYTHING OF THE KIND."
"SHE SAID, QUITE SIMPLY, TO ME..."
YOU LOOK MORE LIKE A PRINCE. I MUST CALL YOU PRINCE CHARMING.

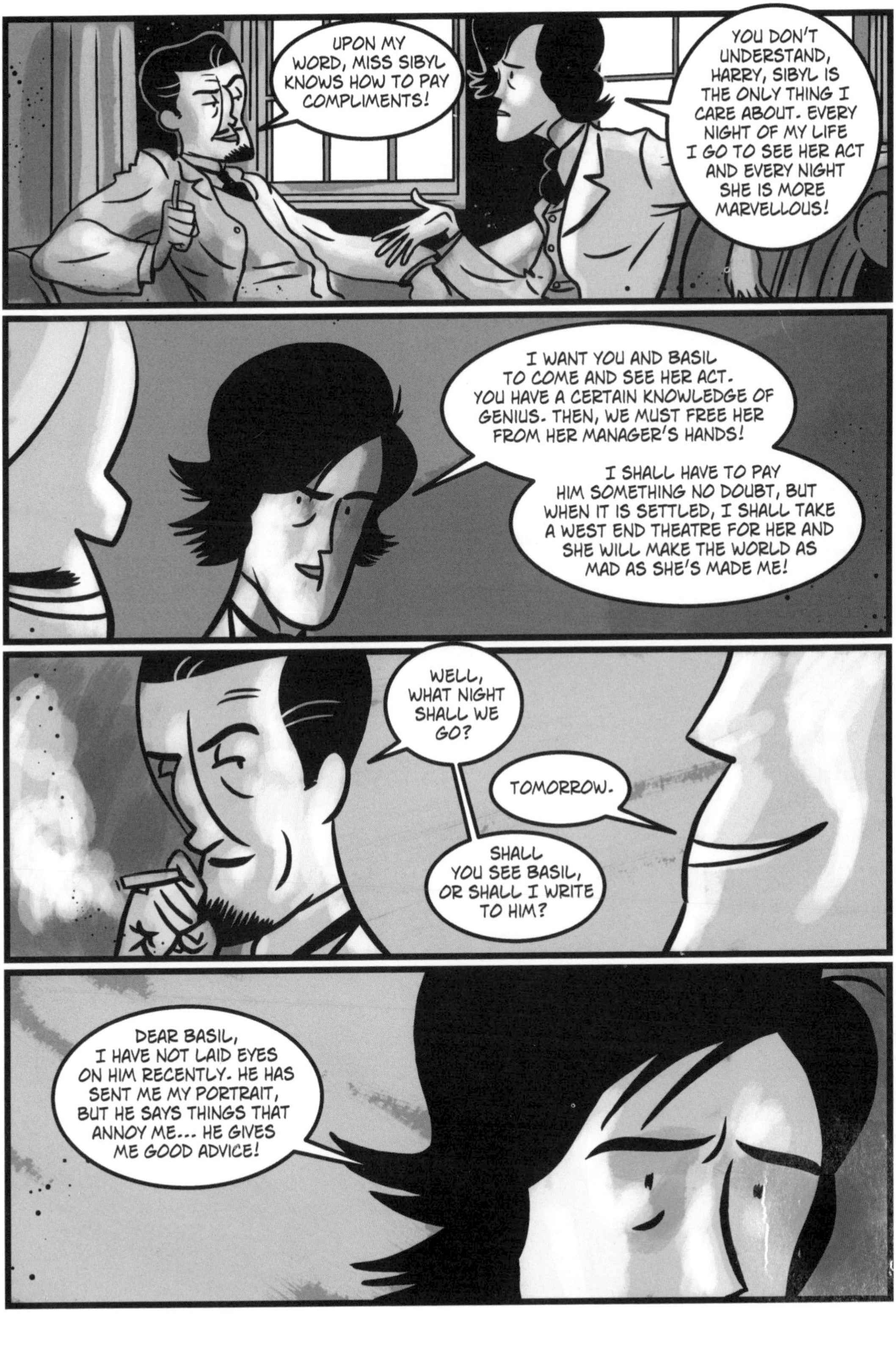
UPON MY WORD, MISS SIBYL KNOWS HOW TO PAY COMPLIMENTS!
YOU DON'T UNDERSTAND, HARRY, SIBYL IS THE ONLY THING I CARE ABOUT. EVERY NIGHT OF MY LIFE I GO TO SEE HER ACT AND EVERY NIGHT SHE IS MORE MARVELLOUS!
I WANT YOU AND BASIL TO COME AND SEE HER ACT. YOU HAVE A CERTAIN KNOWLEDGE OF GENIUS. THEN, WE MUST FREE HER FROM HER MANAGER'S HANDS!
I SHALL HAVE TO PAY HIM SOMETHING NO DOUBT, BUT WHEN IT IS SETTLED, I SHALL TAKE A WEST END THEATRE FOR HER AND SHE WILL MAKE THE WORLD AS MAD AS SHE'S MADE ME!
WELL, WHAT NIGHT SHALL WE GO?
TOMORROW.
SHALL YOU SEE BASIL, OR SHALL I WRITE TO HIM?
DEAR BASIL, I HAVE NOT LAID EYES ON HIM RECENTLY. HE HAS SENT ME MY PORTRAIT, BUT HE SAYS THINGS THAT ANNOY ME... HE GIVES ME GOOD ADVICE!

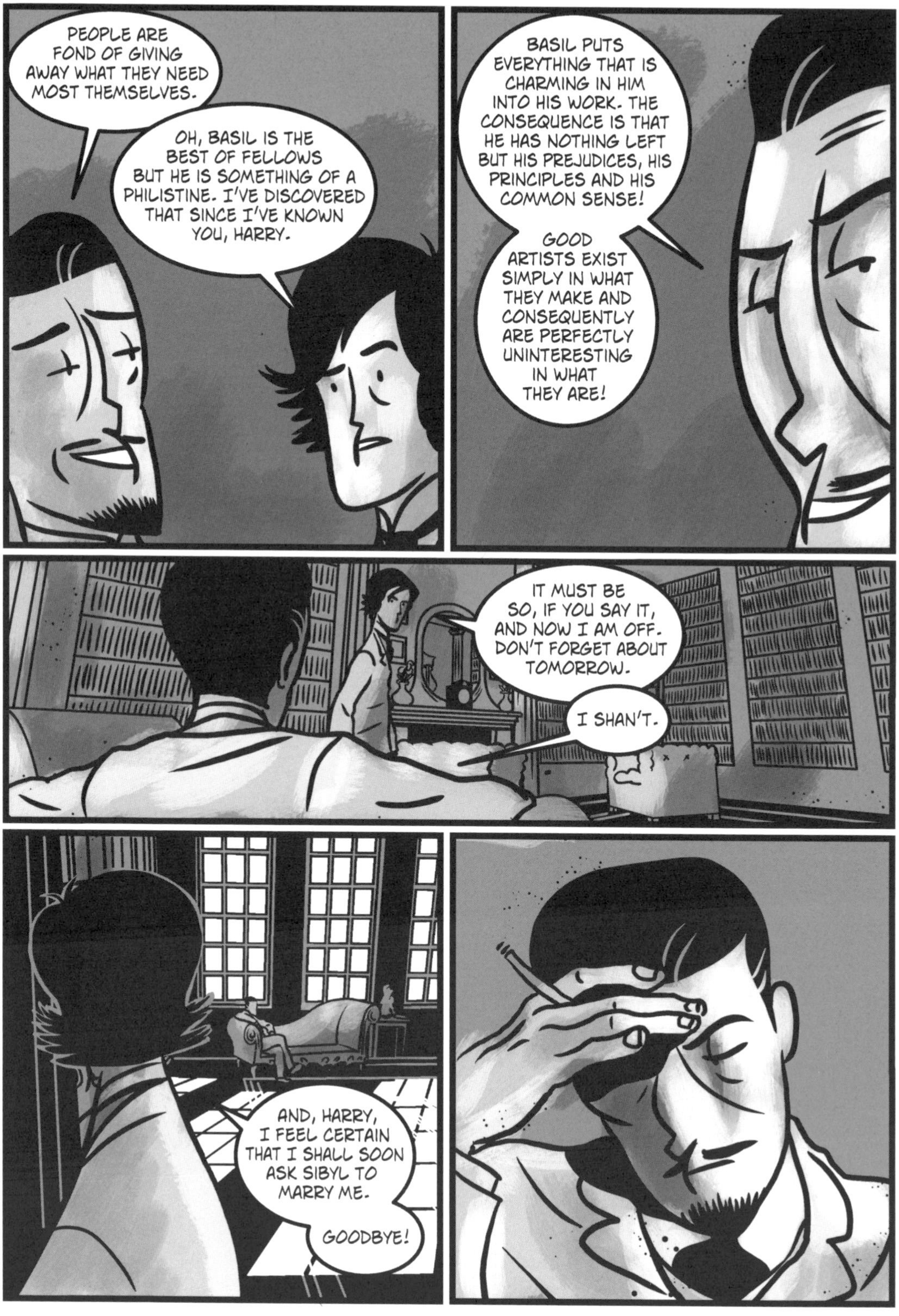
PEOPLE ARE FOND OF GIVING AWAY WHAT THEY NEED MOST THEMSELVES.
OH, BASIL IS THE BEST OF FELLOWS BUT HE IS SOMETHING OF A PHILISTINE. I'VE DISCOVERED THAT SINCE I'VE KNOWN YOU, HARRY.
BASIL PUTS EVERYTHING THAT IS CHARMING IN HIM INTO HIS WORK. THE CONSEQUENCE IS THAT HE HAS NOTHING LEFT BUT HIS PREJUDICES, HIS PRINCIPLES AND HIS COMMON SENSE!
GOOD ARTISTS EXIST SIMPLY IN WHAT THEY MAKE AND CONSEQUENTLY ARE PERFECTLY UNINTERESTING IN WHAT THEY ARE!
IT MUST BE SO, IF YOU SAY IT, AND NOW I AM OFF. DON'T FORGET ABOUT TOMORROW.
I SHAN'T.
AND, HARRY, I FEEL CERTAIN THAT I SHALL SOON ASK SIBYL TO MARRY ME.
GOODBYE!

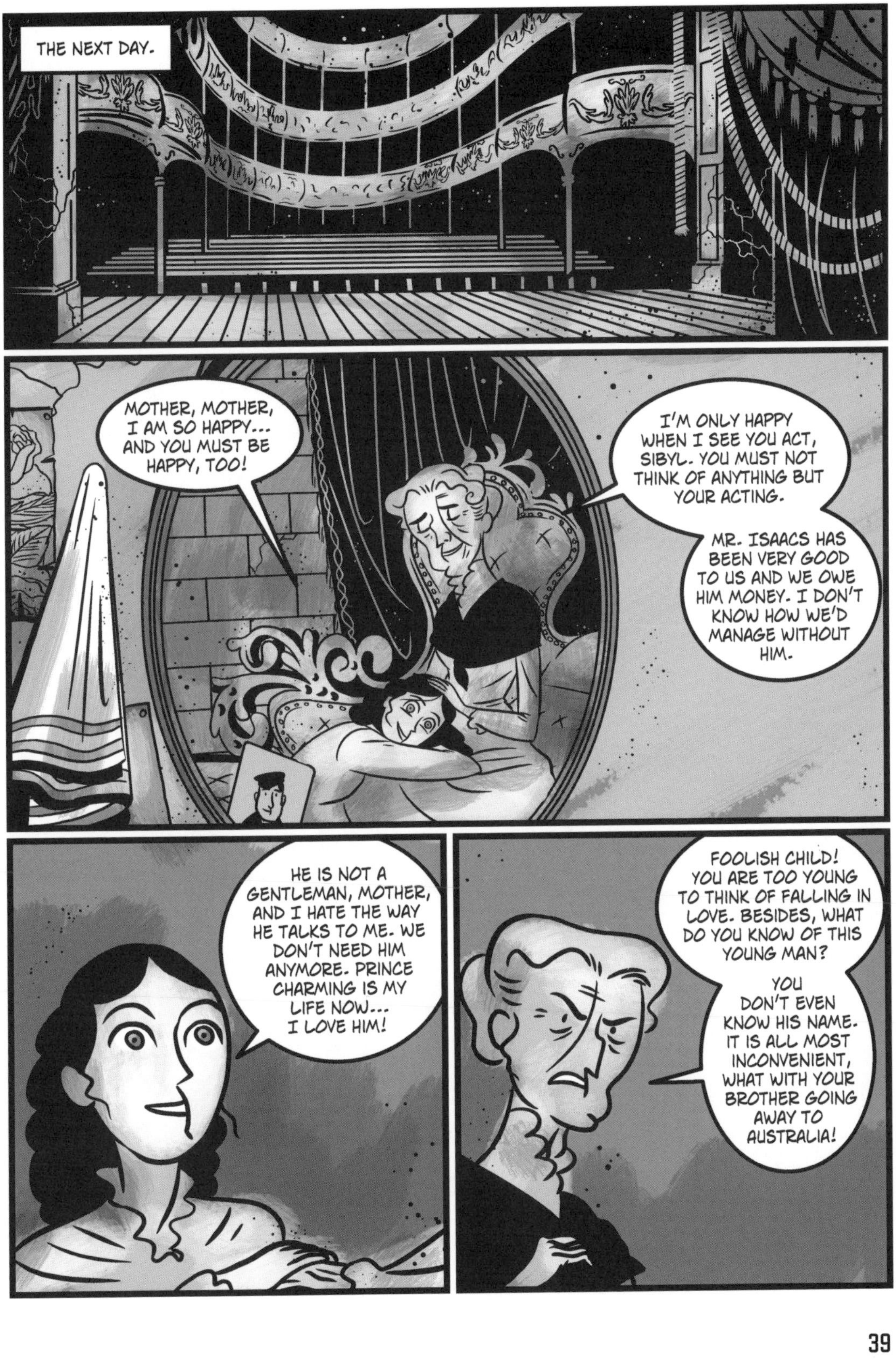
THE NEXT DAY.
MOTHER, MOTHER, I AM SO HAPPY... AND YOU MUST BE HAPPY, TOO!
I'M ONLY HAPPY WHEN I SEE YOU ACT, SIBYL. YOU MUST NOT THINK OF ANYTHING BUT YOUR ACTING.
MR. ISAACS HAS BEEN VERY GOOD TO US AND WE OWE HIM MONEY. I DON'T KNOW HOW WE'D MANAGE WITHOUT HIM.
HE IS NOT A GENTLEMAN, MOTHER, AND I HATE THE WAY HE TALKS TO ME. WE DON'T NEED HIM ANYMORE. PRINCE CHARMING IS MY LIFE NOW... I LOVE HIM!
FOOLISH CHILD! YOU ARE TOO YOUNG TO THINK OF FALLING IN LOVE. BESIDES, WHAT DO YOU KNOW OF THIS YOUNG MAN?
YOU DON'T EVEN KNOW HIS NAME. IT IS ALL MOST INCONVENIENT, WHAT WITH YOUR BROTHER GOING AWAY TO AUSTRALIA!

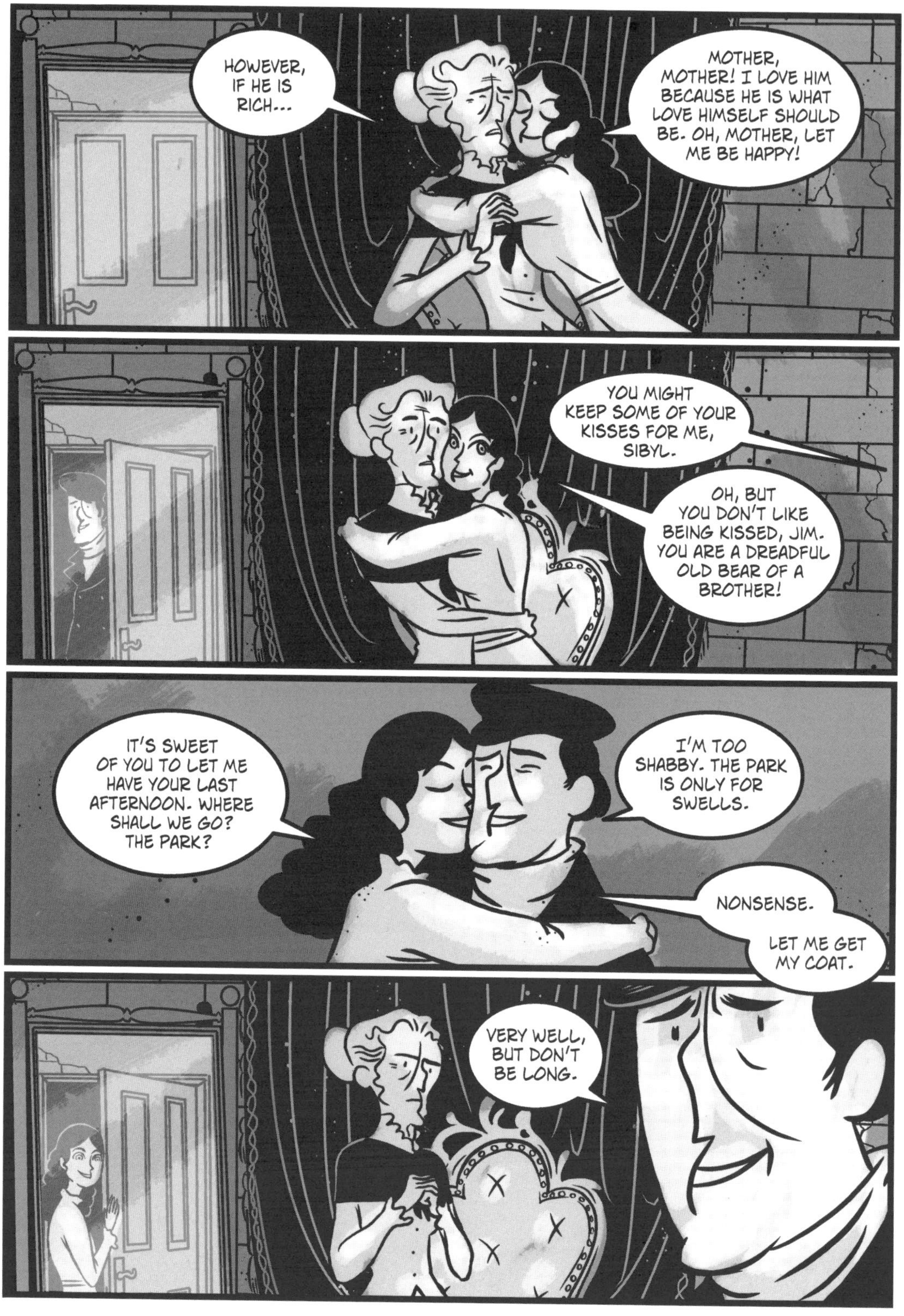
HOWEVER, IF HE IS RICH...
MOTHER, MOTHER! I LOVE HIM BECAUSE HE IS WHAT LOVE HIMSELF SHOULD BE. OH, MOTHER, LET ME BE HAPPY!
YOU MIGHT KEEP SOME OF YOUR KISSES FOR ME, SIBYL.
OH, BUT YOU DON'T LIKE BEING KISSED, JIM. YOU ARE A DREADFUL OLD BEAR OF A BROTHER!
IT'S SWEET OF YOU TO LET ME HAVE YOUR LAST AFTERNOON. WHERE SHALL WE GO? THE PARK?
I'M TOO SHABBY. THE PARK IS ONLY FOR SWELLS.
NONSENSE.
LET ME GET MY COAT.
VERY WELL, BUT DON'T BE LONG.

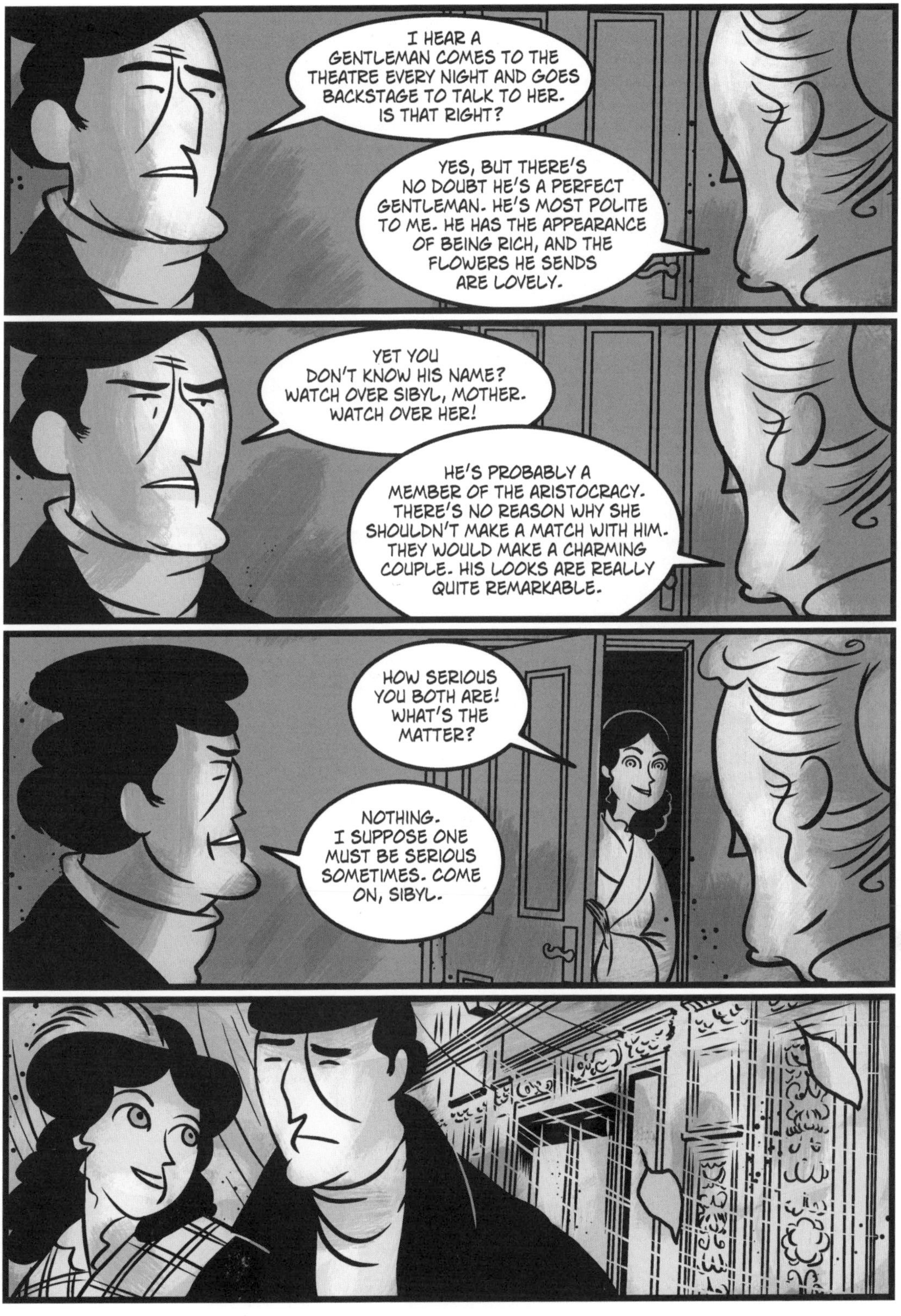
I HEAR A GENTLEMAN COMES TO THE THEATRE EVERY NIGHT AND GOES BACKSTAGE TO TALK TO HER. IS THAT RIGHT?
YES, BUT THERE'S NO DOUBT HE'S A PERFECT GENTLEMAN. HE'S MOST POLITE TO ME. HE HAS THE APPEARANCE OF BEING RICH, AND THE FLOWERS HE SENDS ARE LOVELY.
YET YOU DON'T KNOW HIS NAME? WATCH OVER SIBYL, MOTHER. WATCH OVER HER!
HE'S PROBABLY A MEMBER OF THE ARISTOCRACY. THERE'S NO REASON WHY SHE SHOULDN'T MAKE A MATCH WITH HIM. THEY WOULD MAKE A CHARMING COUPLE. HIS LOOKS ARE REALLY QUITE REMARKABLE.
HOW SERIOUS YOU BOTH ARE! WHAT'S THE MATTER?
NOTHING. I SUPPOSE ONE MUST BE SERIOUS SOMETIMES. COME ON, SIBYL.

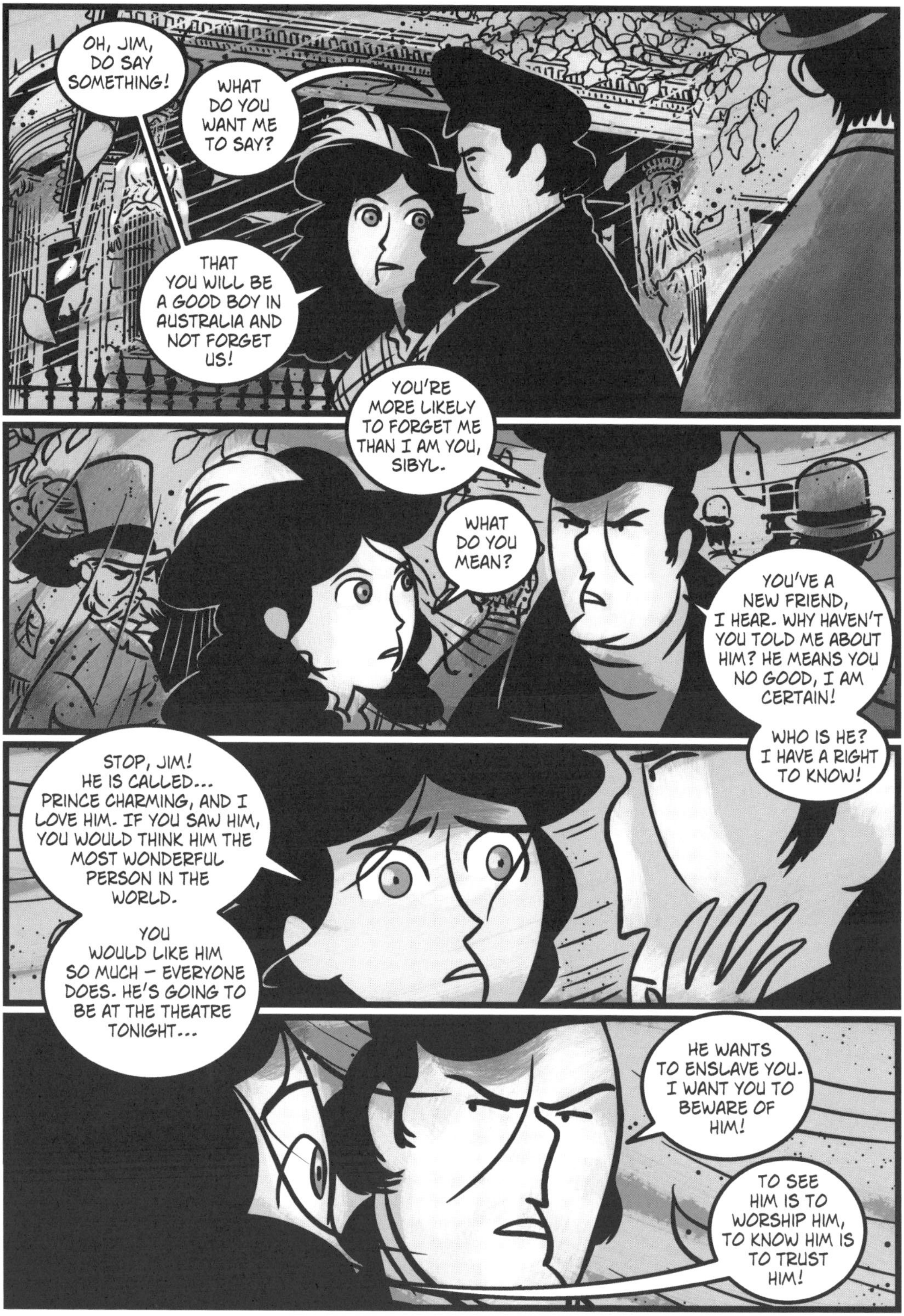
OH, JIM, DO SAY SOMETHING!
WHAT DO YOU WANT ME TO SAY?
THAT YOU WILL BE A GOOD BOY IN AUSTRALIA AND NOT FORGET US!
YOU'RE MORE LIKELY TO FORGET ME THAN I AM YOU, SIBYL.
WHAT DO YOU MEAN?
YOU'VE A NEW FRIEND, I HEAR. WHY HAVEN'T YOU TOLD ME ABOUT HIM? HE MEANS YOU NO GOOD, I AM CERTAIN!
WHO IS HE? I HAVE A RIGHT TO KNOW!
STOP, JIM! HE IS CALLED... PRINCE CHARMING, AND I LOVE HIM. IF YOU SAW HIM, YOU WOULD THINK HIM THE MOST WONDERFUL PERSON IN THE WORLD.
YOU WOULD LIKE HIM SO MUCH – EVERYONE DOES. HE'S GOING TO BE AT THE THEATRE TONIGHT...
HE WANTS TO ENSLAVE YOU. I WANT YOU TO BEWARE OF HIM!
TO SEE HIM IS TO WORSHIP HIM, TO KNOW HIM IS TO TRUST HIM!

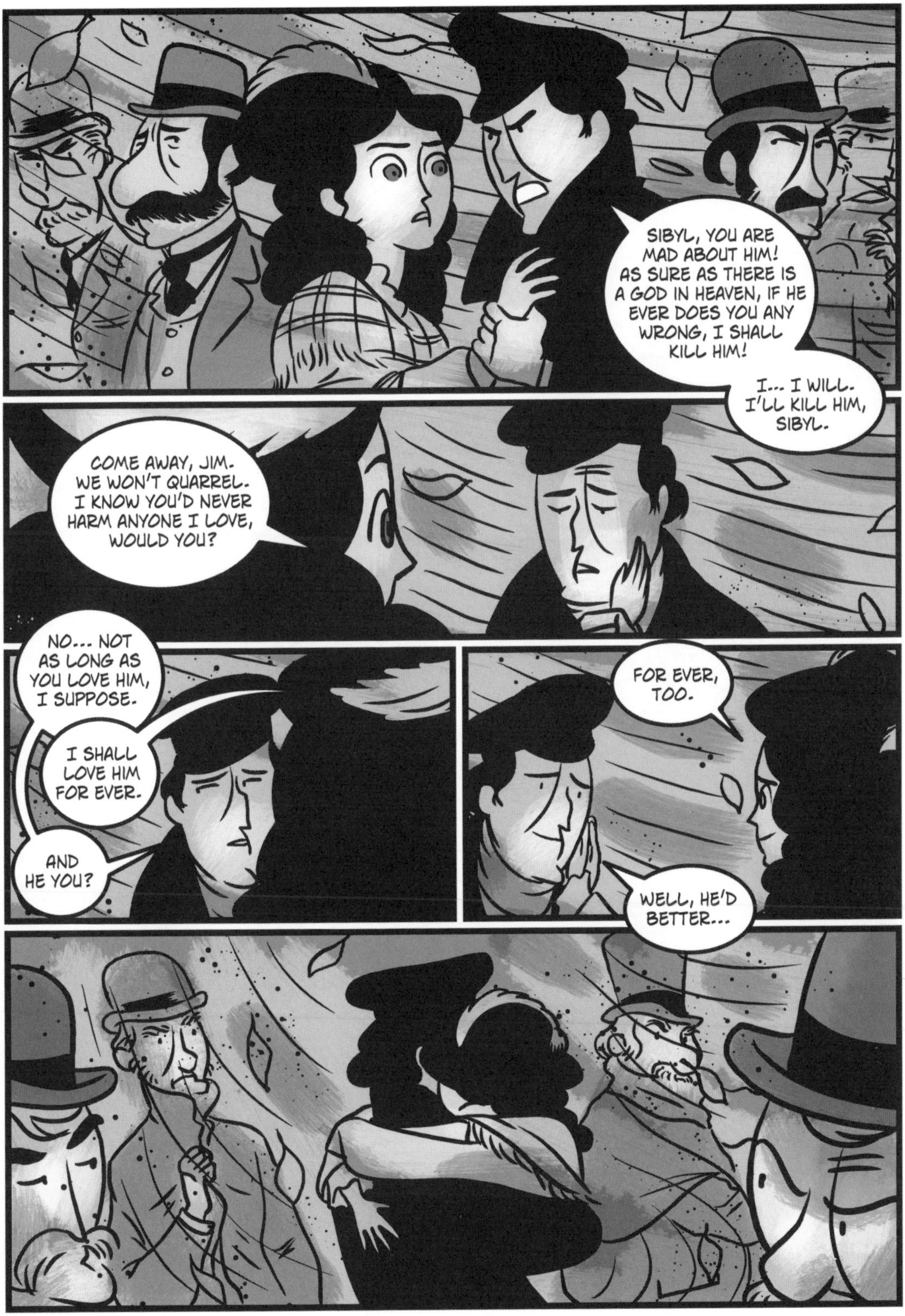
SIBYL, YOU ARE MAD ABOUT HIM! AS SURE AS THERE IS A GOD IN HEAVEN, IF HE EVER DOES YOU ANY WRONG, I SHALL KILL HIM!
I... I WILL. I'LL KILL HIM, SIBYL.
COME AWAY, JIM. WE WON'T QUARREL. I KNOW YOU'D NEVER HARM ANYONE I LOVE, WOULD YOU?
NO... NOT AS LONG AS YOU LOVE HIM, I SUPPOSE.
I SHALL LOVE HIM FOR EVER.
AND HE YOU?
FOR EVER, TOO.
WELL, HE'D BETTER...

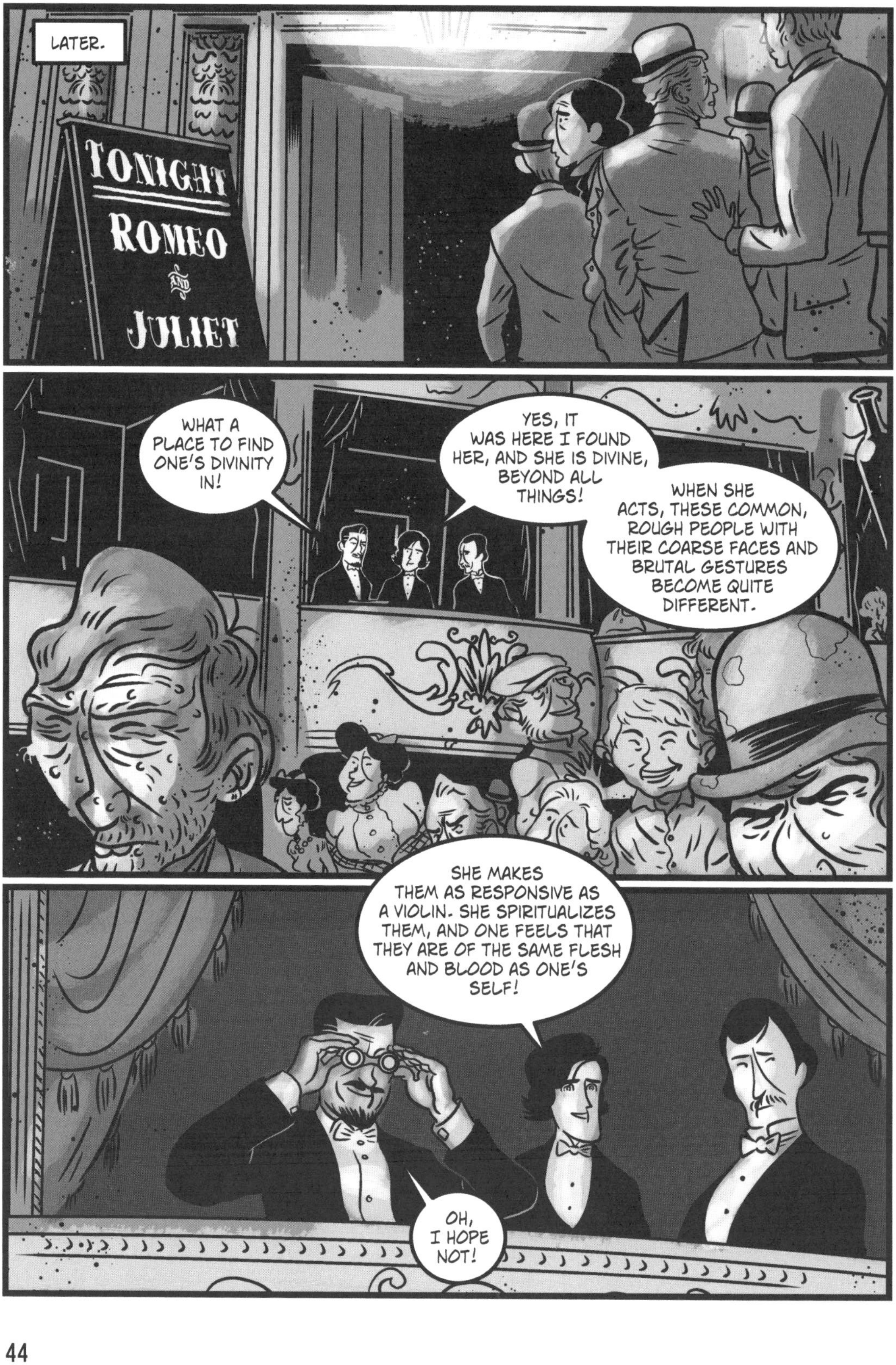
LATER.
TONIGHT ROMEO AND JULIET
WHAT A PLACE TO FIND ONE'S DIVINITY IN!
YES, IT WAS HERE I FOUND HER, AND SHE IS DIVINE, BEYOND ALL THINGS!
WHEN SHE ACTS, THESE COMMON, ROUGH PEOPLE WITH THEIR COARSE FACES AND BRUTAL GESTURES BECOME QUITE DIFFERENT.
SHE MAKES THEM AS RESPONSIVE AS A VIOLIN. SHE SPIRITUALIZES THEM, AND ONE FEELS THAT THEY ARE OF THE SAME FLESH AND BLOOD AS ONE'S SELF!
OH, I HOPE NOT!

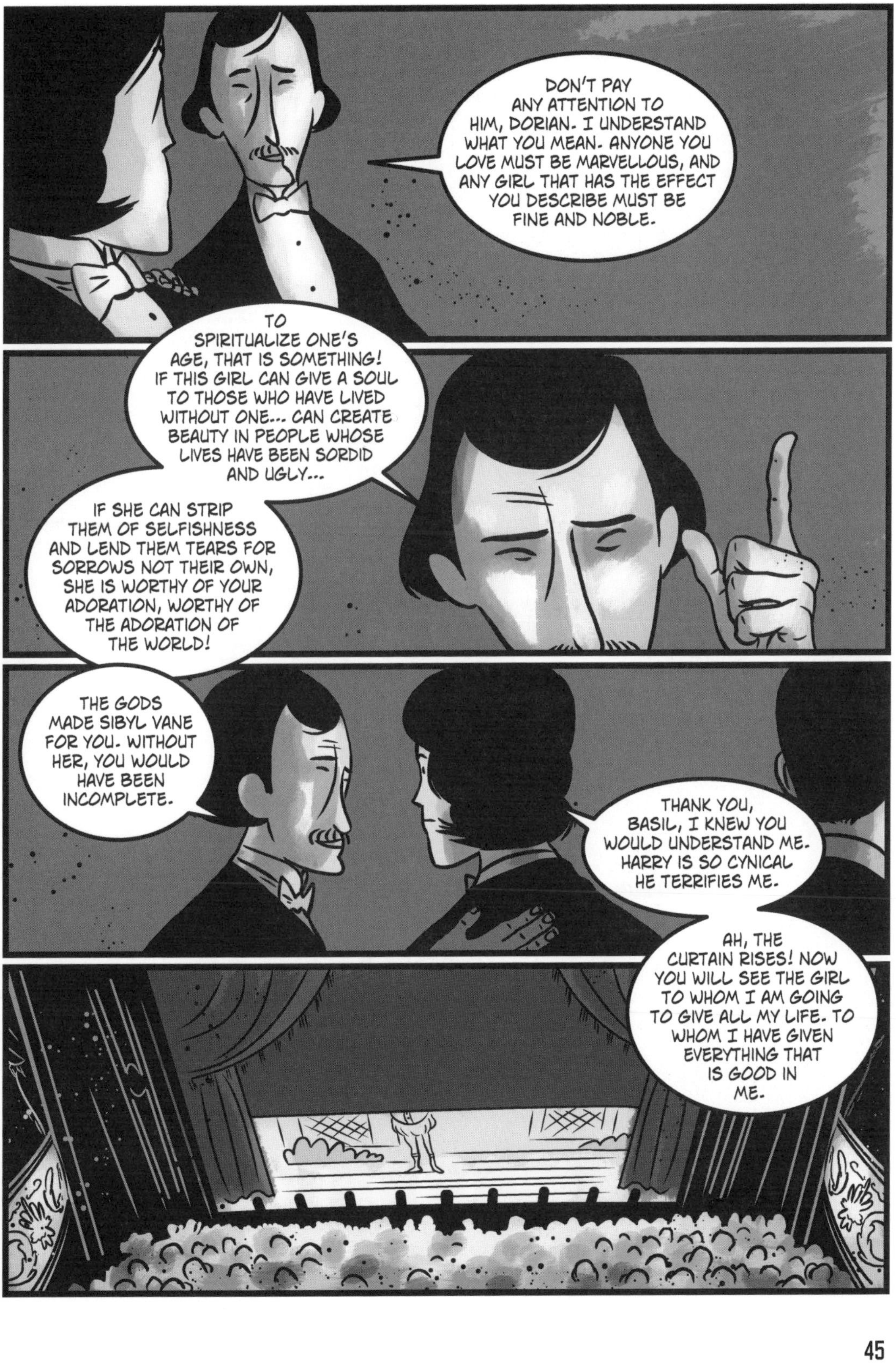
DON'T PAY ANY ATTENTION TO HIM, DORIAN. I UNDERSTAND WHAT YOU MEAN. ANYONE YOU LOVE MUST BE MARVELLOUS, AND ANY GIRL THAT HAS THE EFFECT YOU DESCRIBE MUST BE FINE AND NOBLE.
TO SPIRITUALIZE ONE'S AGE, THAT IS SOMETHING! IF THIS GIRL CAN GIVE A SOUL TO THOSE WHO HAVE LIVED WITHOUT ONE... CAN CREATE BEAUTY IN PEOPLE WHOSE LIVES HAVE BEEN SORDID AND UGLY...
IF SHE CAN STRIP THEM OF SELFISHNESS AND LEND THEM TEARS FOR SORROWS NOT THEIR OWN, SHE IS WORTHY OF YOUR ADORATION, WORTHY OF THE ADORATION OF THE WORLD!
THE GODS MADE SIBYL VANE FOR YOU. WITHOUT HER, YOU WOULD HAVE BEEN INCOMPLETE.
THANK YOU, BASIL, I KNEW YOU WOULD UNDERSTAND ME. HARRY IS SO CYNICAL HE TERRIFIES ME.
AH, THE CURTAIN RISES! NOW YOU WILL SEE THE GIRL TO WHOM I AM GOING TO GIVE ALL MY LIFE. TO WHOM I HAVE GIVEN EVERYTHING THAT IS GOOD IN ME.

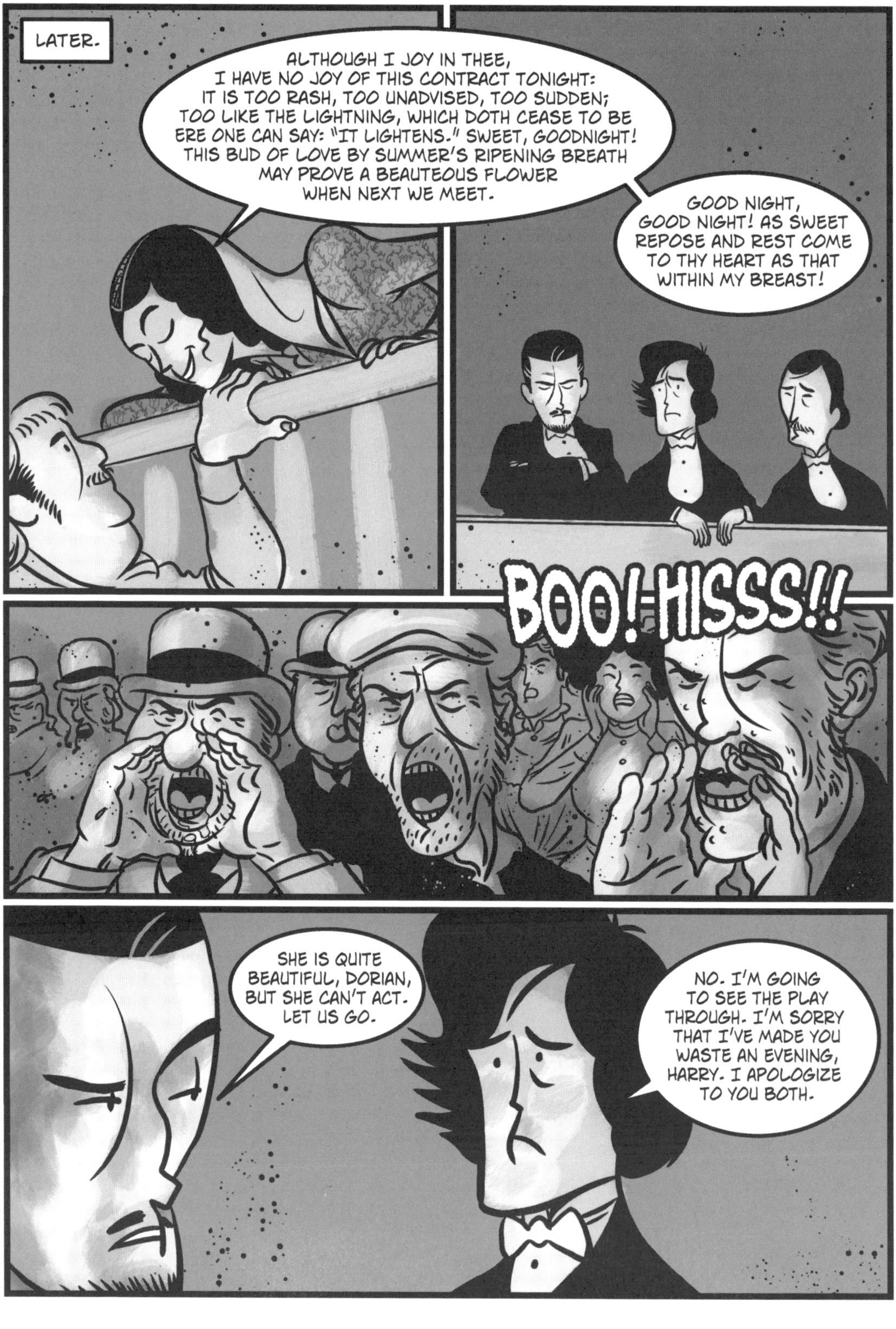
LATER.
ALTHOUGH I JOY IN THEE, I HAVE NO JOY OF THIS CONTRACT TONIGHT: IT IS TOO RASH, TOO UNADVISED, TOO SUDDEN; TOO LIKE THE LIGHTNING, WHICH DOTH CEASE TO BE ERE ONE CAN SAY: "IT LIGHTENS." SWEET, GOODNIGHT! THIS BUD OF LOVE BY SUMMER'S RIPENING BREATH MAY PROVE A BEAUTEOUS FLOWER WHEN NEXT WE MEET.
GOOD NIGHT, GOOD NIGHT! AS SWEET REPOSE AND REST COME TO THY HEART AS THAT WITHIN MY BREAST!
BOO! HISSS!!
SHE IS QUITE BEAUTIFUL, DORIAN, BUT SHE CAN'T ACT. LET US GO.
NO. I'M GOING TO SEE THE PLAY THROUGH. I'M SORRY THAT I'VE MADE YOU WASTE AN EVENING, HARRY. I APOLOGIZE TO YOU BOTH.

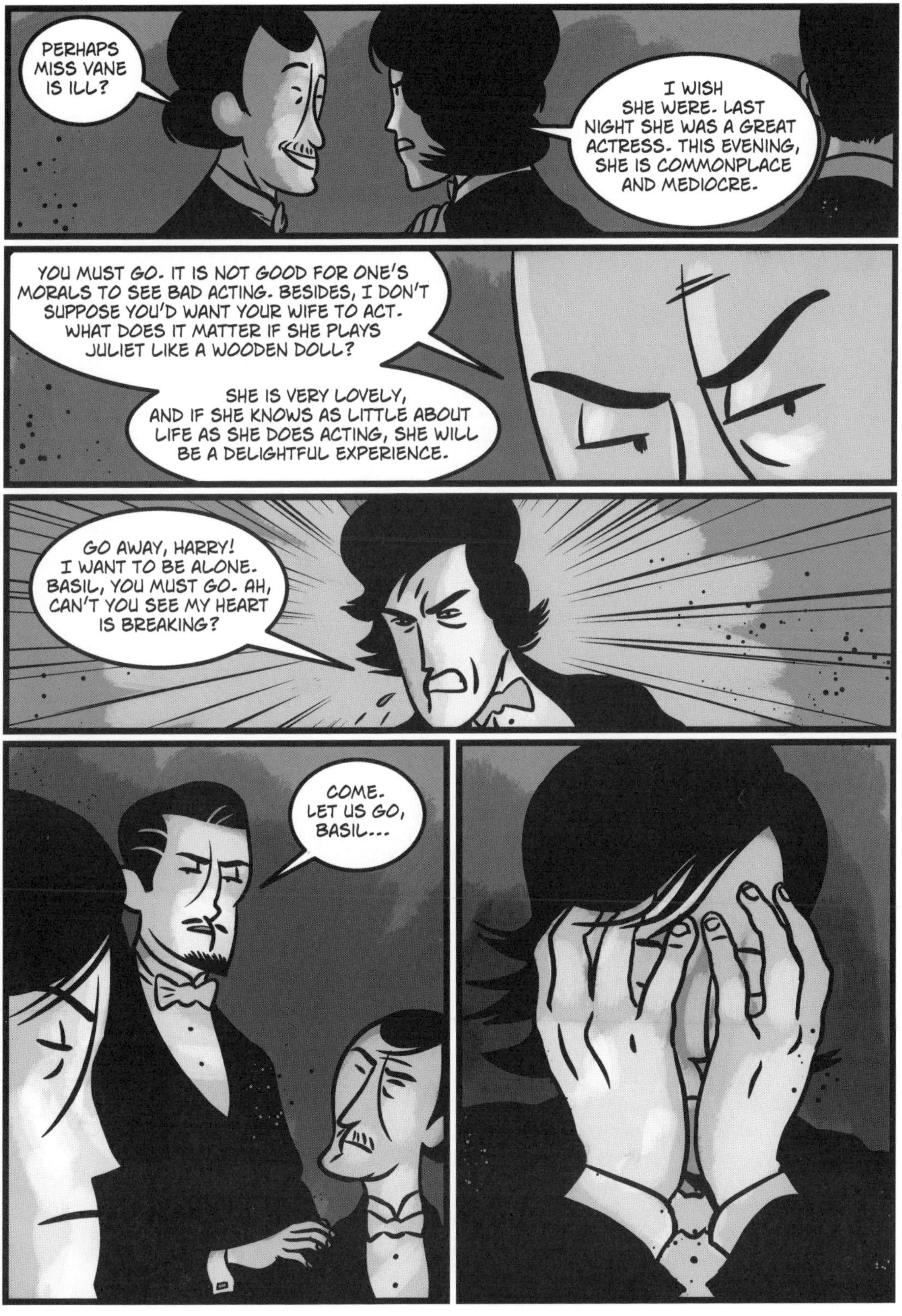
PERHAPS MISS VANE IS ILL?
I WISH SHE WERE. LAST NIGHT SHE WAS A GREAT ACTRESS. THIS EVENING, SHE IS COMMONPLACE AND MEDIOCRE.
YOU MUST GO. IT IS NOT GOOD FOR ONE'S MORALS TO SEE BAD ACTING. BESIDES, I DON'T SUPPOSE YOU'D WANT YOUR WIFE TO ACT. WHAT DOES IT MATTER IF SHE PLAYS JULIET LIKE A WOODEN DOLL?
SHE IS VERY LOVELY, AND IF SHE KNOWS AS LITTLE ABOUT LIFE AS SHE DOES ACTING, SHE WILL BE A DELIGHTFUL EXPERIENCE.
GO AWAY, HARRY! I WANT TO BE ALONE. BASIL, YOU MUST GO. AH, CAN'T YOU SEE MY HEART IS BREAKING?
COME. LET US GO, BASIL...

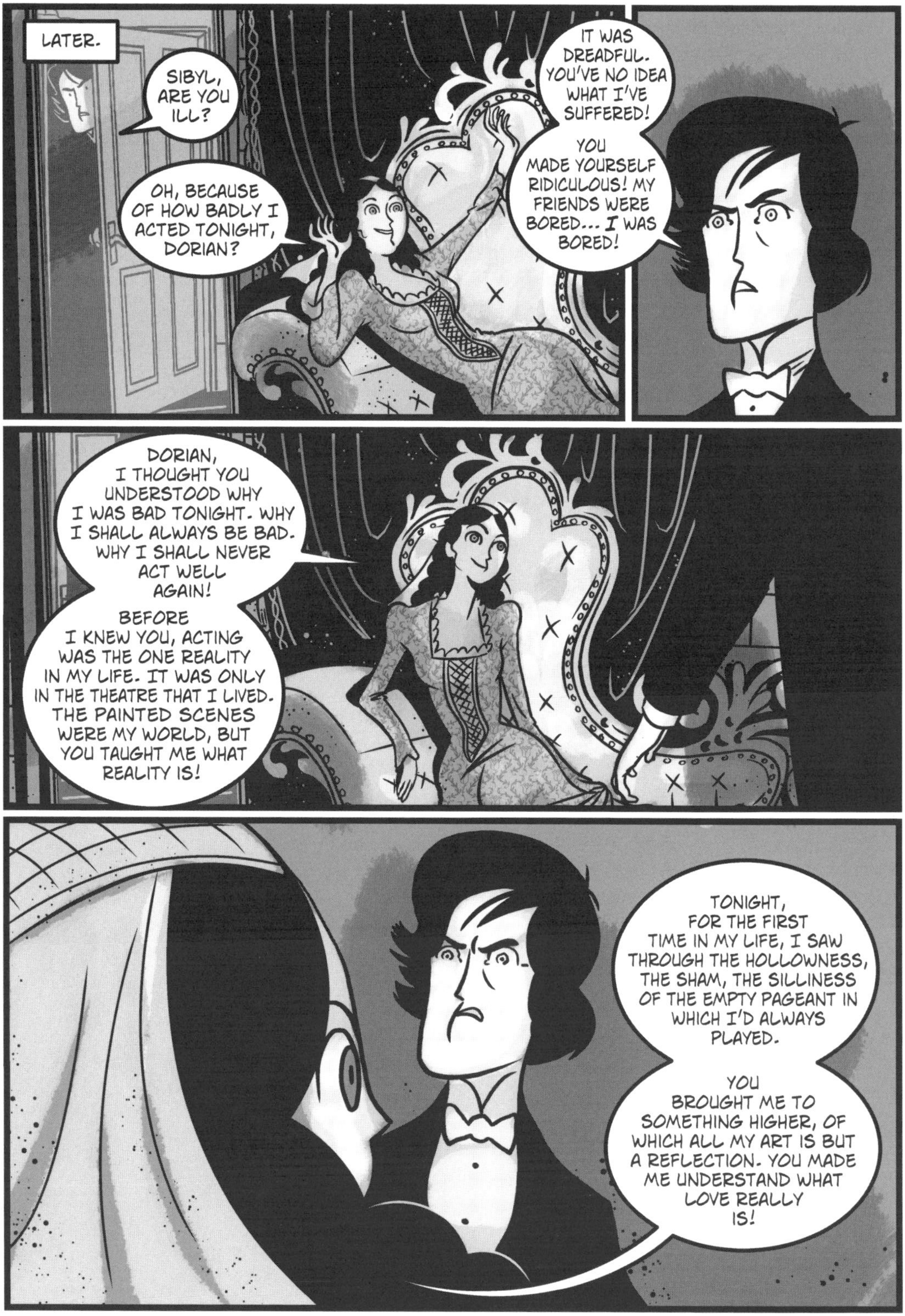
LATER.
SIBYL, ARE YOU ILL?
OH, BECAUSE OF HOW BADLY I ACTED TONIGHT, DORIAN?
IT WAS DREADFUL. YOU'VE NO IDEA WHAT I'VE SUFFERED!
YOU MADE YOURSELF RIDICULOUS! MY FRIENDS WERE BORED... I WAS BORED!
DORIAN, I THOUGHT YOU UNDERSTOOD WHY I WAS BAD TONIGHT. WHY I SHALL ALWAYS BE BAD. WHY I SHALL NEVER ACT WELL AGAIN!
BEFORE I KNEW YOU, ACTING WAS THE ONE REALITY IN MY LIFE. IT WAS ONLY IN THE THEATRE THAT I LIVED. THE PAINTED SCENES WERE MY WORLD, BUT YOU TAUGHT ME WHAT REALITY IS!
TONIGHT, FOR THE FIRST TIME IN MY LIFE, I SAW THROUGH THE HOLLOWNESS, THE SHAM, THE SILLINESS OF THE EMPTY PAGEANT IN WHICH I'D ALWAYS PLAYED.
YOU BROUGHT ME TO SOMETHING HIGHER, OF WHICH ALL MY ART IS BUT A REFLECTION. YOU MADE ME UNDERSTAND WHAT LOVE REALLY IS!

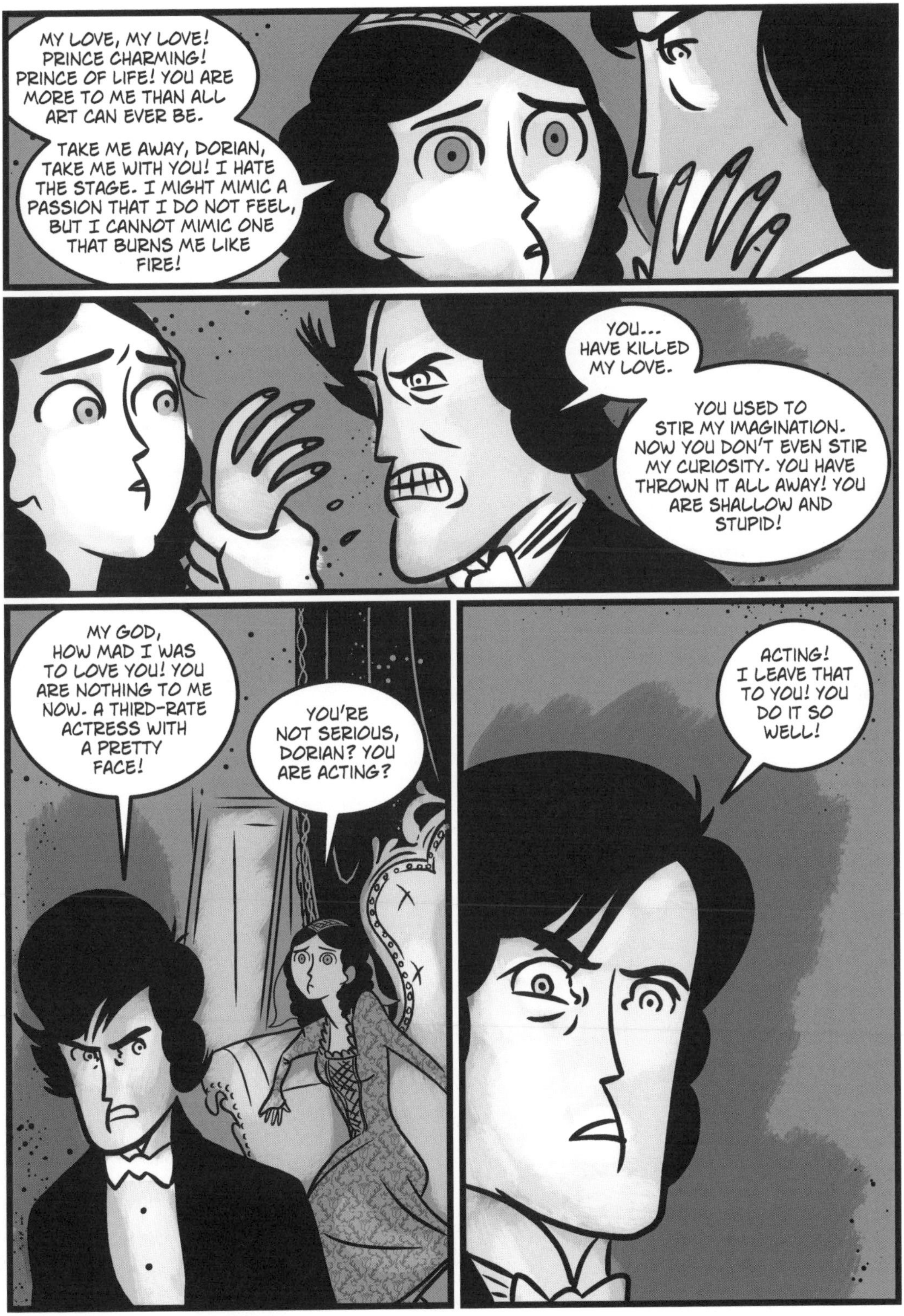
MY LOVE, MY LOVE! PRINCE CHARMING! PRINCE OF LIFE! YOU ARE MORE TO ME THAN ALL ART CAN EVER BE.
TAKE ME AWAY, DORIAN, TAKE ME WITH YOU! I HATE THE STAGE. I MIGHT MIMIC A PASSION THAT I DO NOT FEEL, BUT I CANNOT MIMIC ONE THAT BURNS ME LIKE FIRE!
YOU... HAVE KILLED MY LOVE.
YOU USED TO STIR MY IMAGINATION. NOW YOU DON'T EVEN STIR MY CURIOSITY. YOU HAVE THROWN IT ALL AWAY! YOU ARE SHALLOW AND STUPID!
MY GOD, HOW MAD I WAS TO LOVE YOU! YOU ARE NOTHING TO ME NOW. A THIRD-RATE ACTRESS WITH A PRETTY FACE!
YOU'RE NOT SERIOUS, DORIAN? YOU ARE ACTING?
ACTING! I LEAVE THAT TO YOU! YOU DO IT SO WELL!

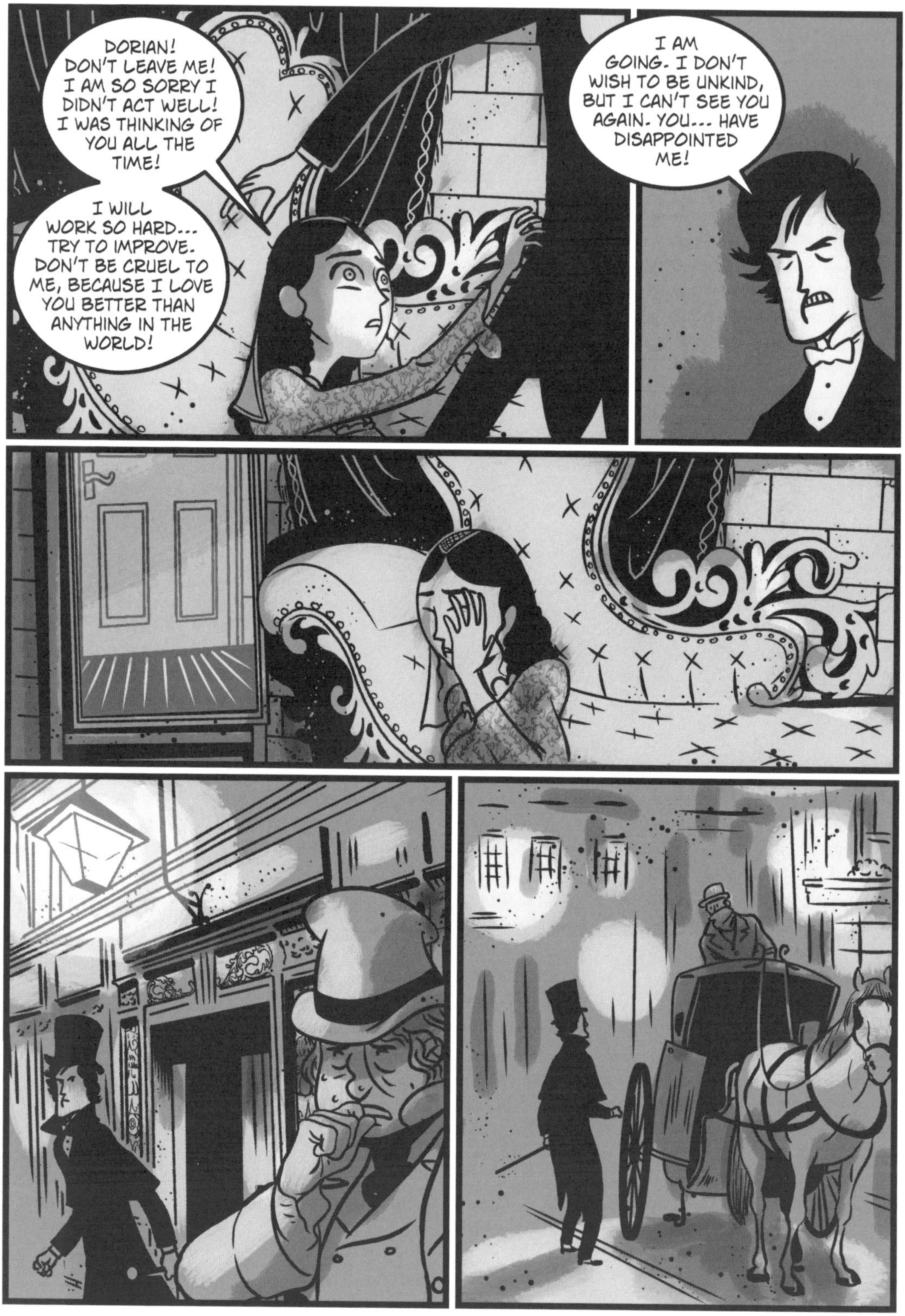
DORIAN! DON'T LEAVE ME! I AM SO SORRY I DIDN'T ACT WELL! I WAS THINKING OF YOU ALL THE TIME!
I WILL WORK SO HARD... TRY TO IMPROVE. DON'T BE CRUEL TO ME, BECAUSE I LOVE YOU BETTER THAN ANYTHING IN THE WORLD!
I AM GOING. I DON'T WISH TO BE UNKIND, BUT I CAN'T SEE YOU AGAIN. YOU... HAVE DISAPPOINTED ME!

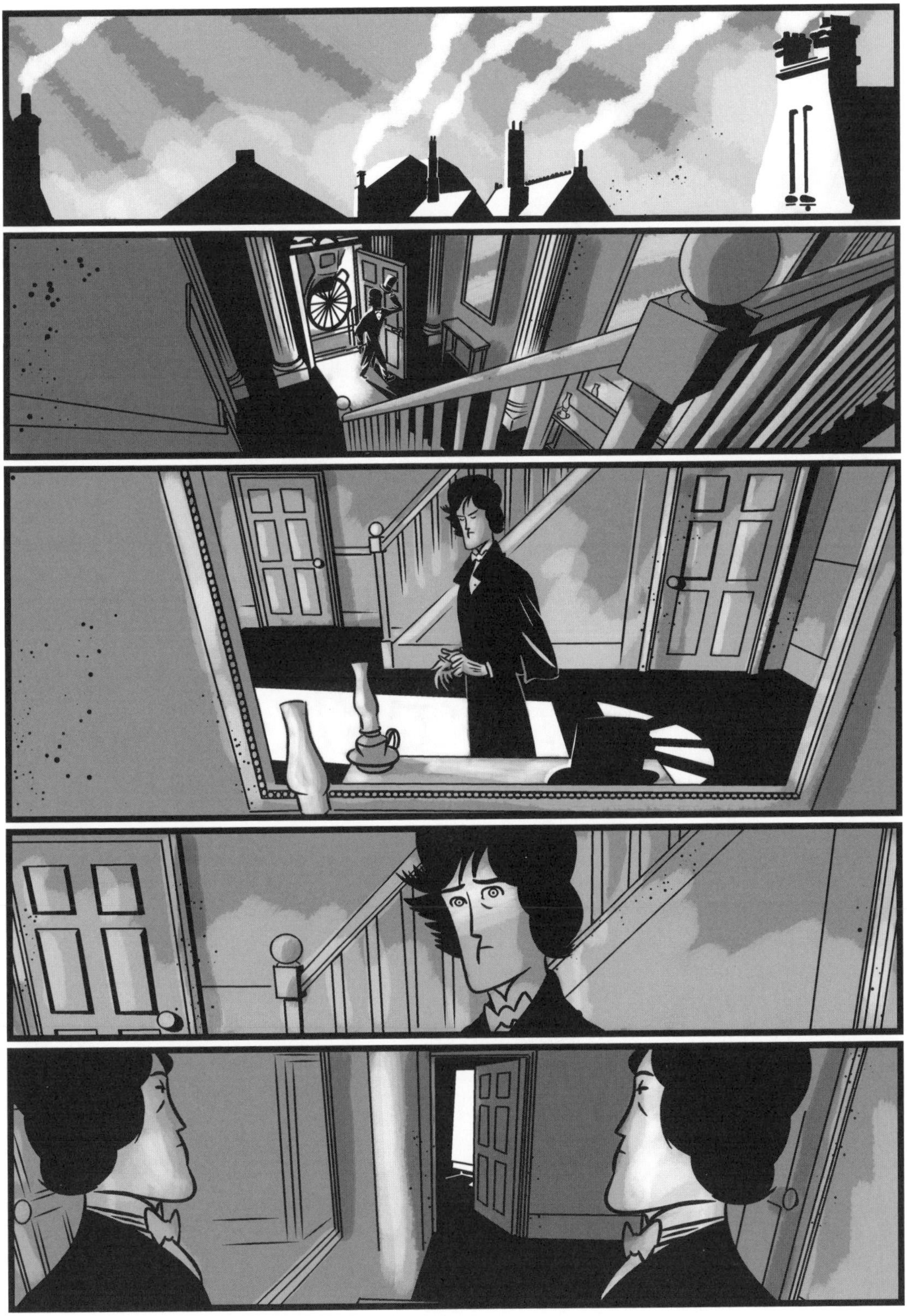

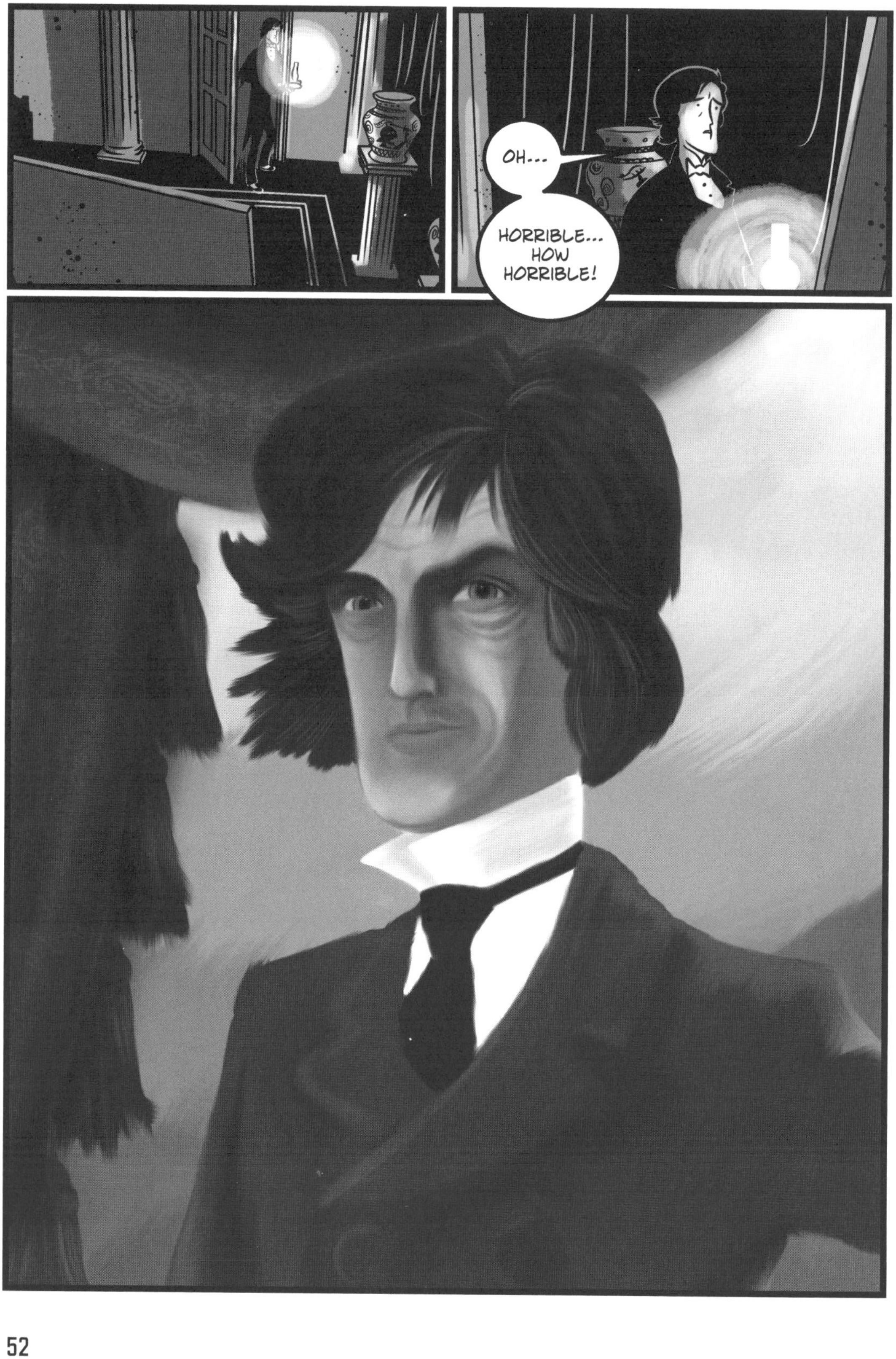
OH...
HORRIBLE... HOW HORRIBLE!

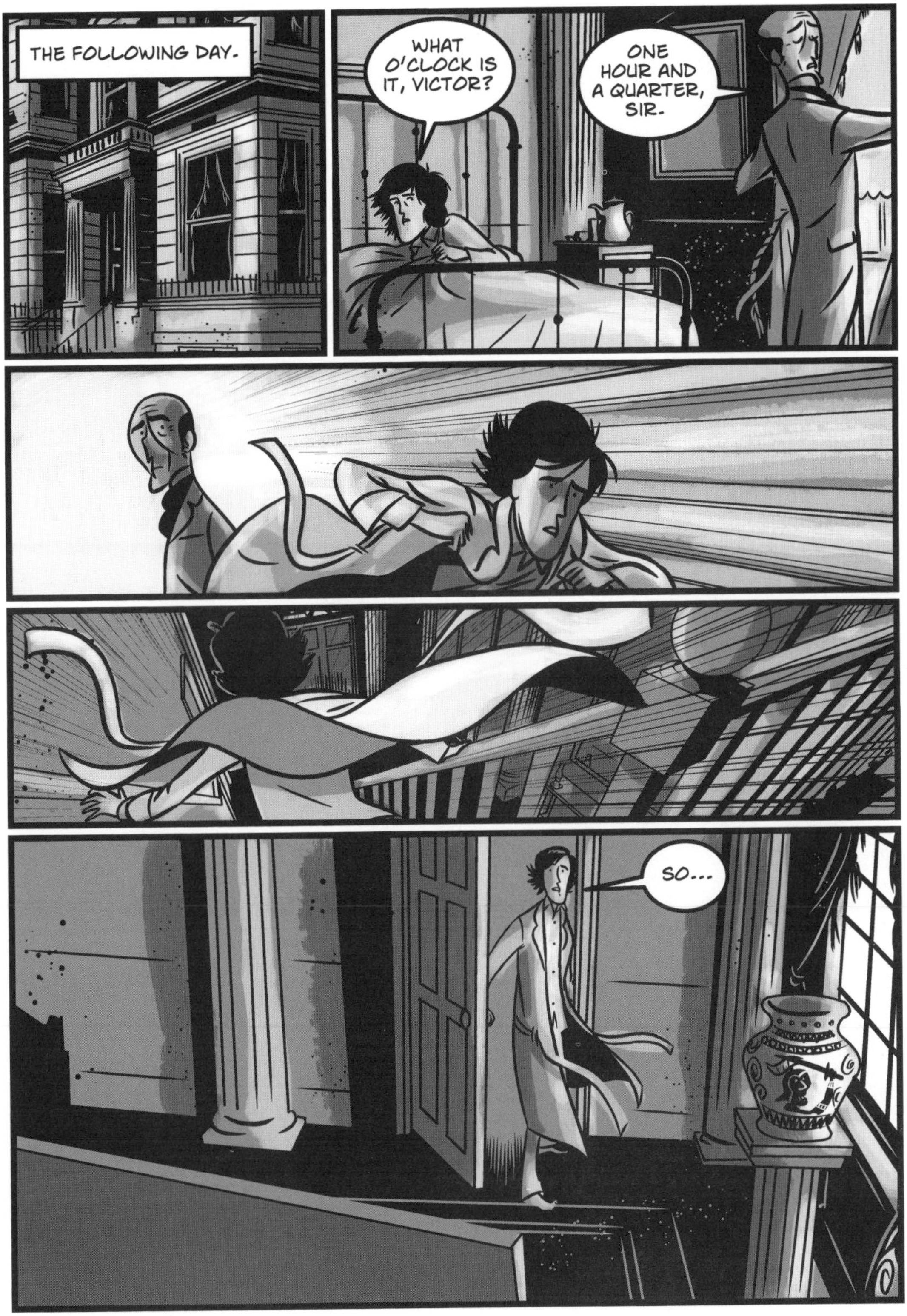
THE FOLLOWING DAY.
WHAT O'CLOCK IS IT, VICTOR?
ONE HOUR AND A QUARTER, SIR.
SO...

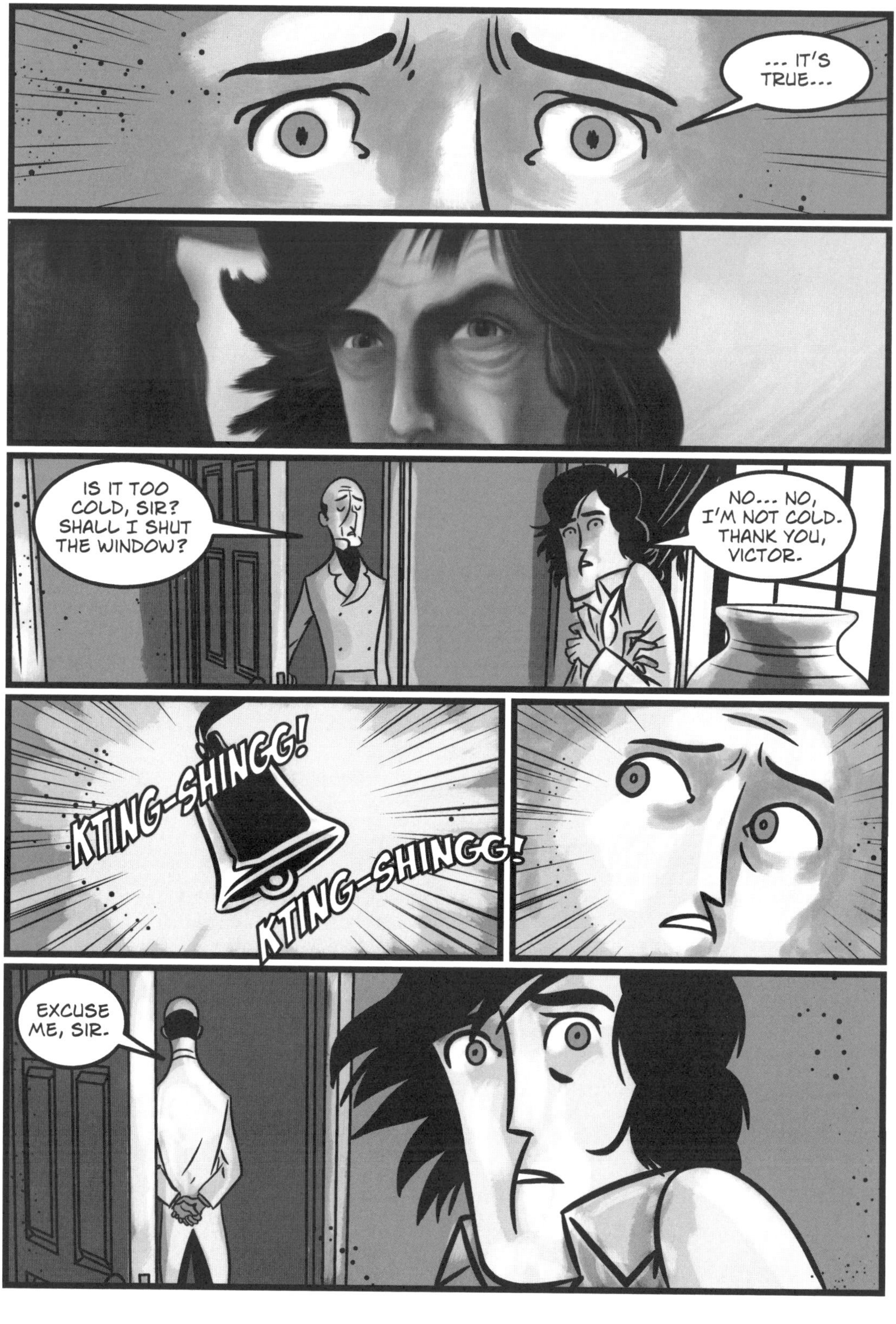
... IT'S TRUE...
IS IT TOO COLD, SIR? SHALL I SHUT THE WINDOW?
NO... NO, I'M NOT COLD. THANK YOU, VICTOR.
KTING-SHINGG!
KTING-SHINGG!
EXCUSE ME, SIR.

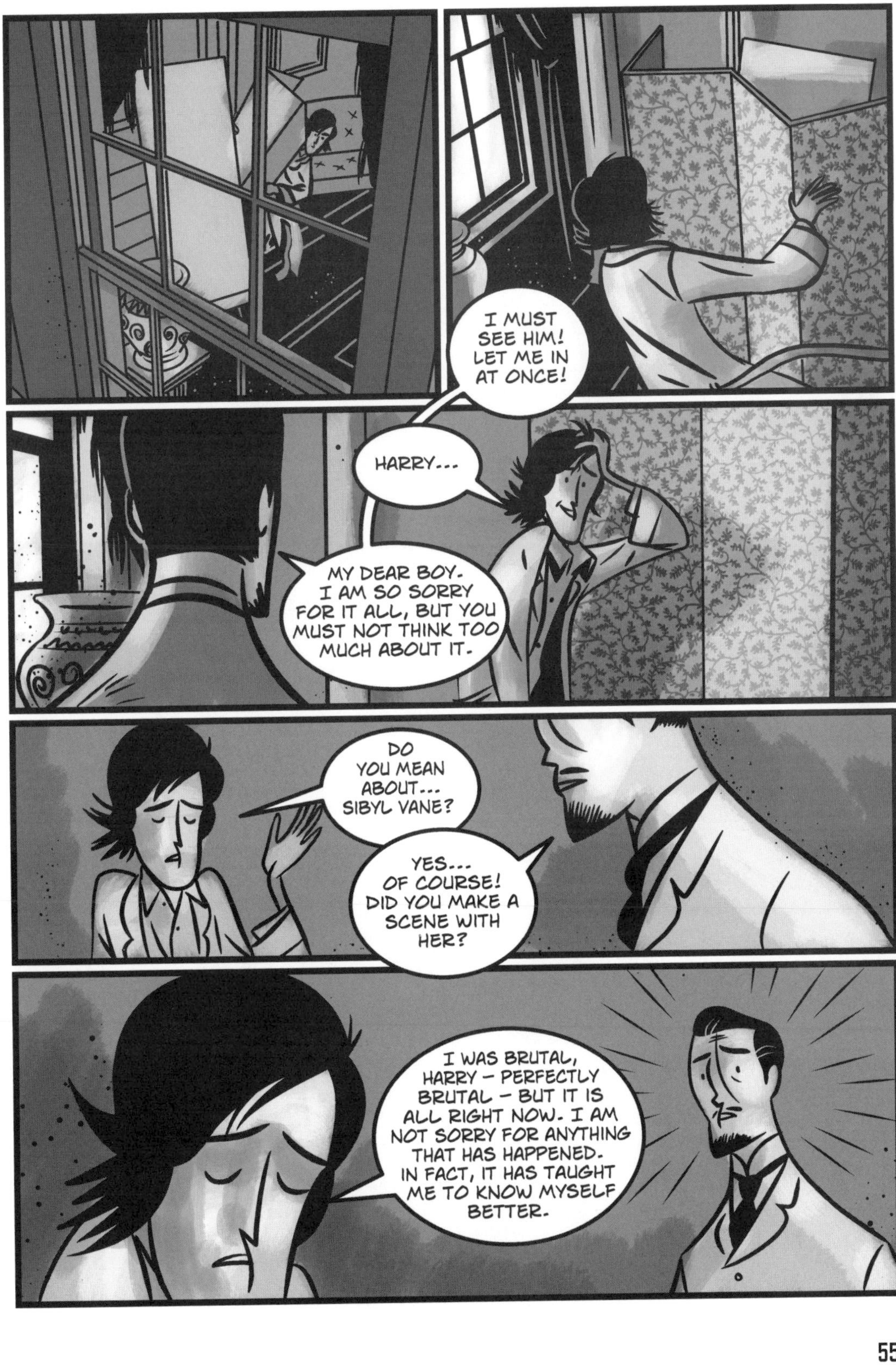
I MUST SEE HIM! LET ME IN AT ONCE!
HARRY...
MY DEAR BOY. I AM SO SORRY FOR IT ALL, BUT YOU MUST NOT THINK TOO MUCH ABOUT IT.
DO YOU MEAN ABOUT... SIBYL VANE?
YES... OF COURSE! DID YOU MAKE A SCENE WITH HER?
I WAS BRUTAL, HARRY – PERFECTLY BRUTAL – BUT IT IS ALL RIGHT NOW. I AM NOT SORRY FOR ANYTHING THAT HAS HAPPENED. IN FACT, IT HAS TAUGHT ME TO KNOW MYSELF BETTER.

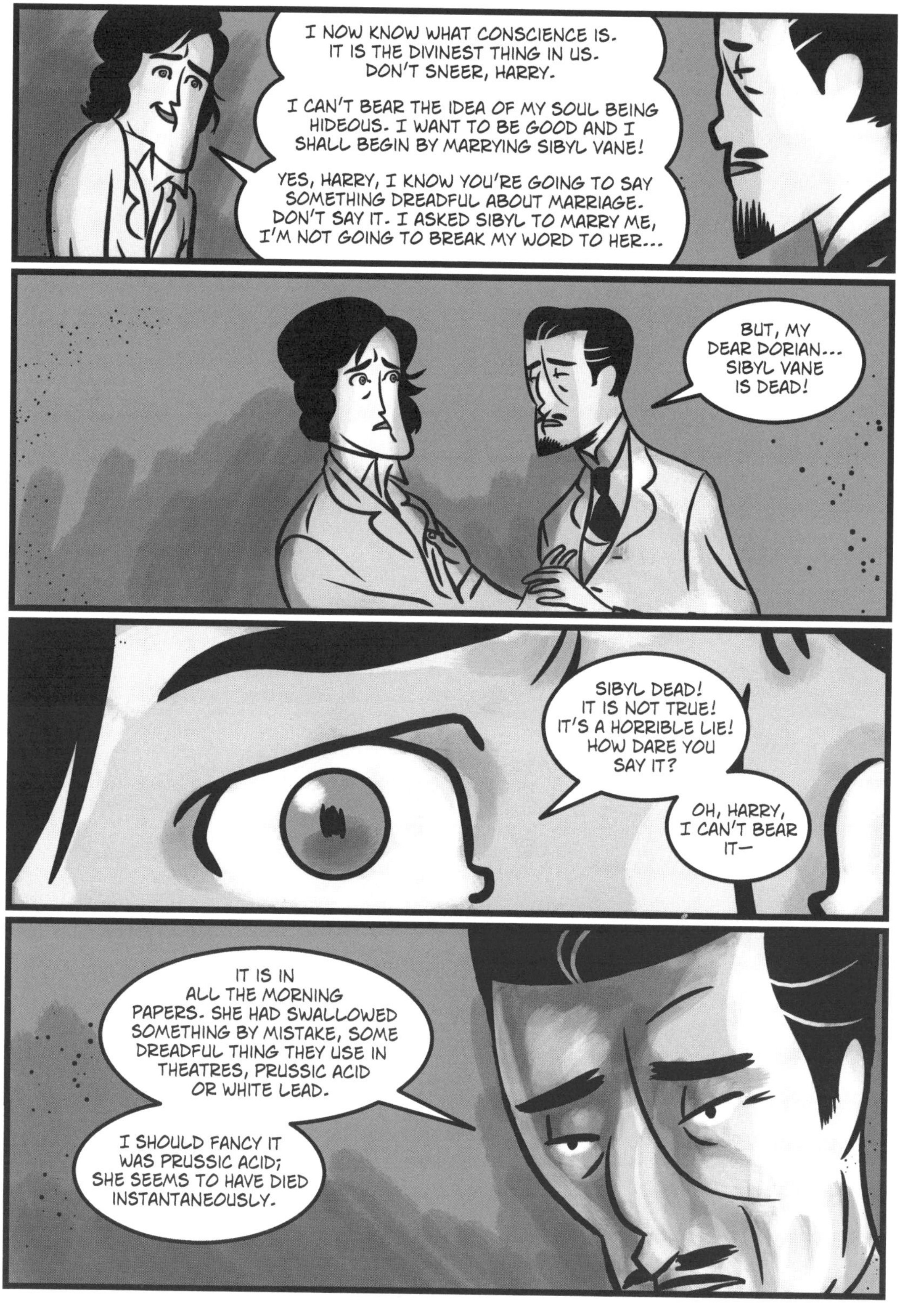
I NOW KNOW WHAT CONSCIENCE IS. IT IS THE DIVINEST THING IN US. DON'T SNEER, HARRY.
I CAN'T BEAR THE IDEA OF MY SOUL BEING HIDEOUS. I WANT TO BE GOOD AND I SHALL BEGIN BY MARRYING SIBYL VANE!
YES, HARRY, I KNOW YOU'RE GOING TO SAY SOMETHING DREADFUL ABOUT MARRIAGE. DON'T SAY IT. I ASKED SIBYL TO MARRY ME, I'M NOT GOING TO BREAK MY WORD TO HER...
BUT, MY DEAR DORIAN... SIBYL VANE IS DEAD!
SIBYL DEAD! IT IS NOT TRUE! IT'S A HORRIBLE LIE! HOW DARE YOU SAY IT?
OH, HARRY, I CAN'T BEAR IT—
IT IS IN ALL THE MORNING PAPERS. SHE HAD SWALLOWED SOMETHING BY MISTAKE, SOME DREADFUL THING THEY USE IN THEATRES, PRUSSIC ACID OR WHITE LEAD.
I SHOULD FANCY IT WAS PRUSSIC ACID; SHE SEEMS TO HAVE DIED INSTANTANEOUSLY.

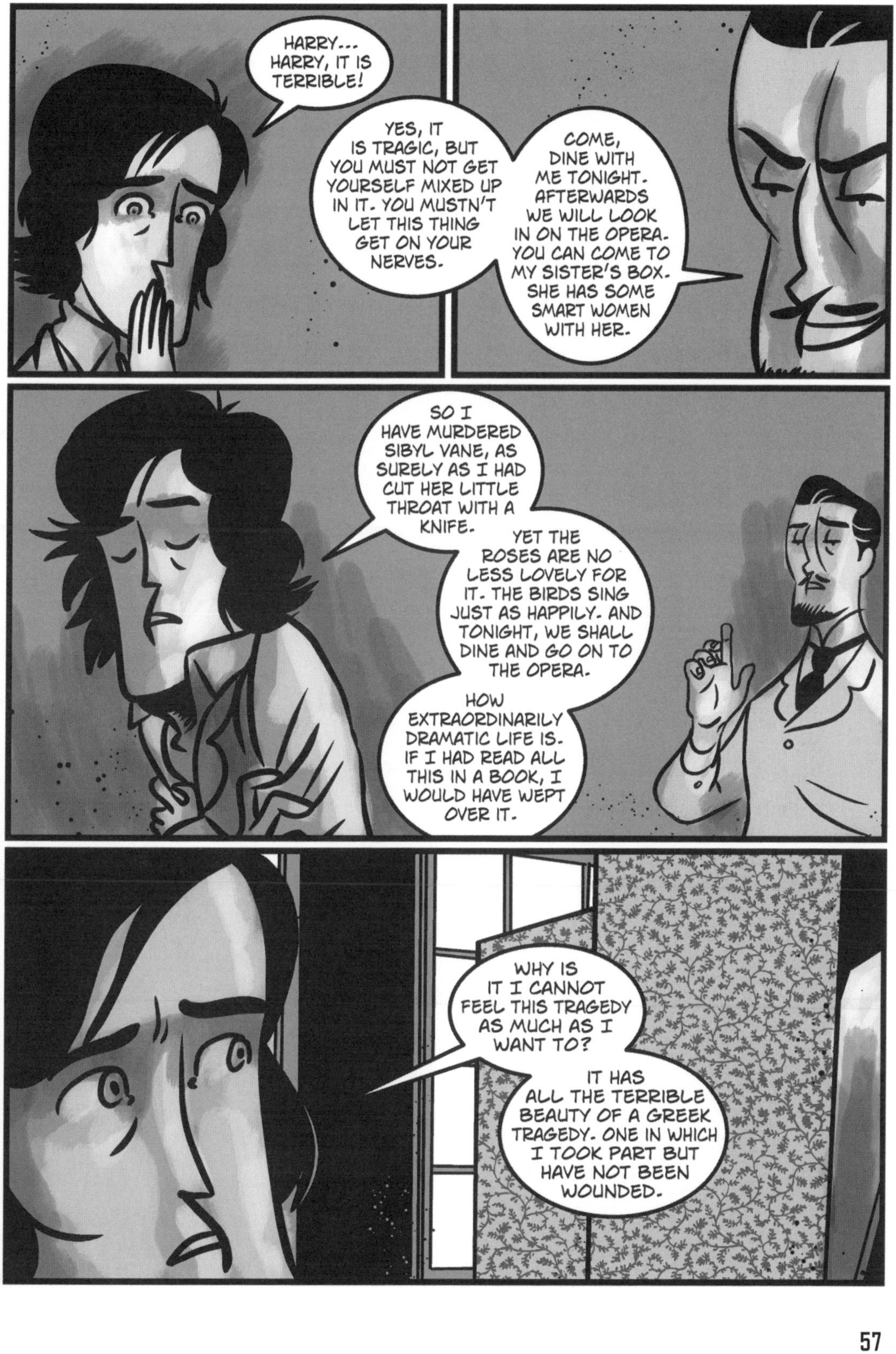
HARRY... HARRY, IT IS TERRIBLE!
YES, IT IS TRAGIC, BUT YOU MUST NOT GET YOURSELF MIXED UP IN IT. YOU MUSTN'T LET THIS THING GET ON YOUR NERVES.
COME, DINE WITH ME TONIGHT. AFTERWARDS WE WILL LOOK IN ON THE OPERA. YOU CAN COME TO MY SISTER'S BOX. SHE HAS SOME SMART WOMEN WITH HER.
SO I HAVE MURDERED SIBYL VANE, AS SURELY AS I HAD CUT HER LITTLE THROAT WITH A KNIFE.
YET THE ROSES ARE NO LESS LOVELY FOR IT. THE BIRDS SING JUST AS HAPPILY. AND TONIGHT, WE SHALL DINE AND GO ON TO THE OPERA.
HOW EXTRAORDINARILY DRAMATIC LIFE IS. IF I HAD READ ALL THIS IN A BOOK, I WOULD HAVE WEPT OVER IT.
WHY IS IT I CANNOT FEEL THIS TRAGEDY AS MUCH AS I WANT TO?
IT HAS ALL THE TERRIBLE BEAUTY OF A GREEK TRAGEDY. ONE IN WHICH I TOOK PART BUT HAVE NOT BEEN WOUNDED.

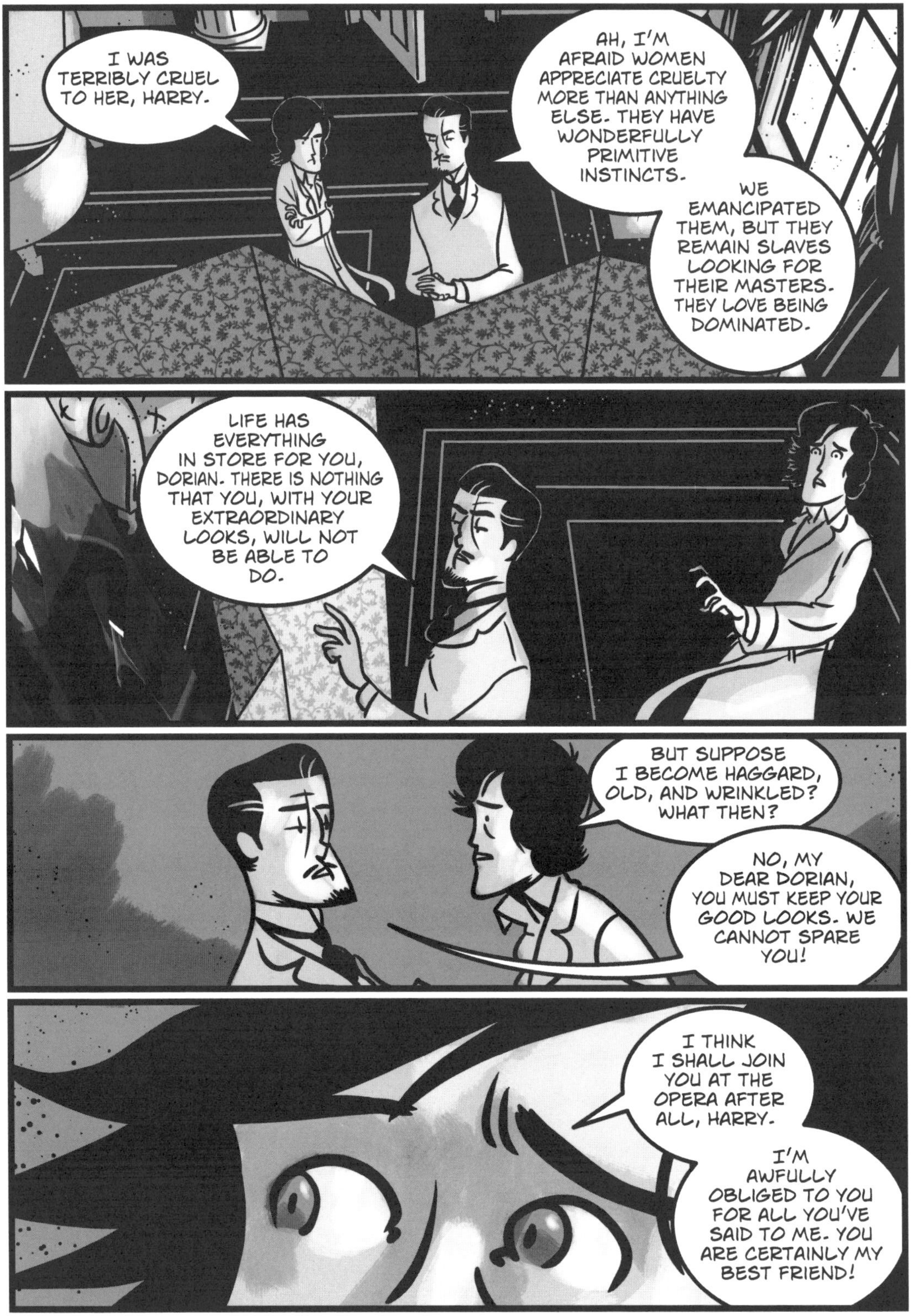
I WAS TERRIBLY CRUEL TO HER, HARRY.
AH, I'M AFRAID WOMEN APPRECIATE CRUELTY MORE THAN ANYTHING ELSE. THEY HAVE WONDERFULLY PRIMITIVE INSTINCTS.
WE EMANCIPATED THEM, BUT THEY REMAIN SLAVES LOOKING FOR THEIR MASTERS. THEY LOVE BEING DOMINATED.
LIFE HAS EVERYTHING IN STORE FOR YOU, DORIAN. THERE IS NOTHING THAT YOU, WITH YOUR EXTRAORDINARY LOOKS, WILL NOT BE ABLE TO DO.
BUT SUPPOSE I BECOME HAGGARD, OLD, AND WRINKLED? WHAT THEN?
NO, MY DEAR DORIAN, YOU MUST KEEP YOUR GOOD LOOKS. WE CANNOT SPARE YOU!
I THINK I SHALL JOIN YOU AT THE OPERA AFTER ALL, HARRY.
I'M AWFULLY OBLIGED TO YOU FOR ALL YOU'VE SAID TO ME. YOU ARE CERTAINLY MY BEST FRIEND!

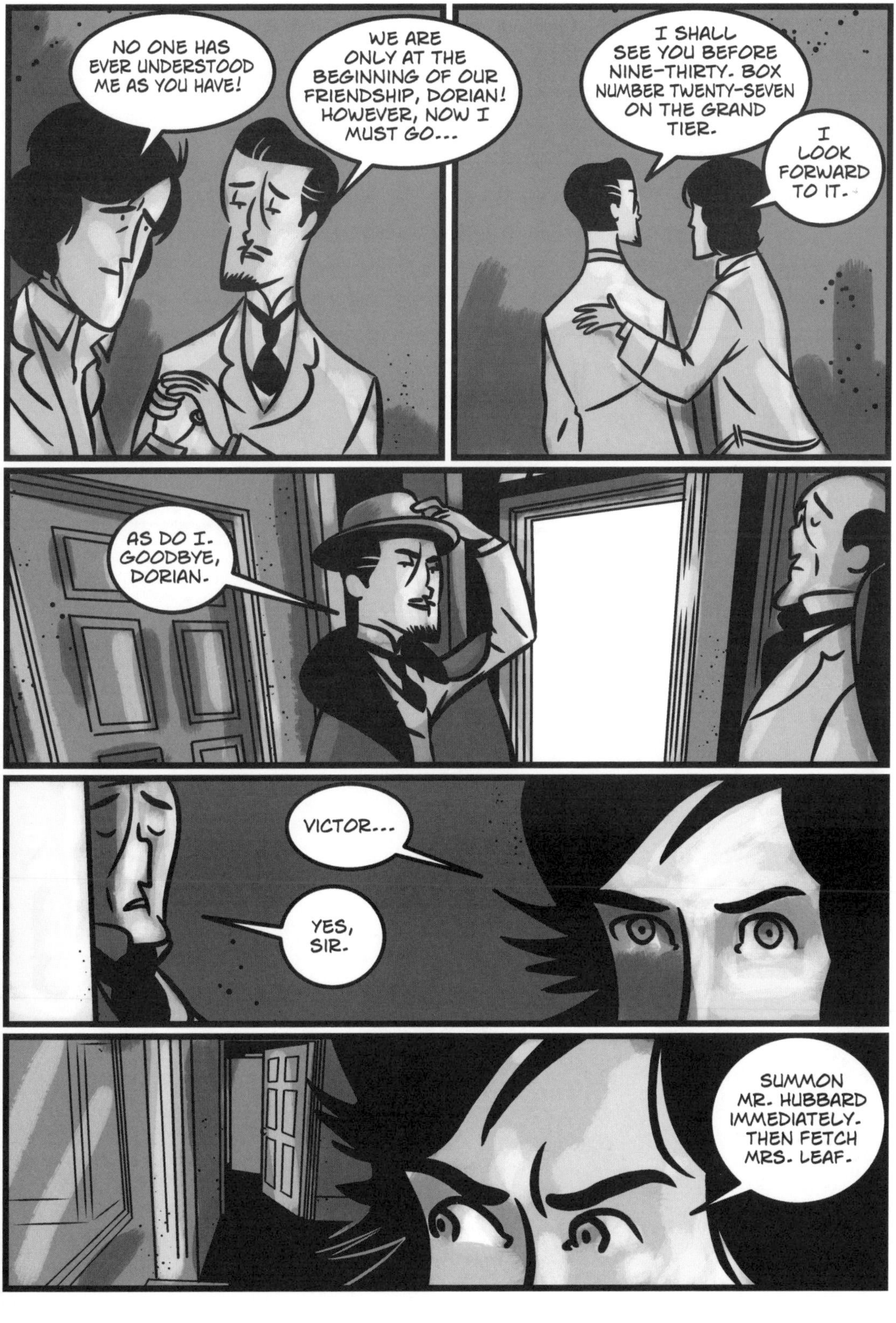
NO ONE HAS EVER UNDERSTOOD ME AS YOU HAVE!
WE ARE ONLY AT THE BEGINNING OF OUR FRIENDSHIP, DORIAN! HOWEVER, NOW I MUST GO...
I SHALL SEE YOU BEFORE NINE-THIRTY. BOX NUMBER TWENTY-SEVEN ON THE GRAND TIER.
I LOOK FORWARD TO IT.
AS DO I. GOODBYE, DORIAN.
VICTOR...
YES, SIR.
SUMMON MR. HUBBARD IMMEDIATELY. THEN FETCH MRS. LEAF.

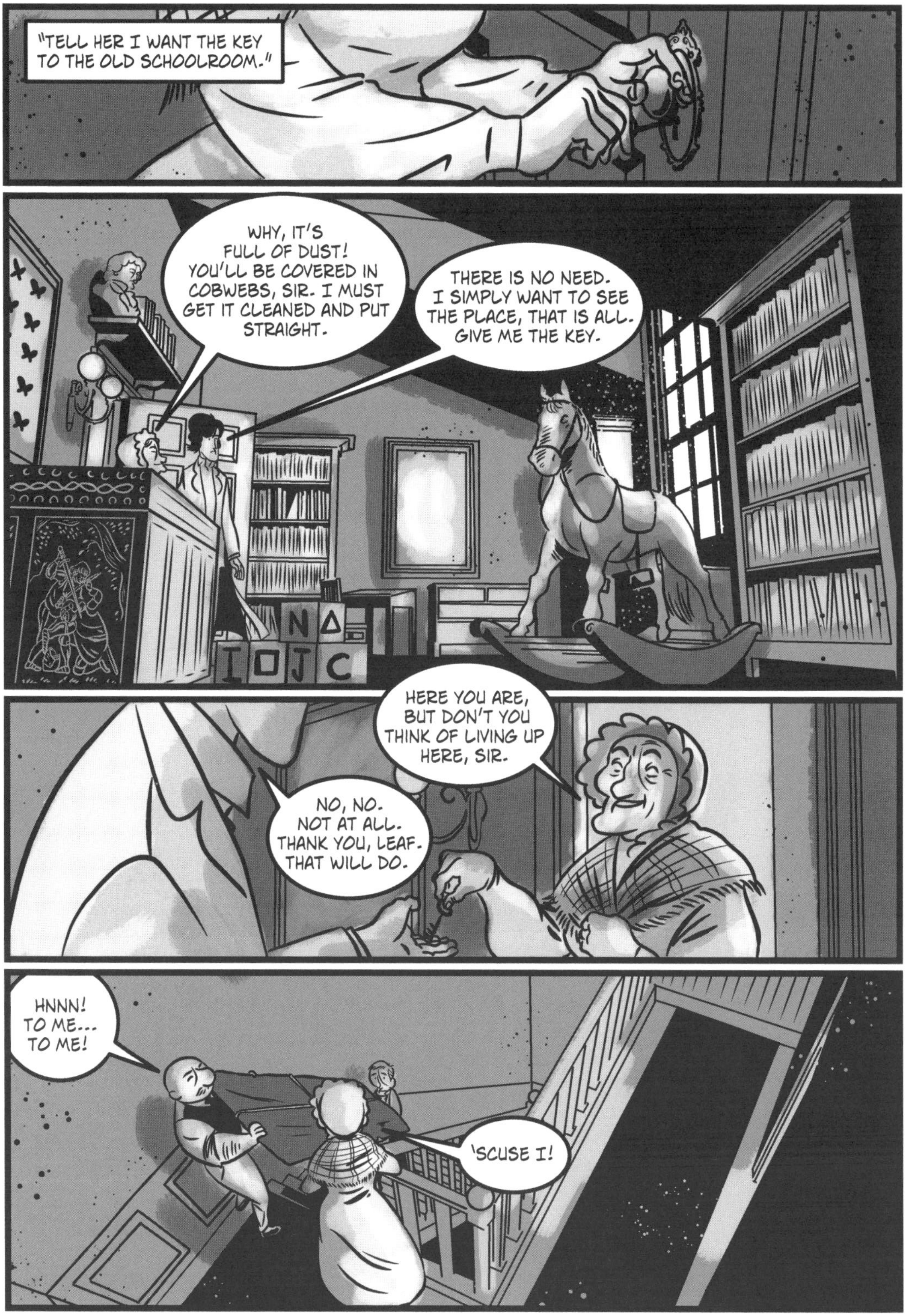
"TELL HER I WANT THE KEY TO THE OLD SCHOOLROOM."
WHY, IT'S FULL OF DUST! YOU'LL BE COVERED IN COBWEBS, SIR. I MUST GET IT CLEANED AND PUT STRAIGHT.
THERE IS NO NEED. I SIMPLY WANT TO SEE THE PLACE, THAT IS ALL. GIVE ME THE KEY.
HERE YOU ARE, BUT DON'T YOU THINK OF LIVING UP HERE, SIR.
NO, NO. NOT AT ALL. THANK YOU, LEAF. THAT WILL DO.
HNNN! TO ME... TO ME!
'SCUSE I!

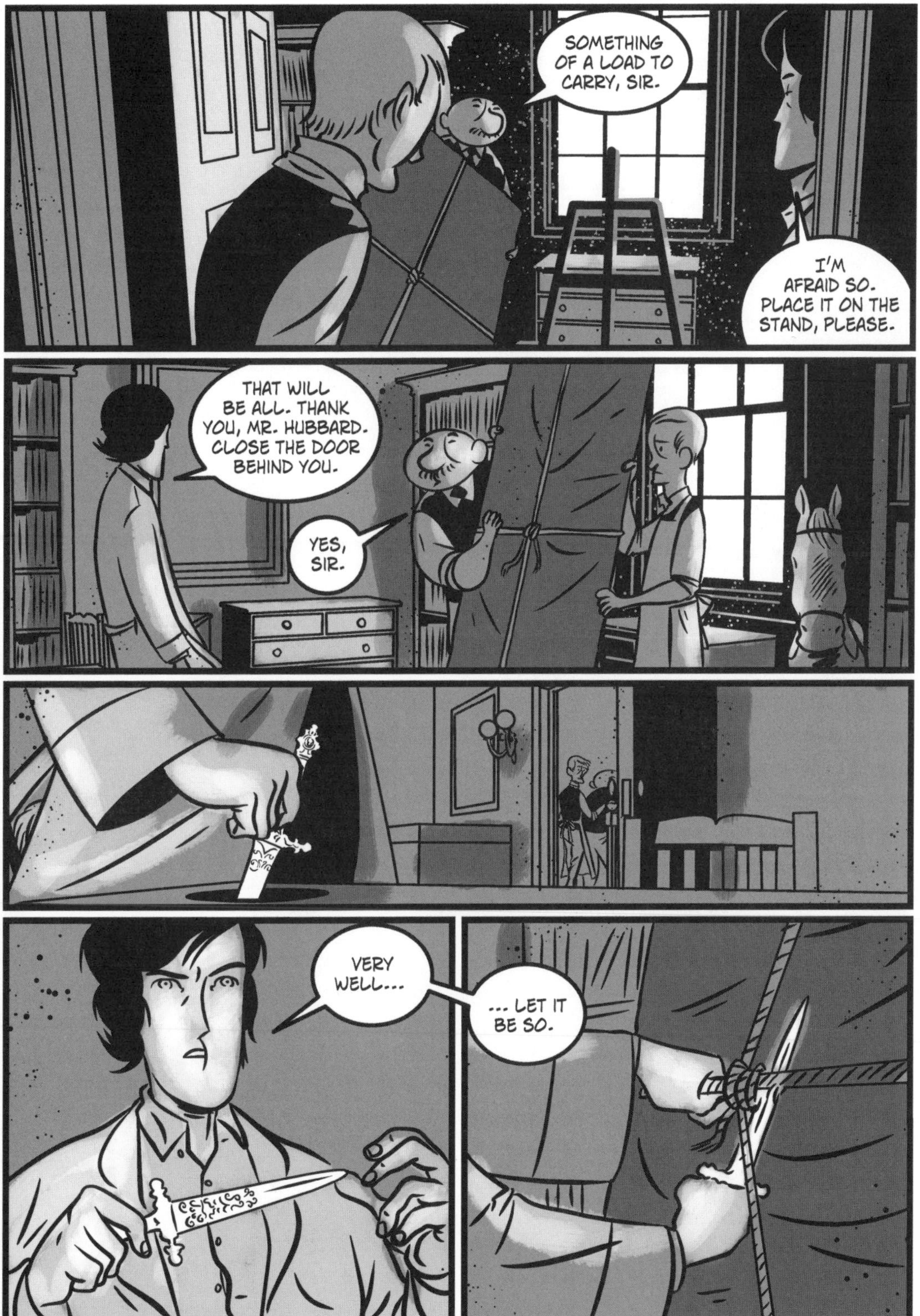
SOMETHING OF A LOAD TO CARRY, SIR.
I'M AFRAID SO. PLACE IT ON THE STAND, PLEASE.
THAT WILL BE ALL. THANK YOU, MR. HUBBARD. CLOSE THE DOOR BEHIND YOU.
YES, SIR.
VERY WELL...
... LET IT BE SO.

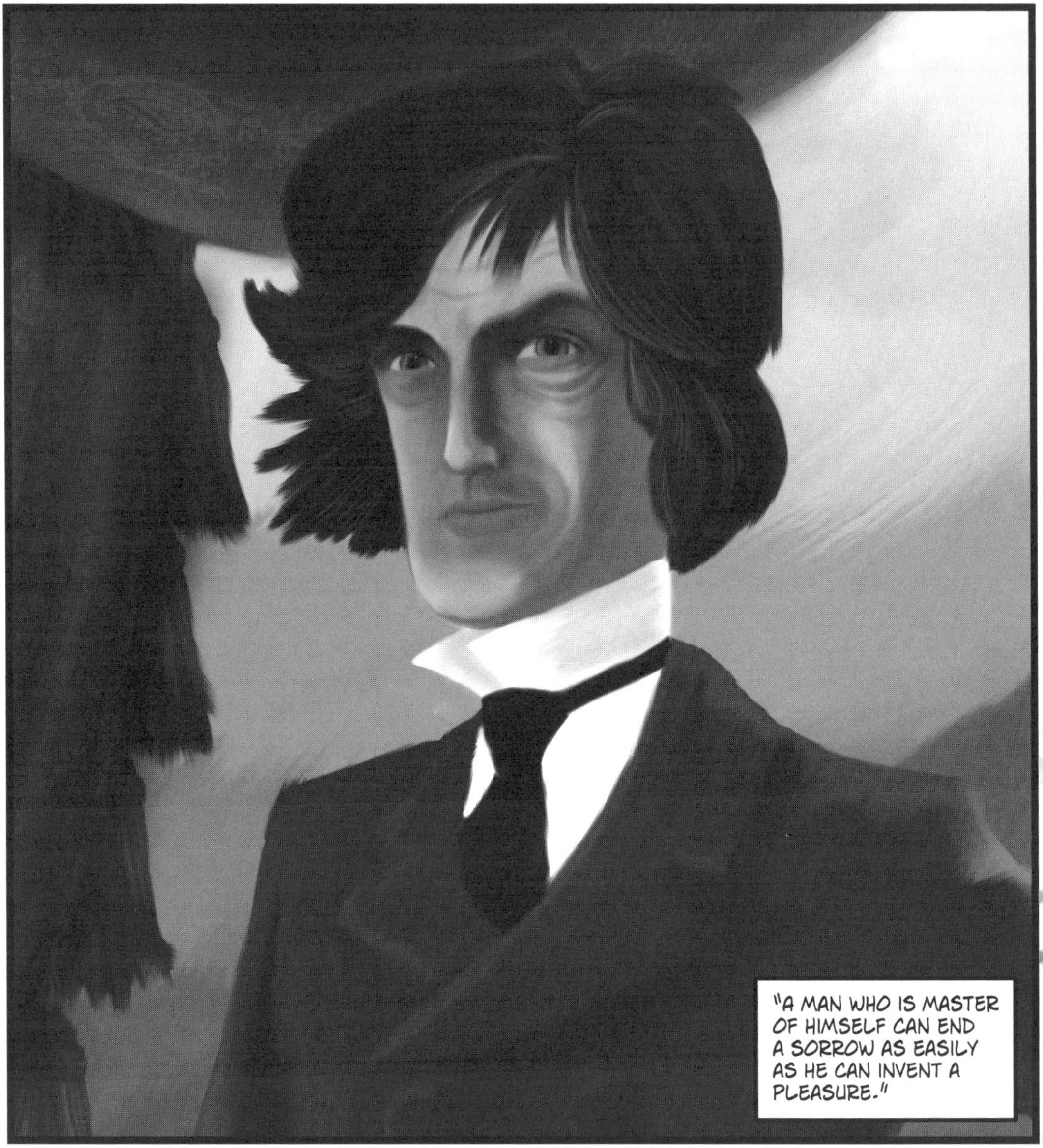
"A MAN WHO IS MASTER OF HIMSELF CAN END A SORROW AS EASILY AS HE CAN INVENT A PLEASURE."

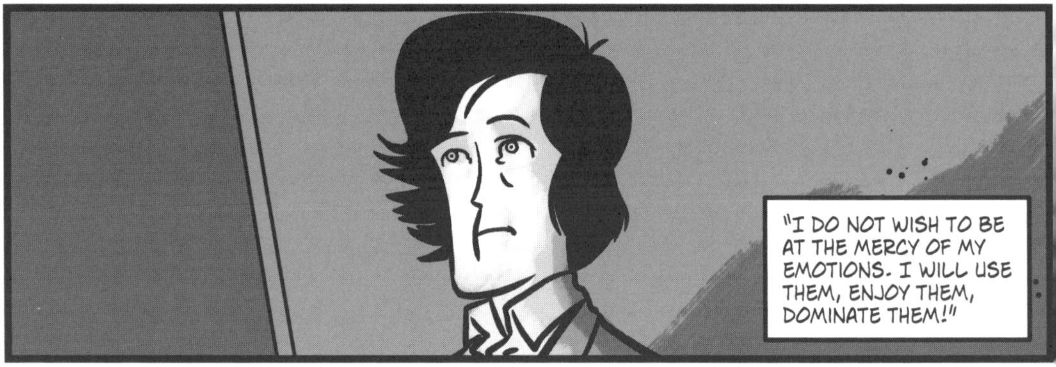
"I DO NOT WISH TO BE AT THE MERCY OF MY EMOTIONS. I WILL USE THEM, ENJOY THEM, DOMINATE THEM!"

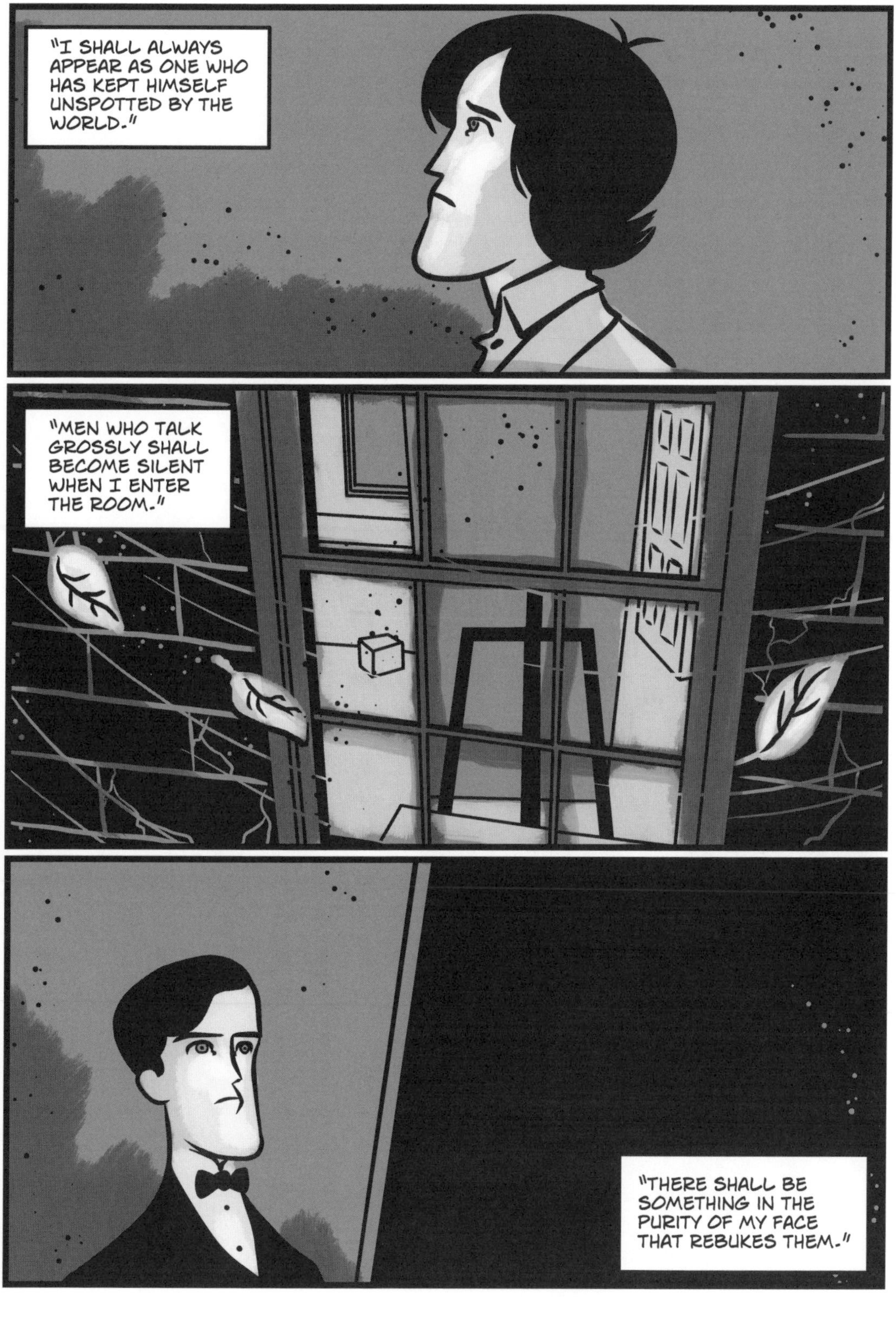
"I SHALL ALWAYS APPEAR AS ONE WHO HAS KEPT HIMSELF UNSPOTTED BY THE WORLD."
"MEN WHO TALK GROSSLY SHALL BECOME SILENT WHEN I ENTER THE ROOM."
"THERE SHALL BE SOMETHING IN THE PURITY OF MY FACE THAT REBUKES THEM."

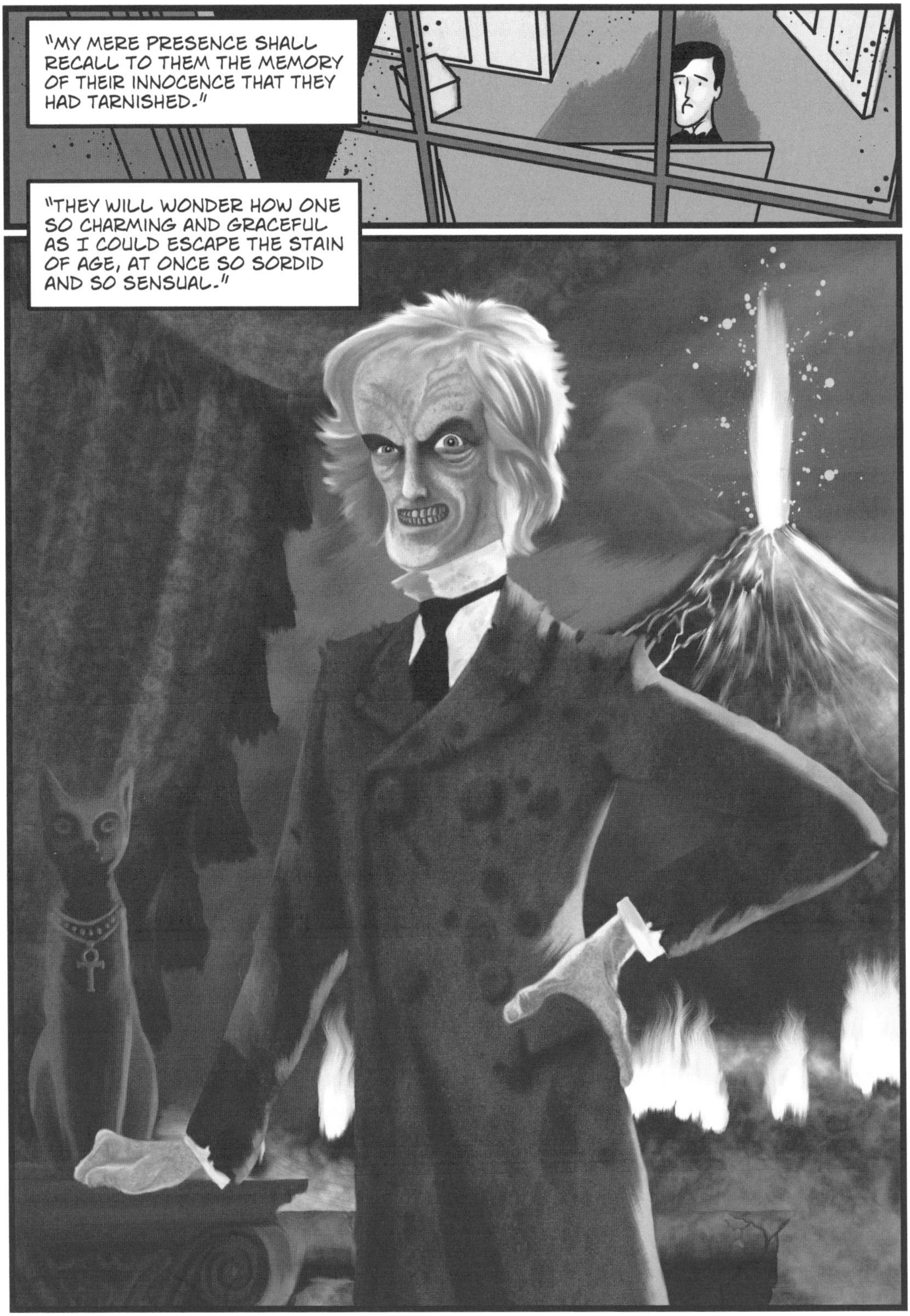
"MY MERE PRESENCE SHALL RECALL TO THEM THE MEMORY OF THEIR INNOCENCE THAT THEY HAD TARNISHED."
"THEY WILL WONDER HOW ONE SO CHARMING AND GRACEFUL AS I COULD ESCAPE THE STAIN OF AGE, AT ONCE SO SORDID AND SO SENSUAL."

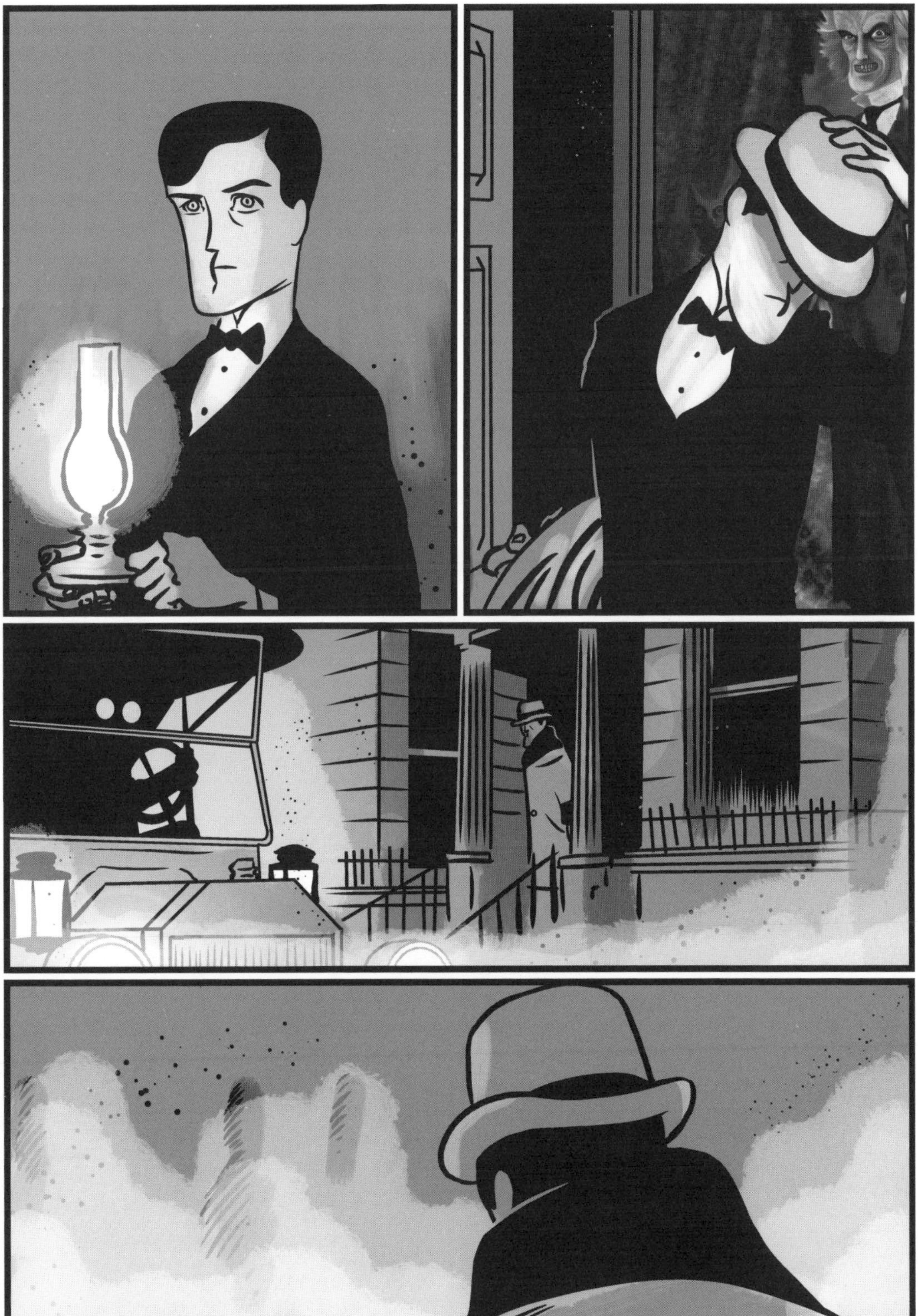

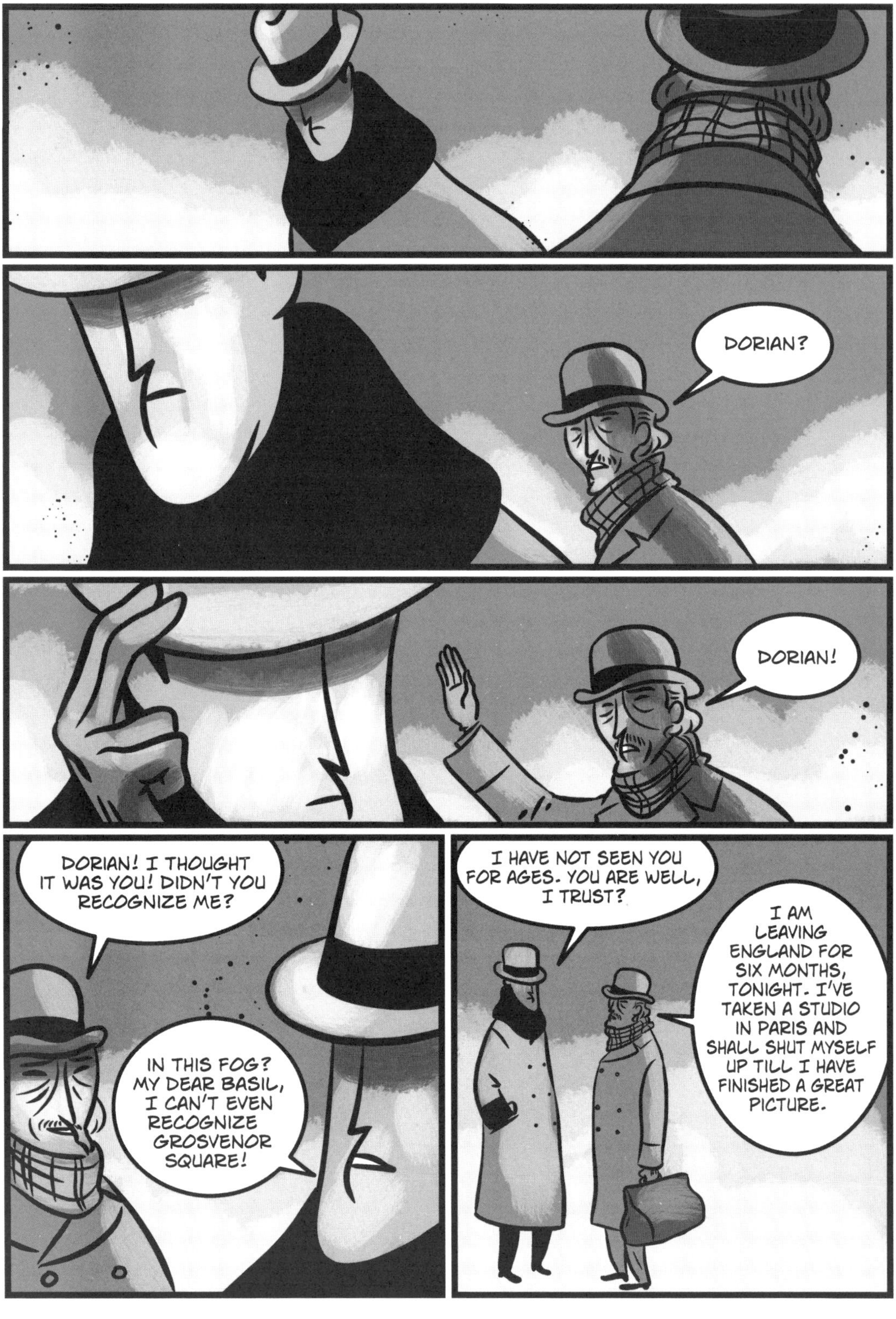
DORIAN?
DORIAN!
DORIAN! I THOUGHT IT WAS YOU! DIDN'T YOU RECOGNIZE ME?
IN THIS FOG? MY DEAR BASIL, I CAN'T EVEN RECOGNIZE GROSVENOR SQUARE!
I HAVE NOT SEEN YOU FOR AGES. YOU ARE WELL, I TRUST?
I AM LEAVING ENGLAND FOR SIX MONTHS, TONIGHT. I'VE TAKEN A STUDIO IN PARIS AND SHALL SHUT MYSELF UP TILL I HAVE FINISHED A GREAT PICTURE.

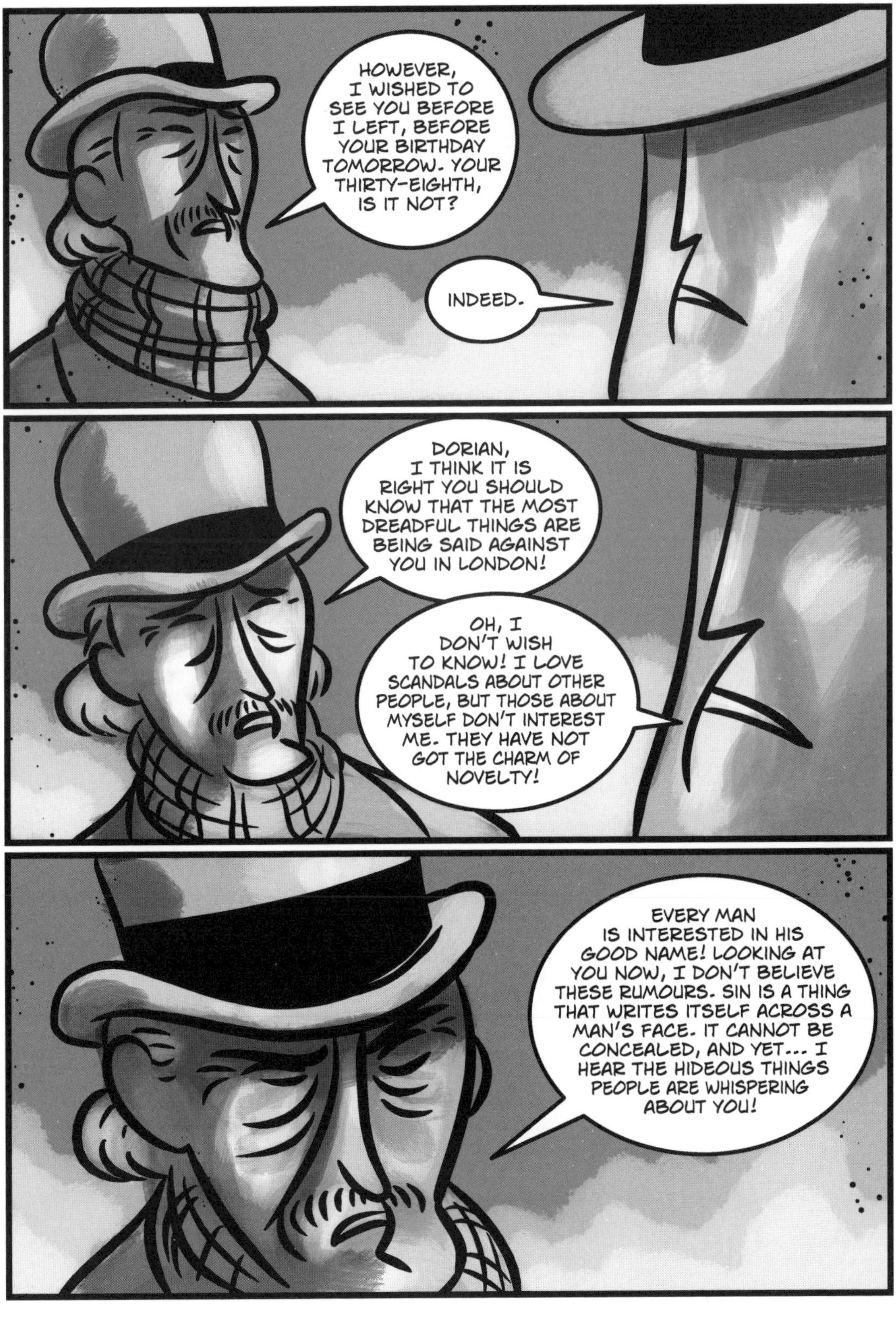
HOWEVER, I WISHED TO SEE YOU BEFORE I LEFT, BEFORE YOUR BIRTHDAY TOMORROW. YOUR THIRTY-EIGHTH, IS IT NOT?
INDEED.
DORIAN, I THINK IT IS RIGHT YOU SHOULD KNOW THAT THE MOST DREADFUL THINGS ARE BEING SAID AGAINST YOU IN LONDON!
OH, I DON'T WISH TO KNOW! I LOVE SCANDALS ABOUT OTHER PEOPLE, BUT THOSE ABOUT MYSELF DON'T INTEREST ME. THEY HAVE NOT GOT THE CHARM OF NOVELTY!
EVERY MAN IS INTERESTED IN HIS GOOD NAME! LOOKING AT YOU NOW, I DON'T BELIEVE THESE RUMOURS. SIN IS A THING THAT WRITES ITSELF ACROSS A MAN'S FACE. IT CANNOT BE CONCEALED, AND YET... I HEAR THE HIDEOUS THINGS PEOPLE ARE WHISPERING ABOUT YOU!

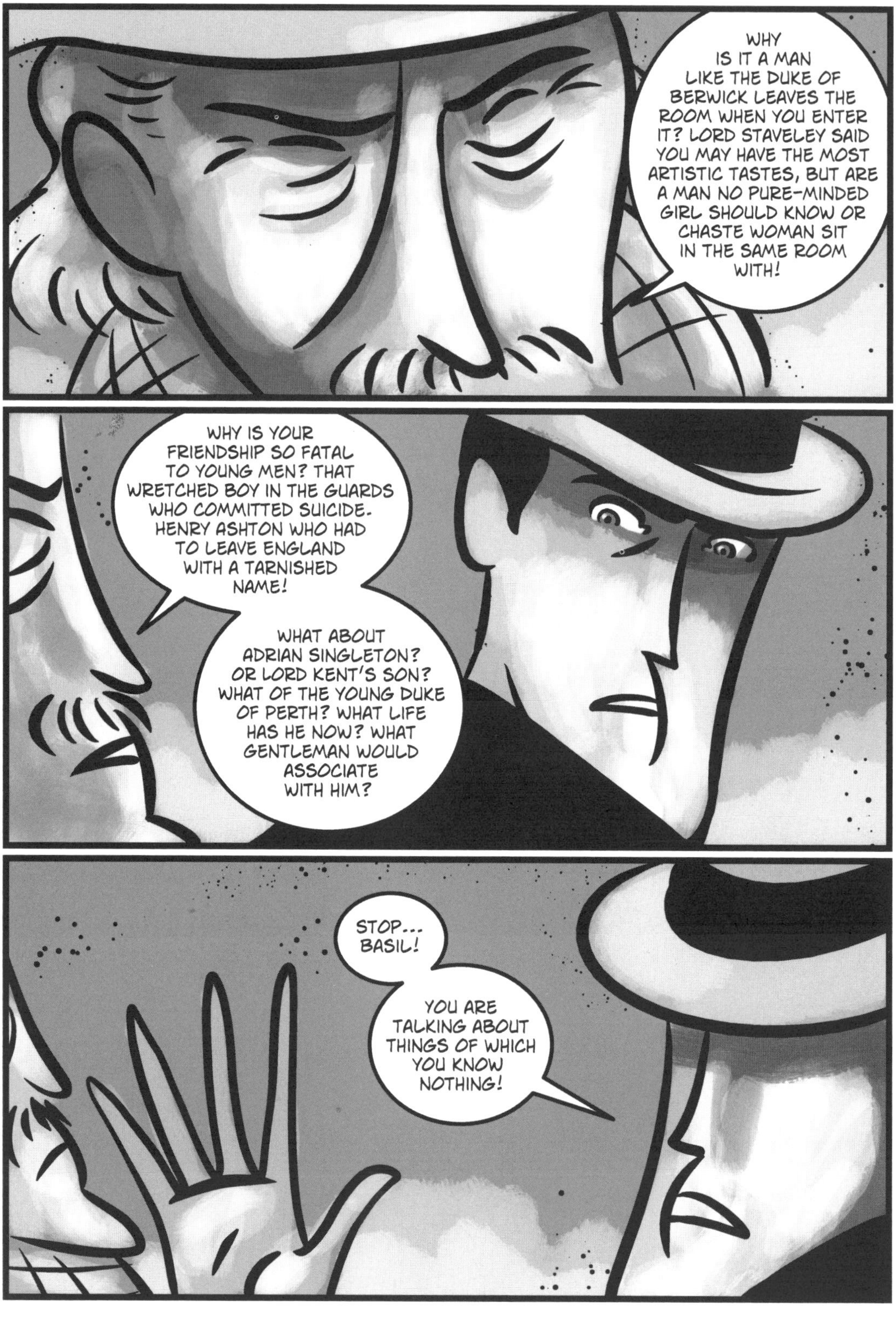
WHY IS IT A MAN LIKE THE DUKE OF BERWICK LEAVES THE ROOM WHEN YOU ENTER IT? LORD STAVELEY SAID YOU MAY HAVE THE MOST ARTISTIC TASTES, BUT ARE A MAN NO PURE-MINDED GIRL SHOULD KNOW OR CHASTE WOMAN SIT IN THE SAME ROOM WITH!
WHY IS YOUR FRIENDSHIP SO FATAL TO YOUNG MEN? THAT WRETCHED BOY IN THE GUARDS WHO COMMITTED SUICIDE. HENRY ASHTON WHO HAD TO LEAVE ENGLAND WITH A TARNISHED NAME!
WHAT ABOUT ADRIAN SINGLETON? OR LORD KENT'S SON? WHAT OF THE YOUNG DUKE OF PERTH? WHAT LIFE HAS HE NOW? WHAT GENTLEMAN WOULD ASSOCIATE WITH HIM?
STOP... BASIL!
YOU ARE TALKING ABOUT THINGS OF WHICH YOU KNOW NOTHING!

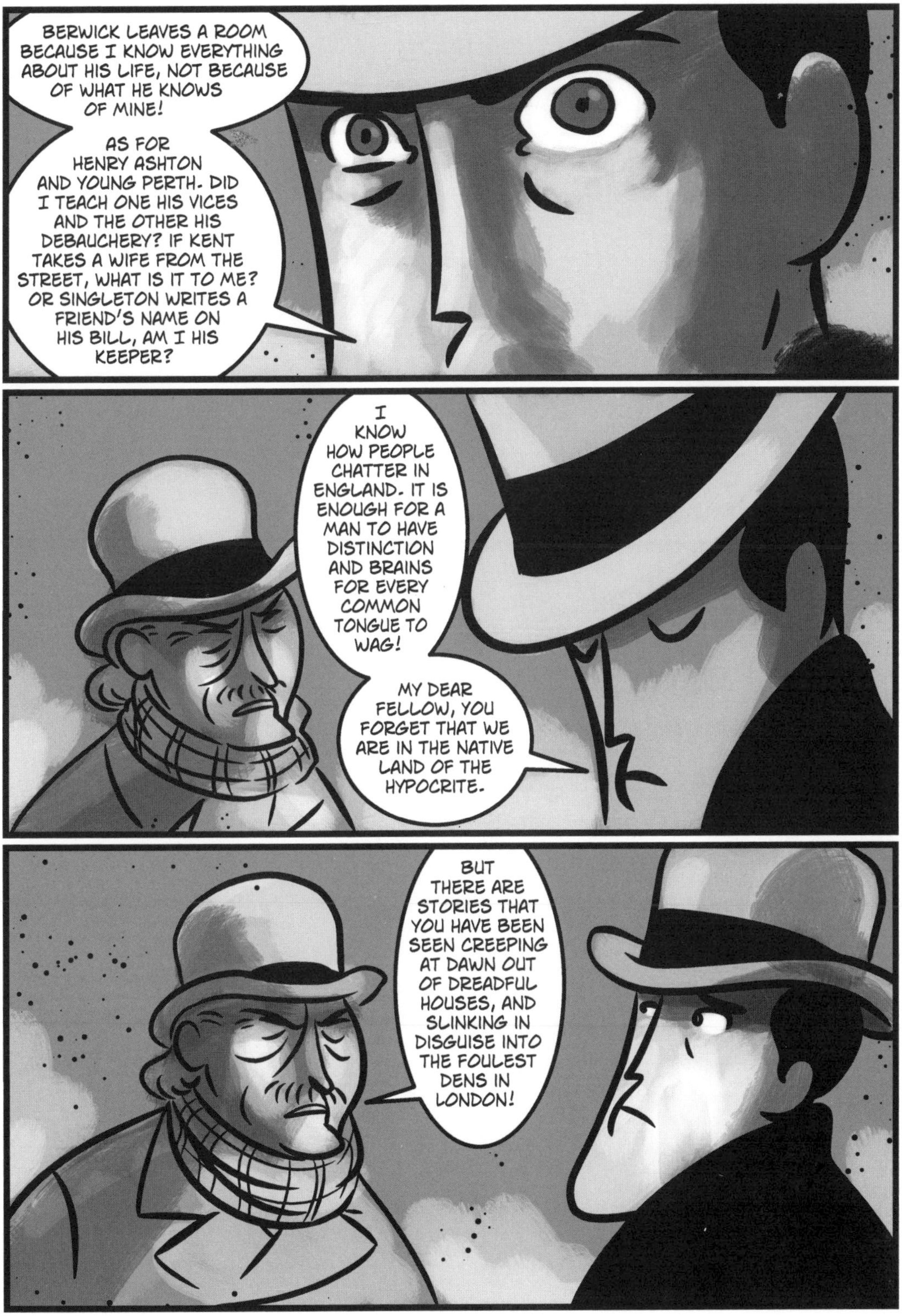
BERWICK LEAVES A ROOM BECAUSE I KNOW EVERYTHING ABOUT HIS LIFE, NOT BECAUSE OF WHAT HE KNOWS OF MINE!
AS FOR HENRY ASHTON AND YOUNG PERTH. DID I TEACH ONE HIS VICES AND THE OTHER HIS DEBAUCHERY? IF KENT TAKES A WIFE FROM THE STREET, WHAT IS IT TO ME? OR SINGLETON WRITES A FRIEND'S NAME ON HIS BILL, AM I HIS KEEPER?
I KNOW HOW PEOPLE CHATTER IN ENGLAND. IT IS ENOUGH FOR A MAN TO HAVE DISTINCTION AND BRAINS FOR EVERY COMMON TONGUE TO WAG!
MY DEAR FELLOW, YOU FORGET THAT WE ARE IN THE NATIVE LAND OF THE HYPOCRITE.
BUT THERE ARE STORIES THAT YOU HAVE BEEN SEEN CREEPING AT DAWN OUT OF DREADFUL HOUSES, AND SLINKING IN DISGUISE INTO THE FOULEST DENS IN LONDON!

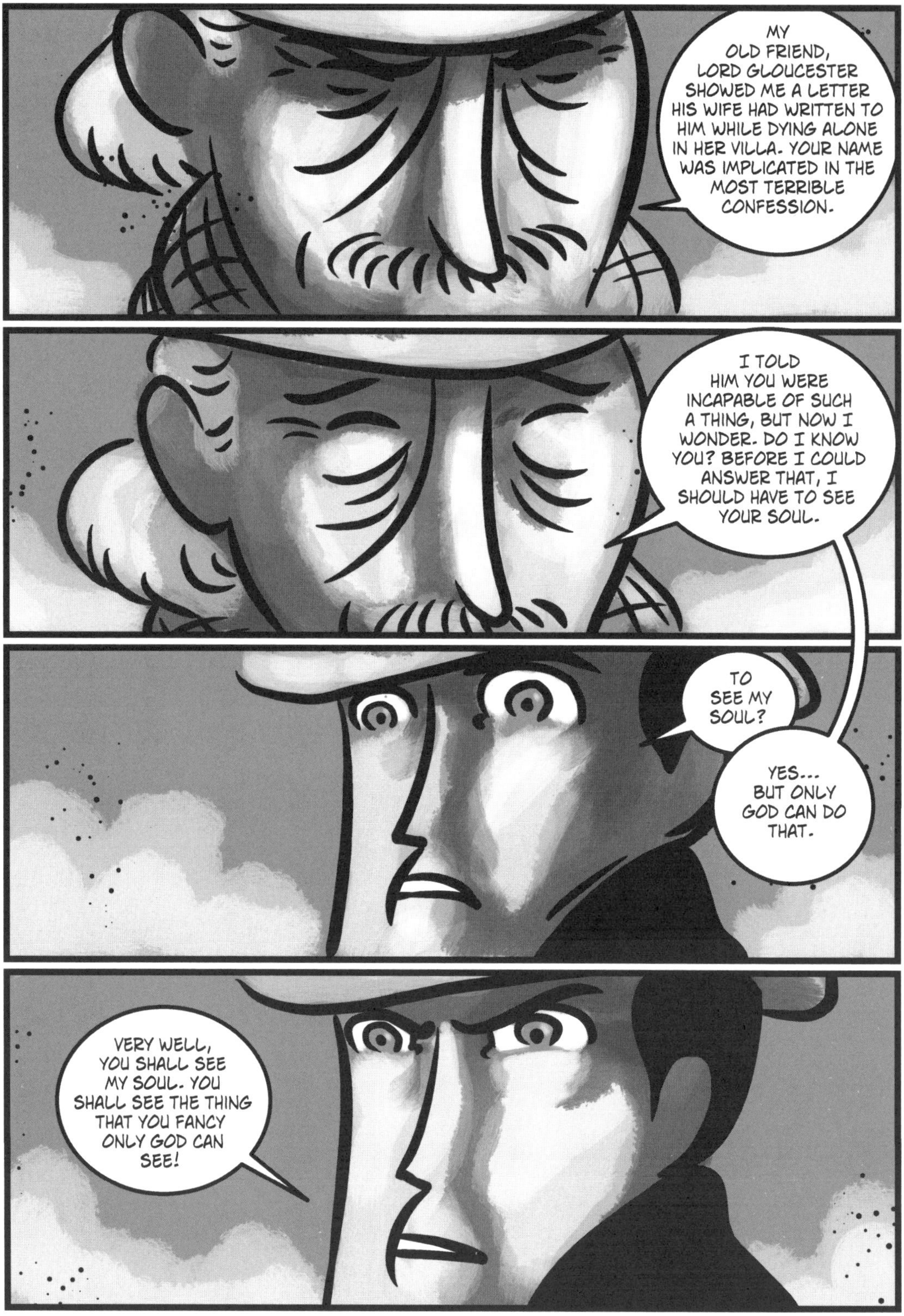
MY OLD FRIEND, LORD GLOUCESTER SHOWED ME A LETTER HIS WIFE HAD WRITTEN TO HIM WHILE DYING ALONE IN HER VILLA. YOUR NAME WAS IMPLICATED IN THE MOST TERRIBLE CONFESSION.
I TOLD HIM YOU WERE INCAPABLE OF SUCH A THING, BUT NOW I WONDER. DO I KNOW YOU? BEFORE I COULD ANSWER THAT, I SHOULD HAVE TO SEE YOUR SOUL.
TO SEE MY SOUL?
YES... BUT ONLY GOD CAN DO THAT.
VERY WELL, YOU SHALL SEE MY SOUL. YOU SHALL SEE THE THING THAT YOU FANCY ONLY GOD CAN SEE!

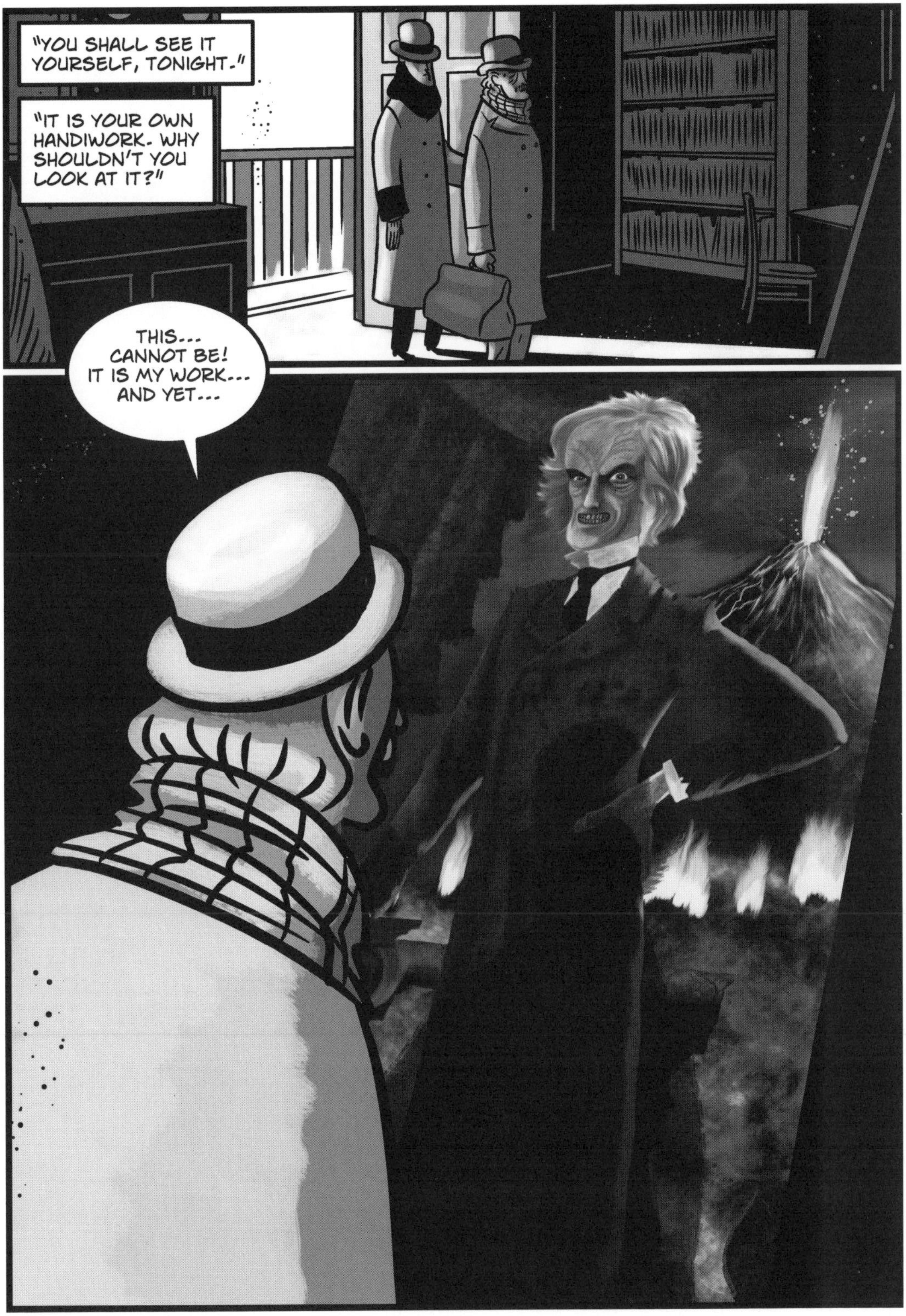
"YOU SHALL SEE IT YOURSELF, TONIGHT."
"IT IS YOUR OWN HANDIWORK. WHY SHOULDN'T YOU LOOK AT IT?"
THIS... CANNOT BE! IT IS MY WORK... AND YET...

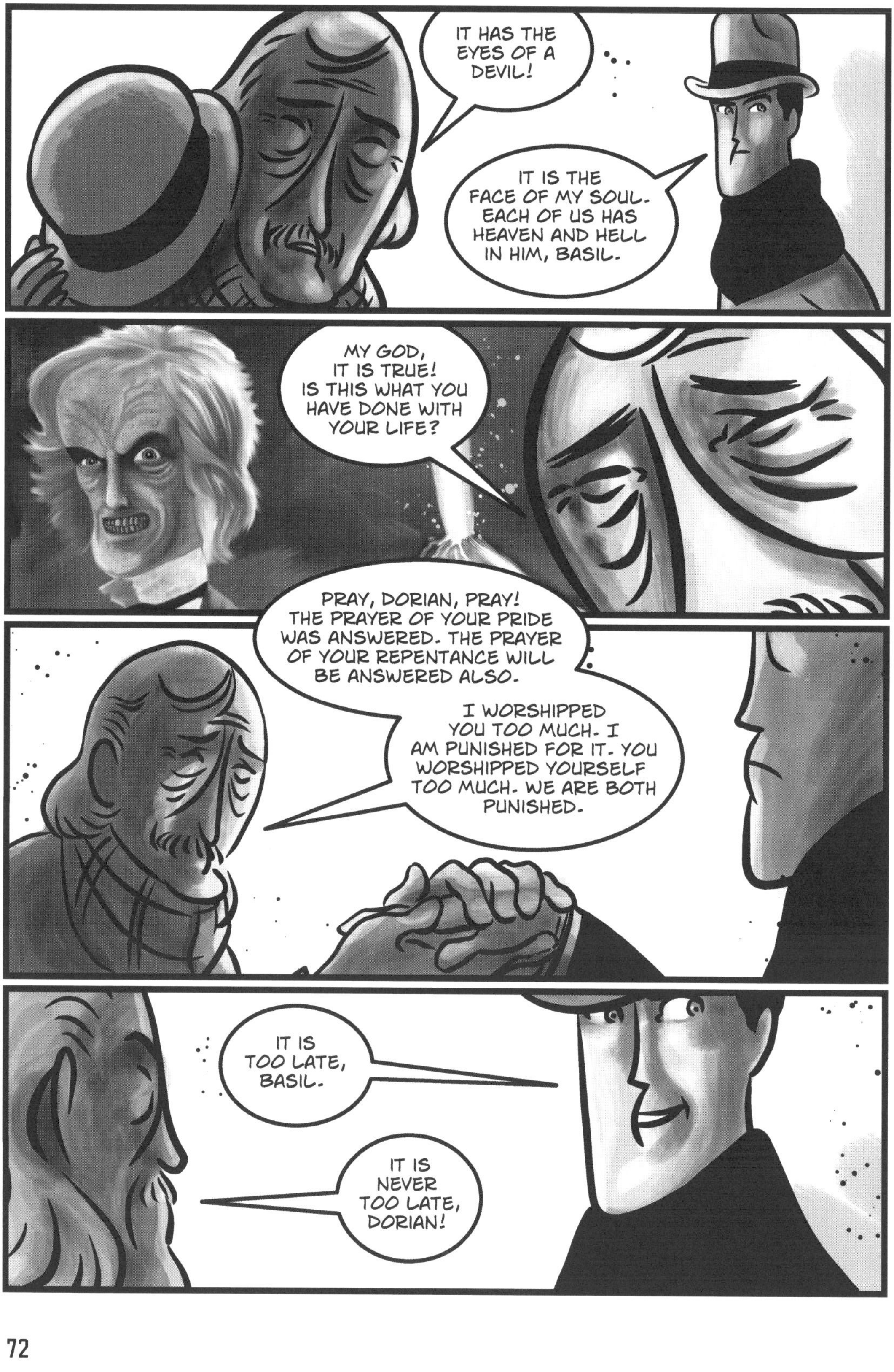
IT HAS THE EYES OF A DEVIL!
IT IS THE FACE OF MY SOUL. EACH OF US HAS HEAVEN AND HELL IN HIM, BASIL.
MY GOD, IT IS TRUE! IS THIS WHAT YOU HAVE DONE WITH YOUR LIFE?
PRAY, DORIAN, PRAY! THE PRAYER OF YOUR PRIDE WAS ANSWERED. THE PRAYER OF YOUR REPENTANCE WILL BE ANSWERED ALSO.
I WORSHIPPED YOU TOO MUCH. I AM PUNISHED FOR IT. YOU WORSHIPPED YOURSELF TOO MUCH. WE ARE BOTH PUNISHED.
IT IS TOO LATE, BASIL.
IT IS NEVER TOO LATE, DORIAN!

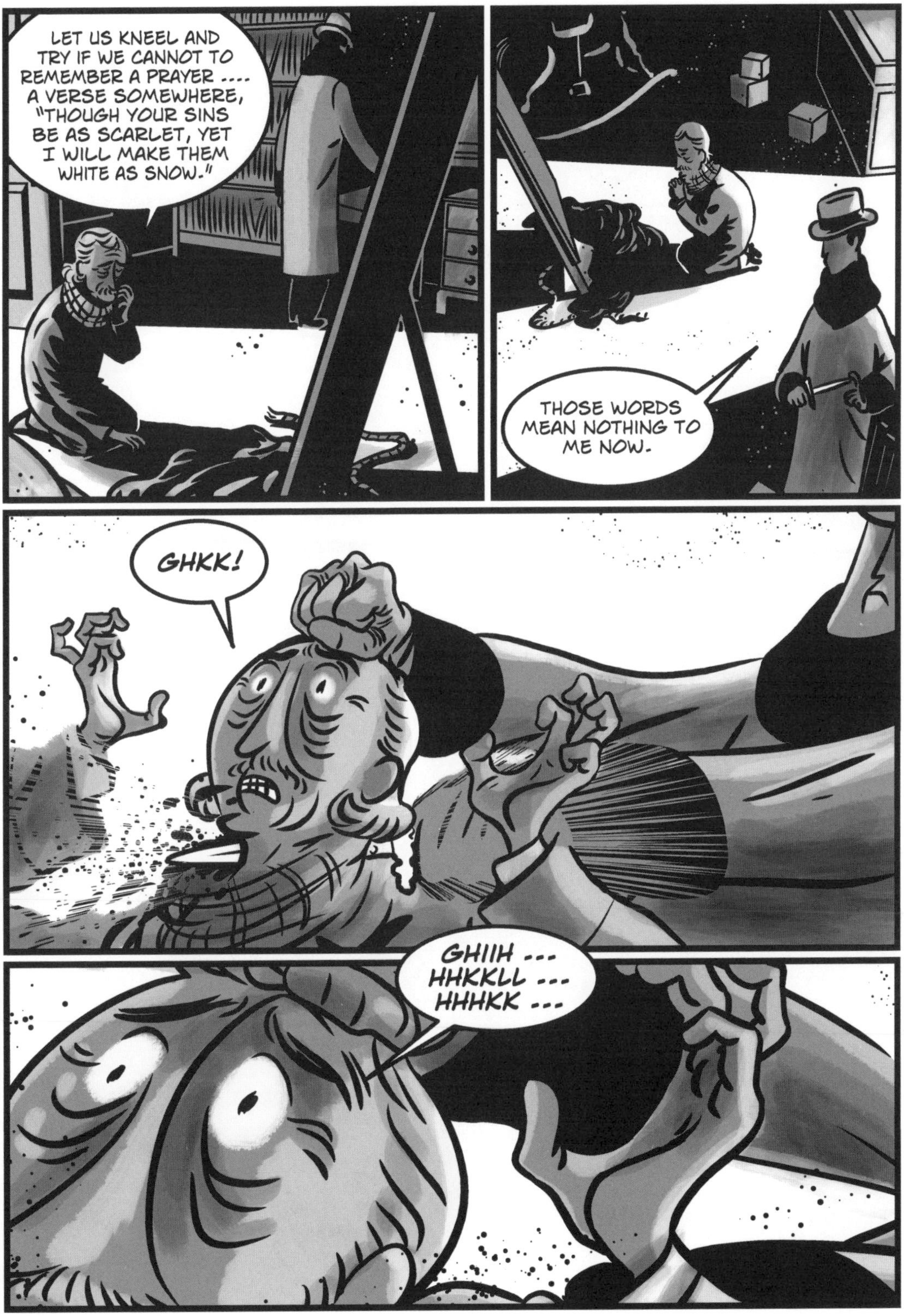
LET US KNEEL AND TRY IF WE CANNOT TO REMEMBER A PRAYER .... A VERSE SOMEWHERE, "THOUGH YOUR SINS BE AS SCARLET, YET I WILL MAKE THEM WHITE AS SNOW."
THOSE WORDS MEAN NOTHING TO ME NOW.
GHKK!
GHIIH ... HHKKLL ... HHHKK ...

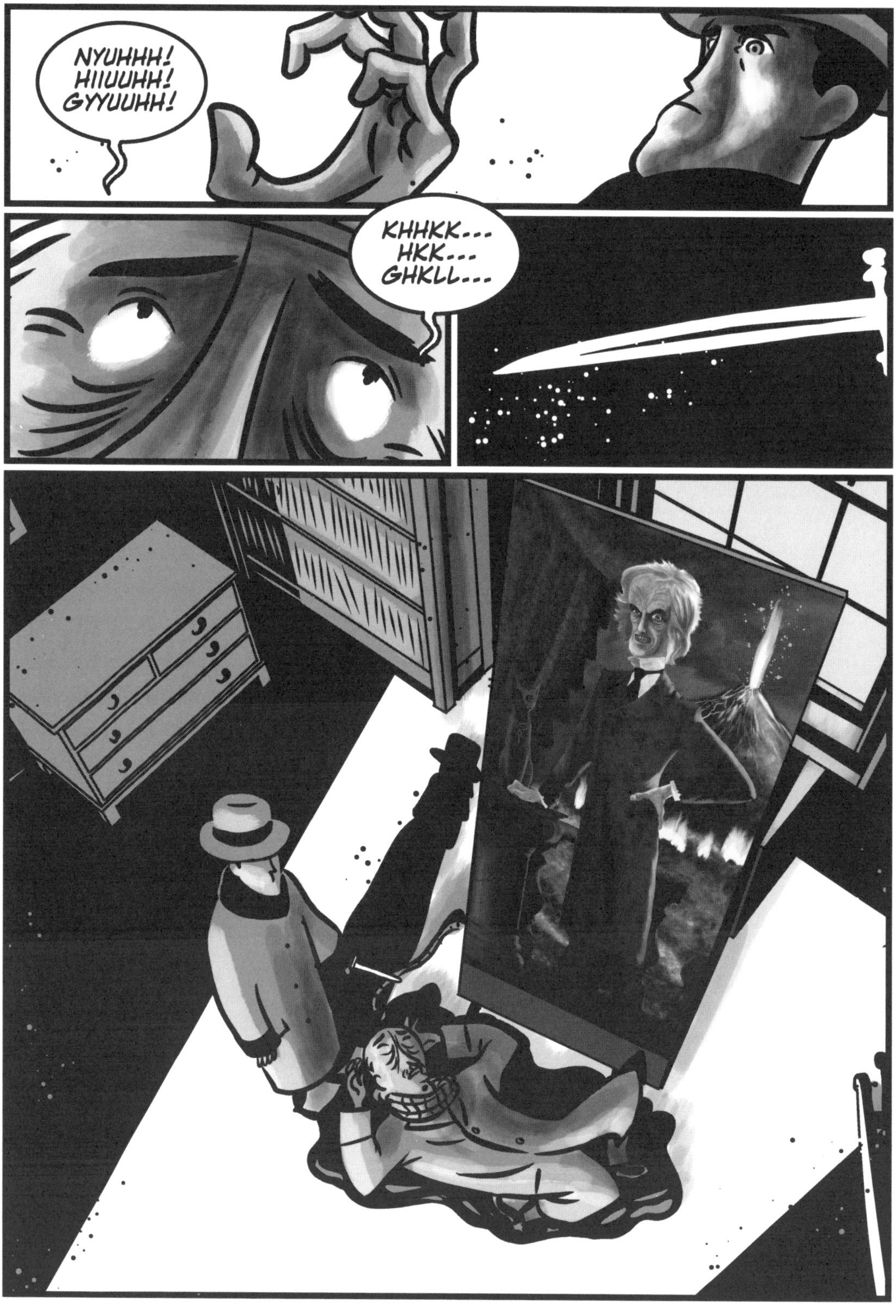
NYUHHH!
HIIUUHH!
GYYUUHH!
KHHKK...
HKK...
GHKLL...

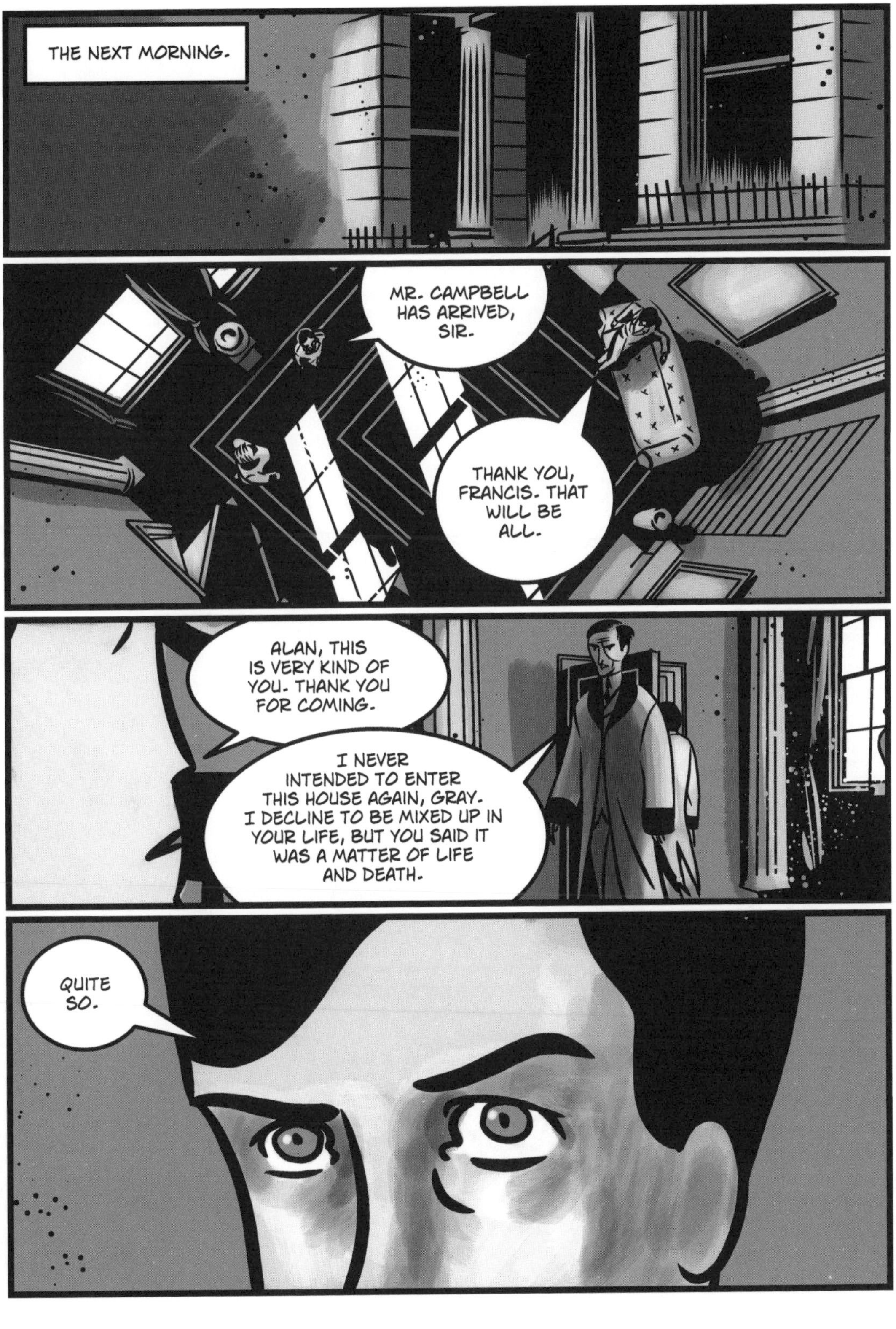
THE NEXT MORNING.
MR. CAMPBELL HAS ARRIVED, SIR.
THANK YOU, FRANCIS. THAT WILL BE ALL.
ALAN, THIS IS VERY KIND OF YOU. THANK YOU FOR COMING.
I NEVER INTENDED TO ENTER THIS HOUSE AGAIN, GRAY. I DECLINE TO BE MIXED UP IN YOUR LIFE, BUT YOU SAID IT WAS A MATTER OF LIFE AND DEATH.
QUITE SO.

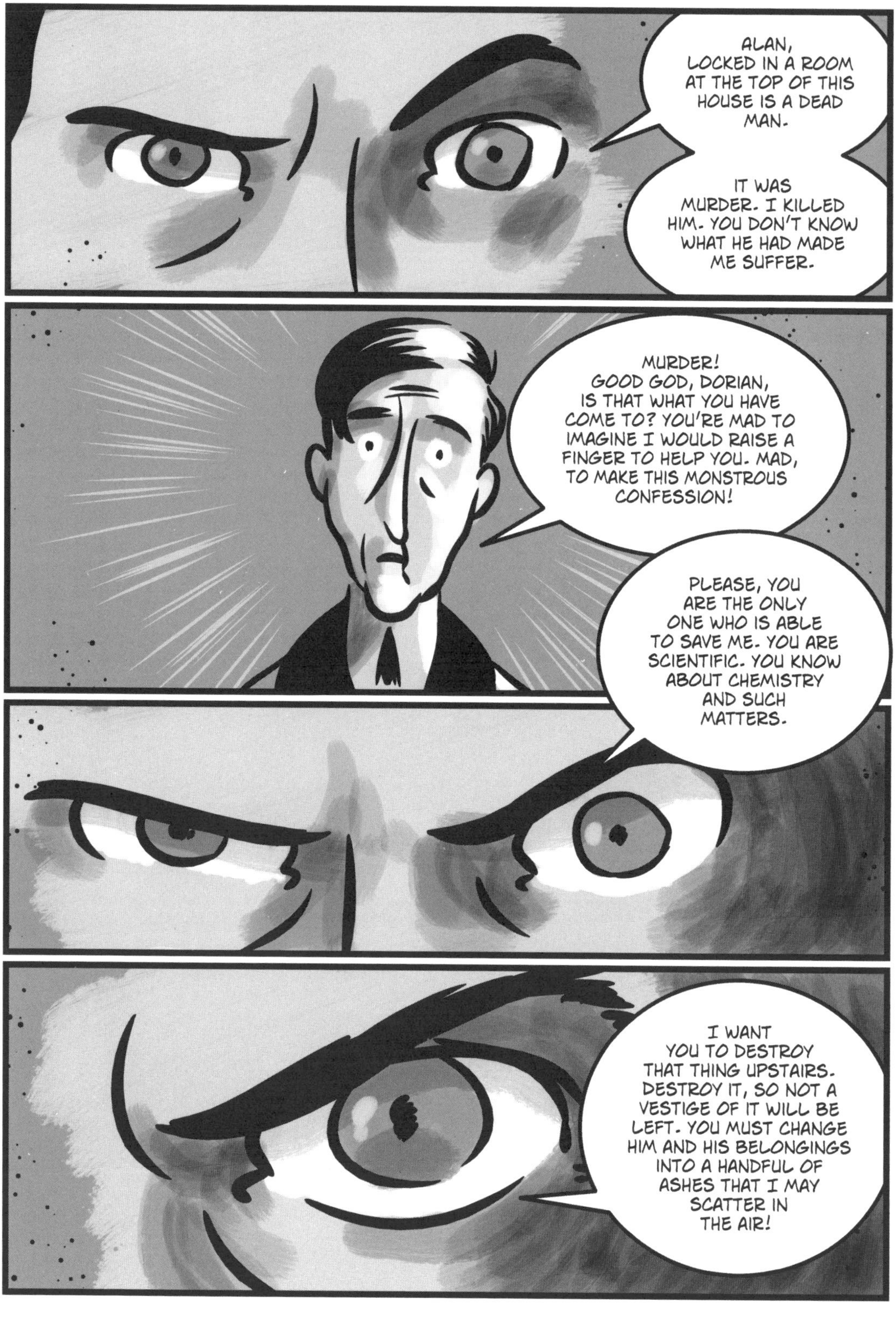
ALAN, LOCKED IN A ROOM AT THE TOP OF THIS HOUSE IS A DEAD MAN.
IT WAS MURDER. I KILLED HIM. YOU DON'T KNOW WHAT HE HAD MADE ME SUFFER.
MURDER! GOOD GOD, DORIAN, IS THAT WHAT YOU HAVE COME TO? YOU'RE MAD TO IMAGINE I WOULD RAISE A FINGER TO HELP YOU. MAD, TO MAKE THIS MONSTROUS CONFESSION!
PLEASE, YOU ARE THE ONLY ONE WHO IS ABLE TO SAVE ME. YOU ARE SCIENTIFIC. YOU KNOW ABOUT CHEMISTRY AND SUCH MATTERS.
I WANT YOU TO DESTROY THAT THING UPSTAIRS. DESTROY IT, SO NOT A VESTIGE OF IT WILL BE LEFT. YOU MUST CHANGE HIM AND HIS BELONGINGS INTO A HANDFUL OF ASHES THAT I MAY SCATTER IN THE AIR!

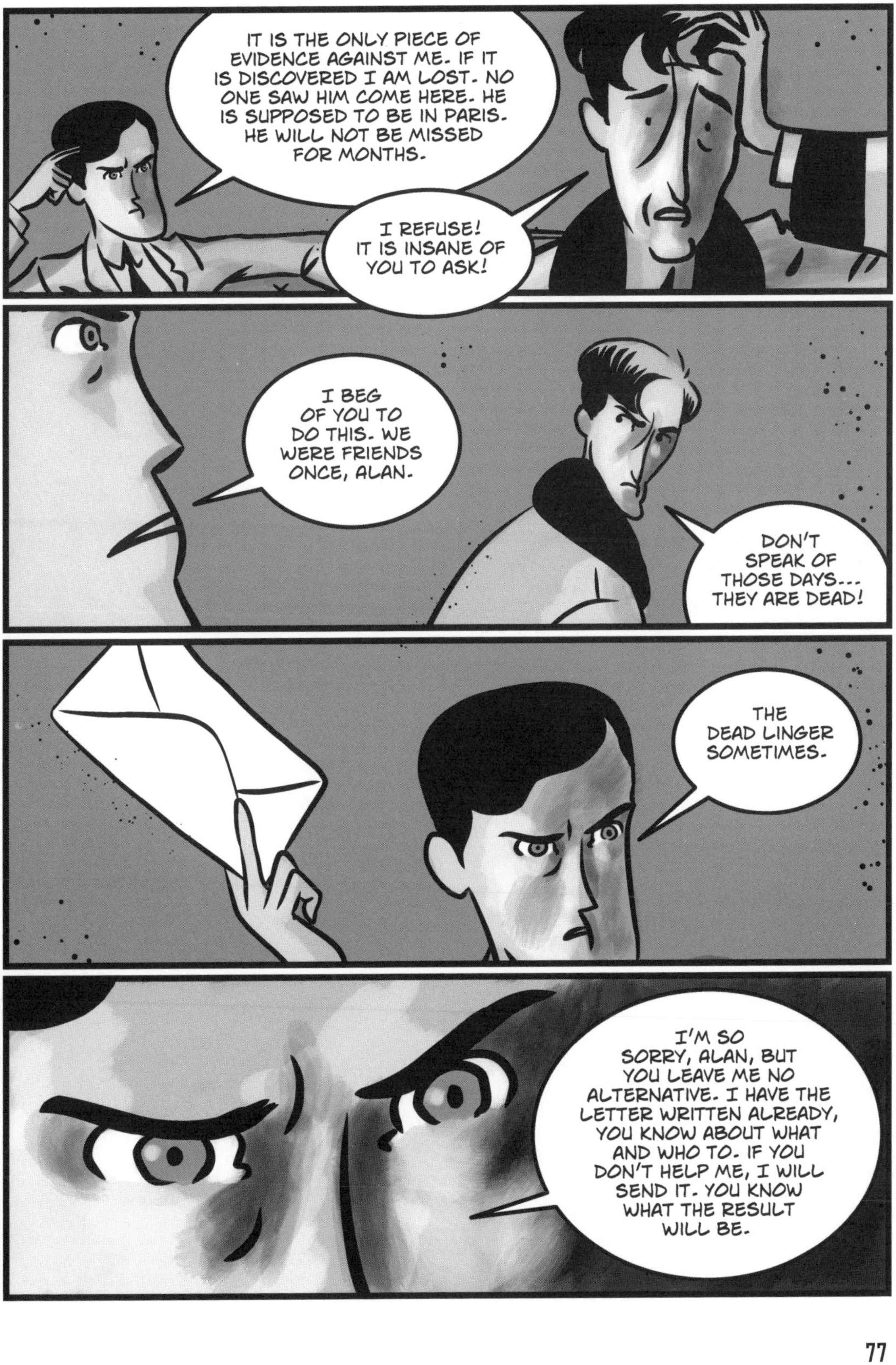
IT IS THE ONLY PIECE OF EVIDENCE AGAINST ME. IF IT IS DISCOVERED I AM LOST. NO ONE SAW HIM COME HERE. HE IS SUPPOSED TO BE IN PARIS. HE WILL NOT BE MISSED FOR MONTHS.
I REFUSE! IT IS INSANE OF YOU TO ASK!
I BEG OF YOU TO DO THIS. WE WERE FRIENDS ONCE, ALAN.
DON'T SPEAK OF THOSE DAYS... THEY ARE DEAD!
THE DEAD LINGER SOMETIMES.
I'M SO SORRY, ALAN, BUT YOU LEAVE ME NO ALTERNATIVE. I HAVE THE LETTER WRITTEN ALREADY, YOU KNOW ABOUT WHAT AND WHO TO. IF YOU DON'T HELP ME, I WILL SEND IT. YOU KNOW WHAT THE RESULT WILL BE.

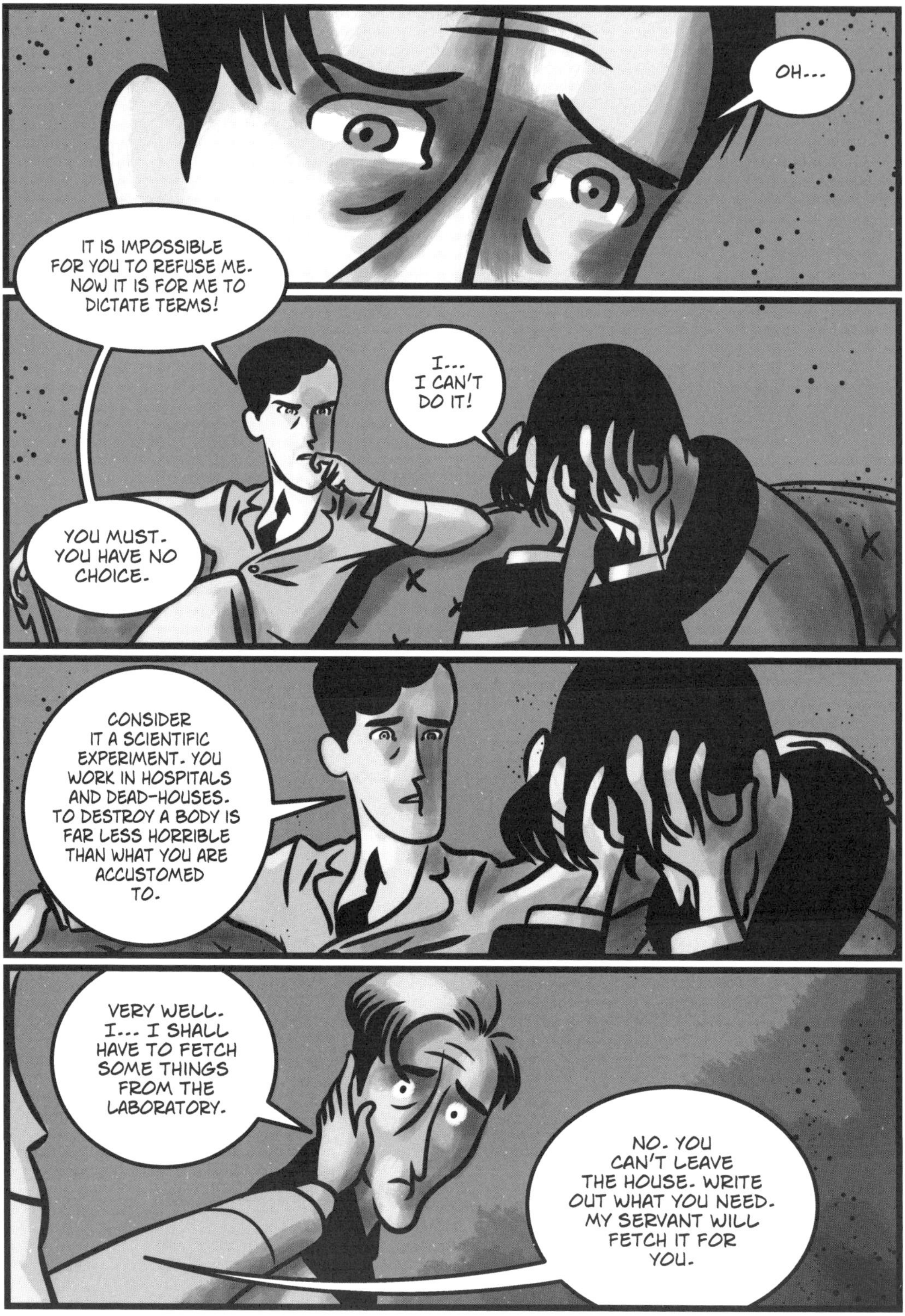
OH...
IT IS IMPOSSIBLE FOR YOU TO REFUSE ME. NOW IT IS FOR ME TO DICTATE TERMS!
I... I CAN'T DO IT!
YOU MUST. YOU HAVE NO CHOICE.
CONSIDER IT A SCIENTIFIC EXPERIMENT. YOU WORK IN HOSPITALS AND DEAD-HOUSES. TO DESTROY A BODY IS FAR LESS HORRIBLE THAN WHAT YOU ARE ACCUSTOMED TO.
VERY WELL. I... I SHALL HAVE TO FETCH SOME THINGS FROM THE LABORATORY.
NO. YOU CAN'T LEAVE THE HOUSE. WRITE OUT WHAT YOU NEED. MY SERVANT WILL FETCH IT FOR YOU.

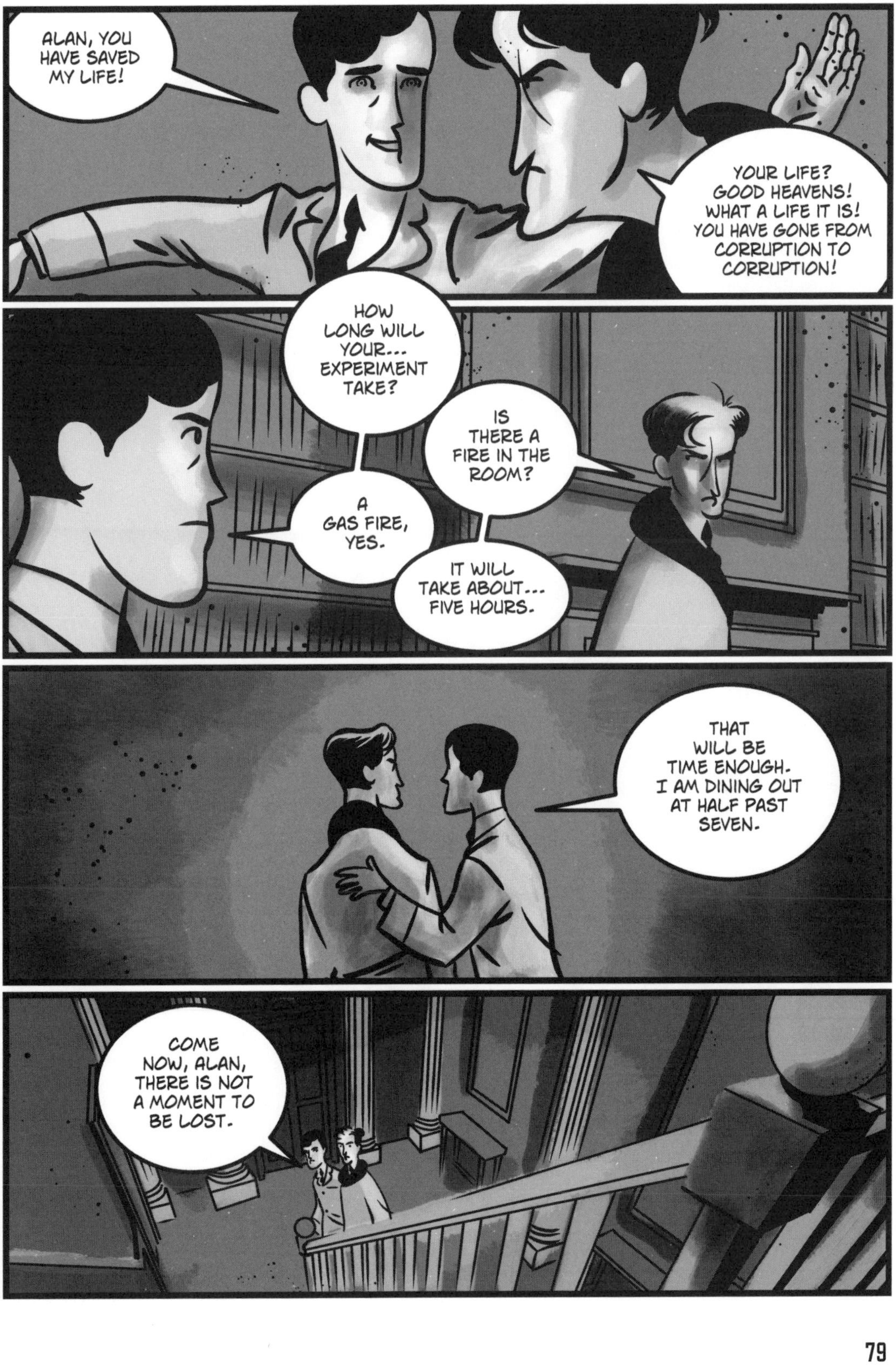
ALAN, YOU HAVE SAVED MY LIFE!
YOUR LIFE? GOOD HEAVENS! WHAT A LIFE IT IS! YOU HAVE GONE FROM CORRUPTION TO CORRUPTION!
HOW LONG WILL YOUR... EXPERIMENT TAKE?
IS THERE A FIRE IN THE ROOM?
A GAS FIRE, YES.
IT WILL TAKE ABOUT... FIVE HOURS.
THAT WILL BE TIME ENOUGH. I AM DINING OUT AT HALF PAST SEVEN.
COME NOW, ALAN, THERE IS NOT A MOMENT TO BE LOST.

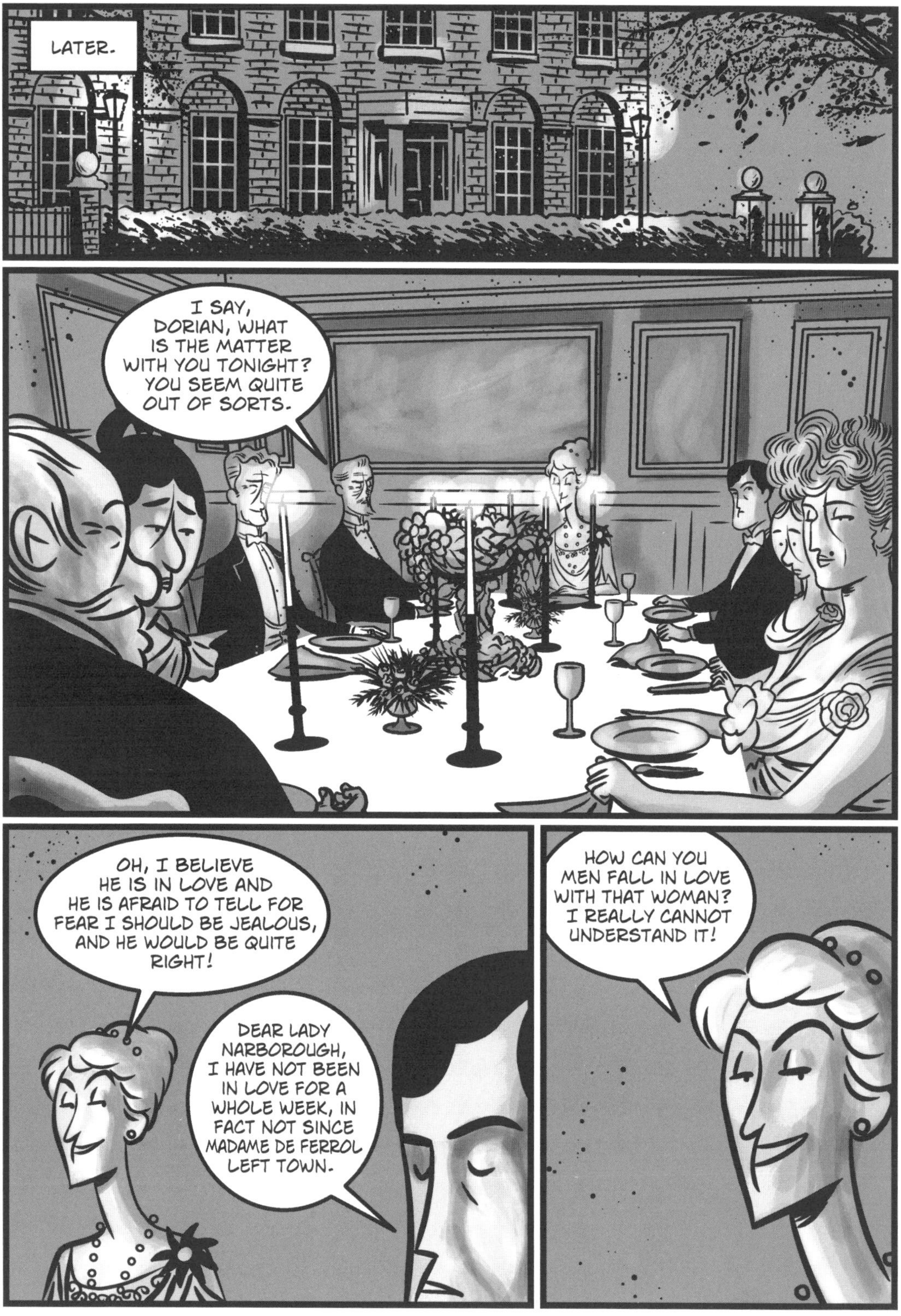
LATER.
I SAY, DORIAN, WHAT IS THE MATTER WITH YOU TONIGHT? YOU SEEM QUITE OUT OF SORTS.
OH, I BELIEVE HE IS IN LOVE AND HE IS AFRAID TO TELL FOR FEAR I SHOULD BE JEALOUS, AND HE WOULD BE QUITE RIGHT!
DEAR LADY NARBOROUGH, I HAVE NOT BEEN IN LOVE FOR A WHOLE WEEK, IN FACT NOT SINCE MADAME DE FERROL LEFT TOWN.
HOW CAN YOU MEN FALL IN LOVE WITH THAT WOMAN? I REALLY CANNOT UNDERSTAND IT!

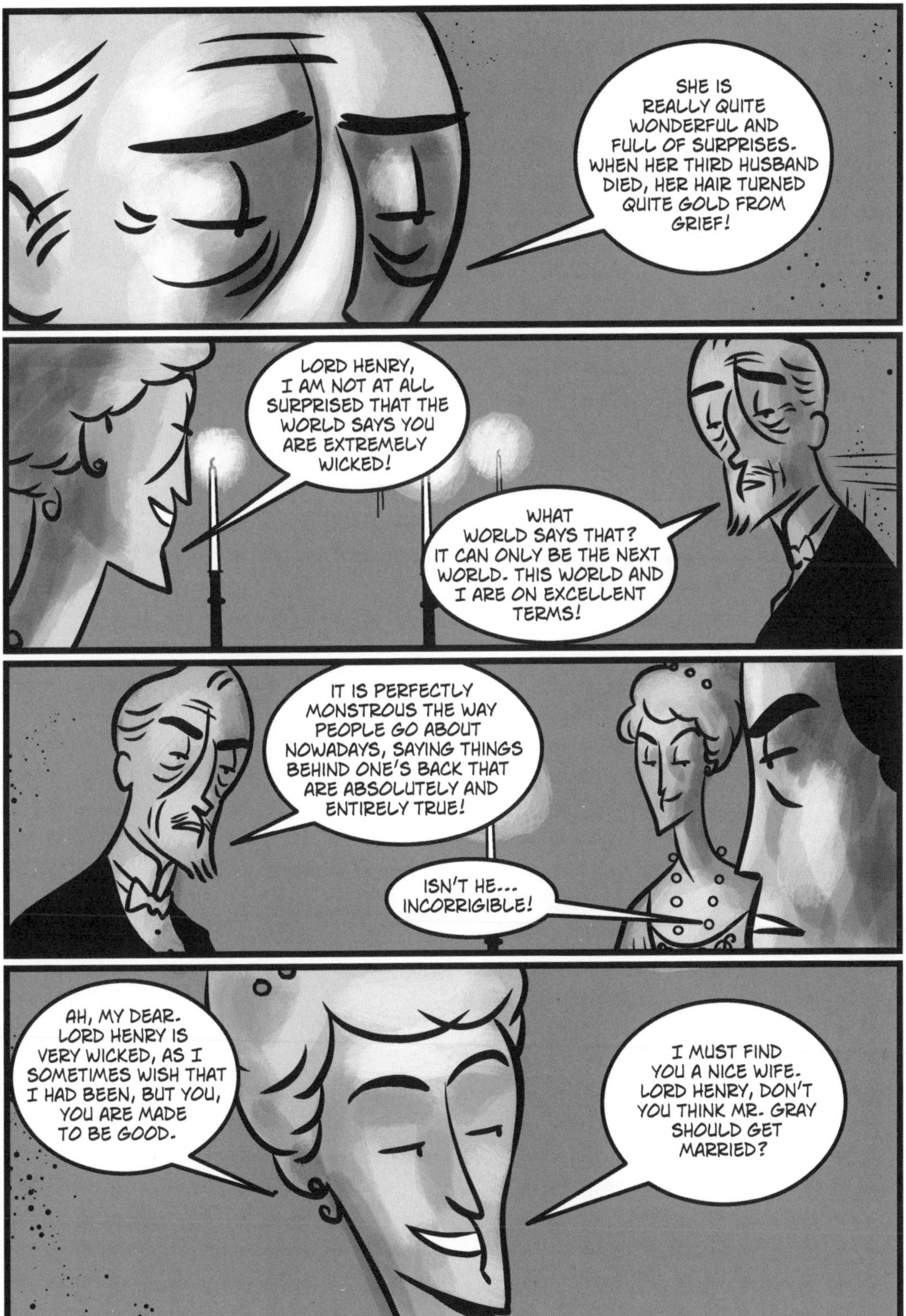
SHE IS REALLY QUITE WONDERFUL AND FULL OF SURPRISES. WHEN HER THIRD HUSBAND DIED, HER HAIR TURNED QUITE GOLD FROM GRIEF!
LORD HENRY, I AM NOT AT ALL SURPRISED THAT THE WORLD SAYS YOU ARE EXTREMELY WICKED!
WHAT WORLD SAYS THAT? IT CAN ONLY BE THE NEXT WORLD. THIS WORLD AND I ARE ON EXCELLENT TERMS!
IT IS PERFECTLY MONSTROUS THE WAY PEOPLE GO ABOUT NOWADAYS, SAYING THINGS BEHIND ONE'S BACK THAT ARE ABSOLUTELY AND ENTIRELY TRUE!
ISN'T HE... INCORRIGIBLE!
AH, MY DEAR. LORD HENRY IS VERY WICKED, AS I SOMETIMES WISH THAT I HAD BEEN, BUT YOU, YOU ARE MADE TO BE GOOD.
I MUST FIND YOU A NICE WIFE. LORD HENRY, DON'T YOU THINK MR. GRAY SHOULD GET MARRIED?

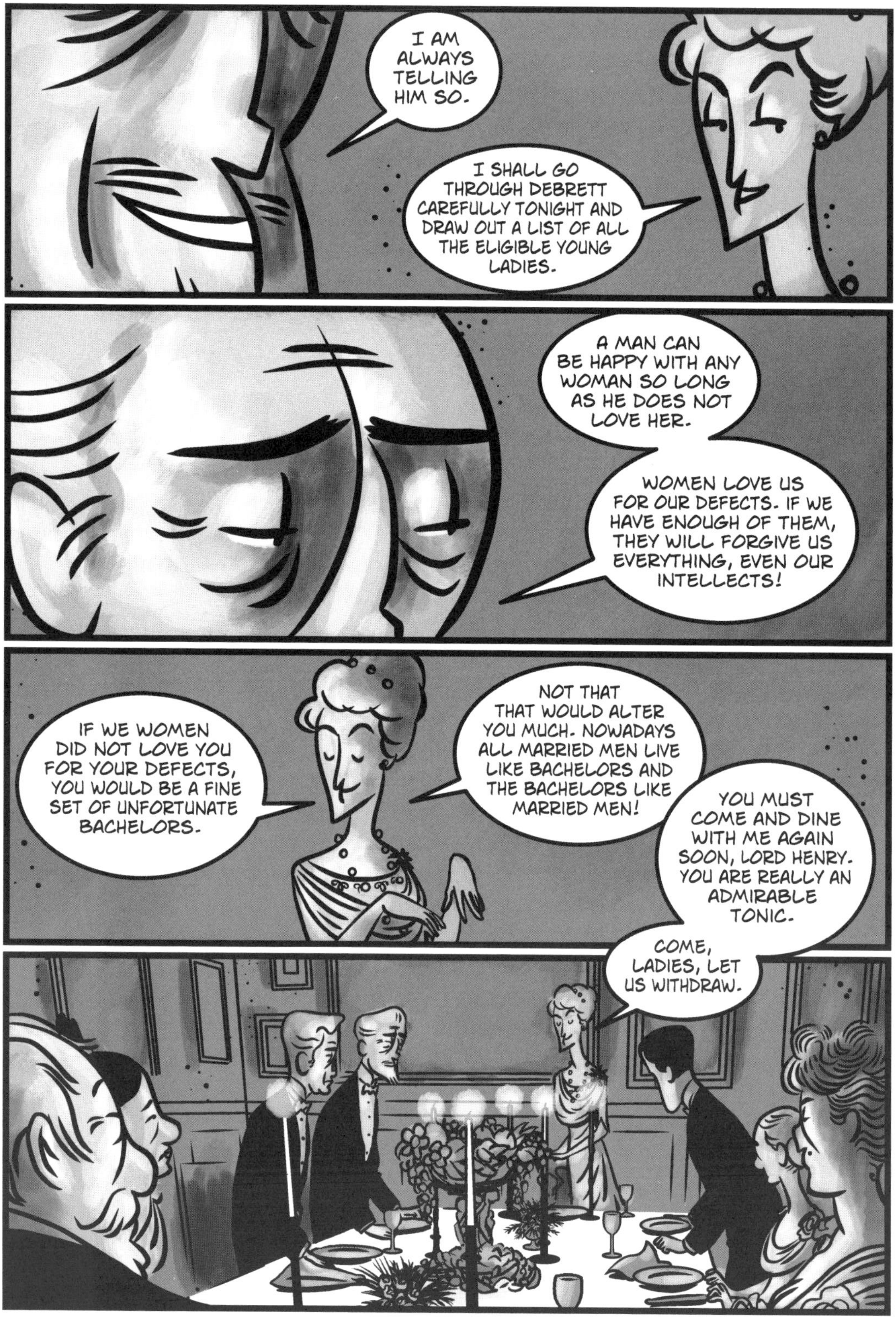
I AM ALWAYS TELLING HIM SO.
I SHALL GO THROUGH DEBRETT CAREFULLY TONIGHT AND DRAW OUT A LIST OF ALL THE ELIGIBLE YOUNG LADIES.
A MAN CAN BE HAPPY WITH ANY WOMAN SO LONG AS HE DOES NOT LOVE HER.
WOMEN LOVE US FOR OUR DEFECTS. IF WE HAVE ENOUGH OF THEM, THEY WILL FORGIVE US EVERYTHING, EVEN OUR INTELLECTS!
IF WE WOMEN DID NOT LOVE YOU FOR YOUR DEFECTS, YOU WOULD BE A FINE SET OF UNFORTUNATE BACHELORS.
NOT THAT THAT WOULD ALTER YOU MUCH. NOWADAYS ALL MARRIED MEN LIVE LIKE BACHELORS AND THE BACHELORS LIKE MARRIED MEN!
YOU MUST COME AND DINE WITH ME AGAIN SOON, LORD HENRY. YOU ARE REALLY AN ADMIRABLE TONIC.
COME, LADIES, LET US WITHDRAW.

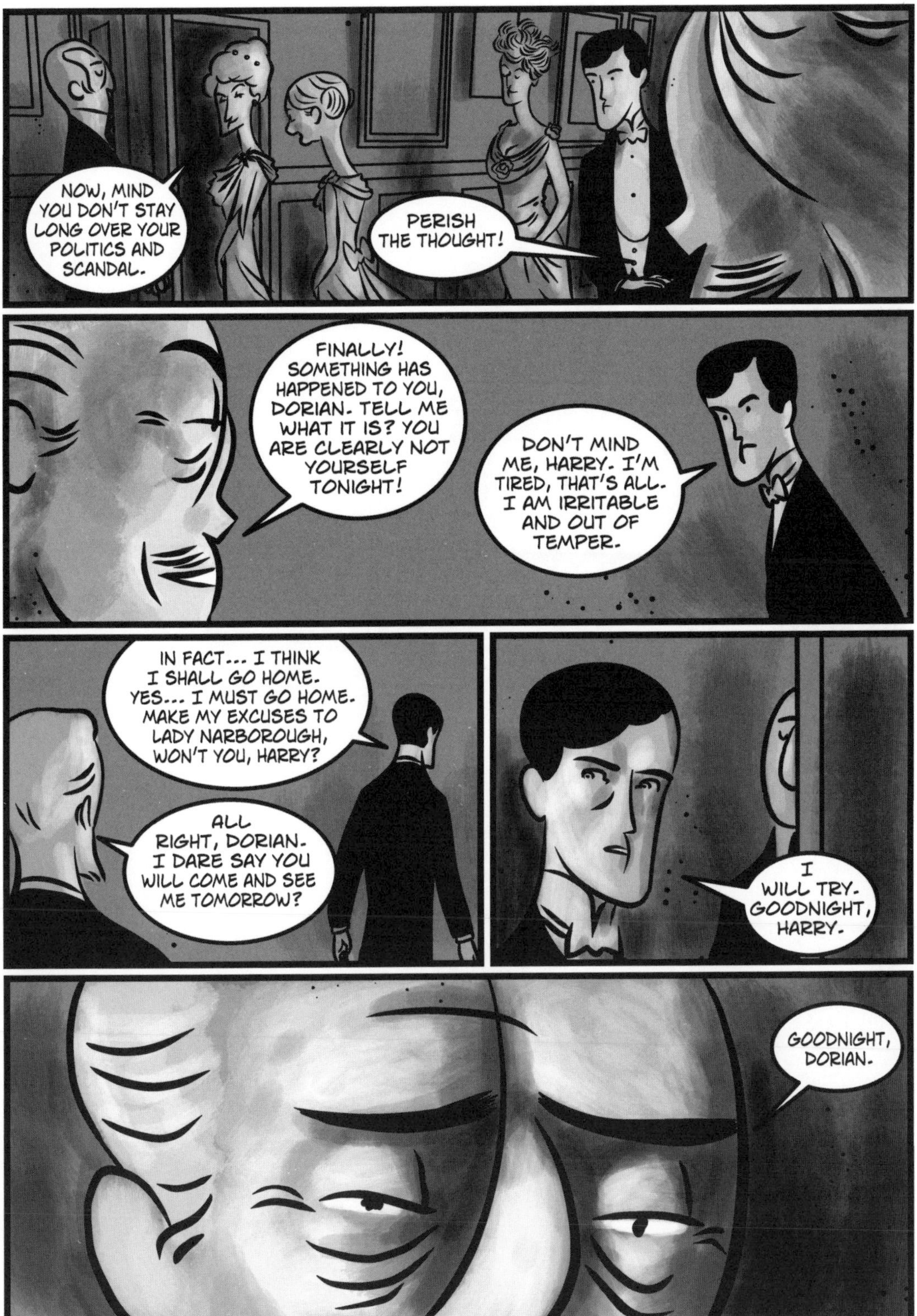
NOW, MIND YOU DON'T STAY LONG OVER YOUR POLITICS AND SCANDAL.
PERISH THE THOUGHT!
FINALLY! SOMETHING HAS HAPPENED TO YOU, DORIAN. TELL ME WHAT IT IS? YOU ARE CLEARLY NOT YOURSELF TONIGHT!
DON'T MIND ME, HARRY. I'M TIRED, THAT'S ALL. I AM IRRITABLE AND OUT OF TEMPER.
IN FACT... I THINK I SHALL GO HOME. YES... I MUST GO HOME. MAKE MY EXCUSES TO LADY NARBOROUGH, WON'T YOU, HARRY?
ALL RIGHT, DORIAN. I DARE SAY YOU WILL COME AND SEE ME TOMORROW?
I WILL TRY. GOODNIGHT, HARRY.
GOODNIGHT, DORIAN.

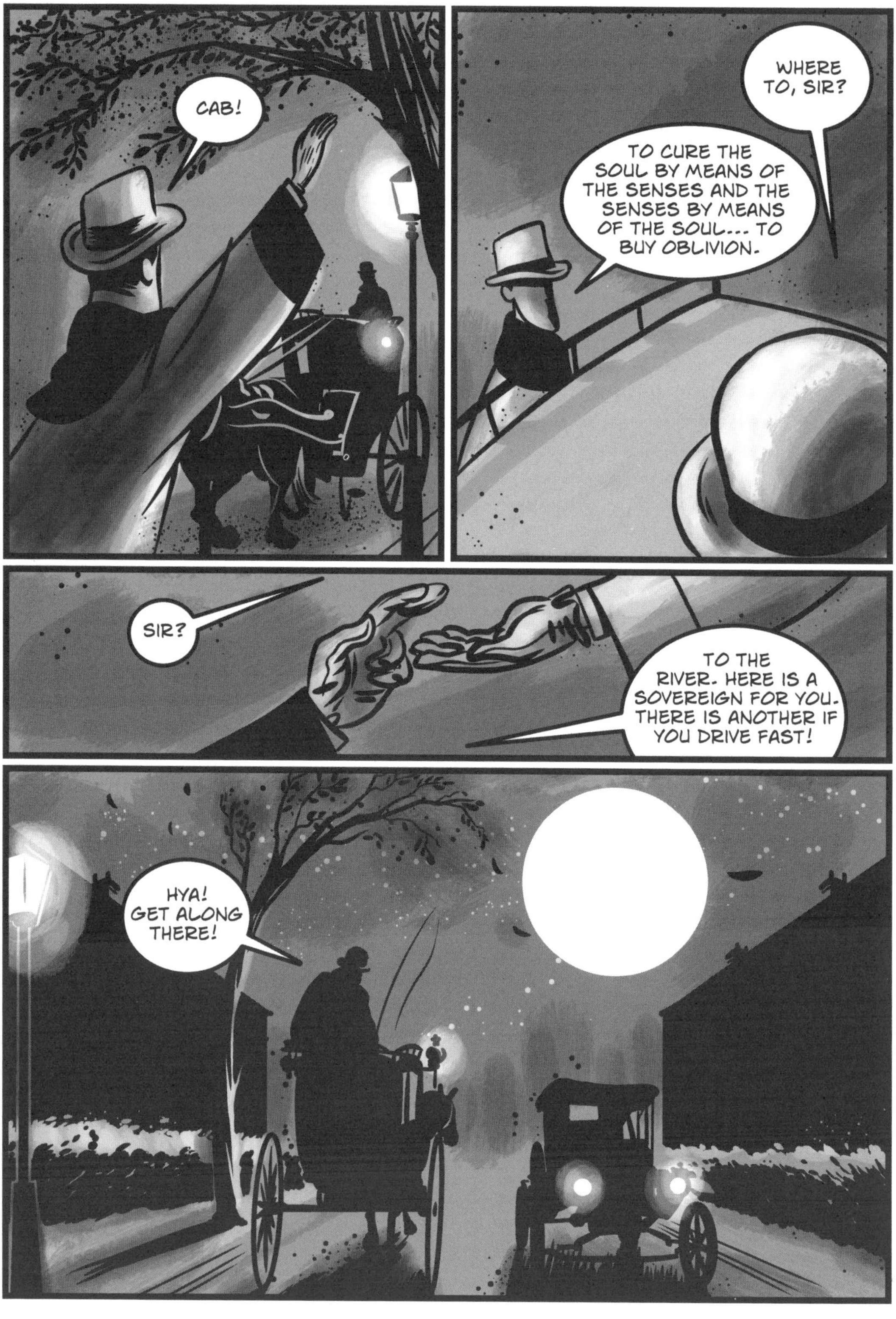
CAB!
WHERE TO, SIR?
TO CURE THE SOUL BY MEANS OF THE SENSES AND THE SENSES BY MEANS OF THE SOUL... TO BUY OBLIVION.
SIR?
TO THE RIVER. HERE IS A SOVEREIGN FOR YOU. THERE IS ANOTHER IF YOU DRIVE FAST!
HYA! GET ALONG THERE!

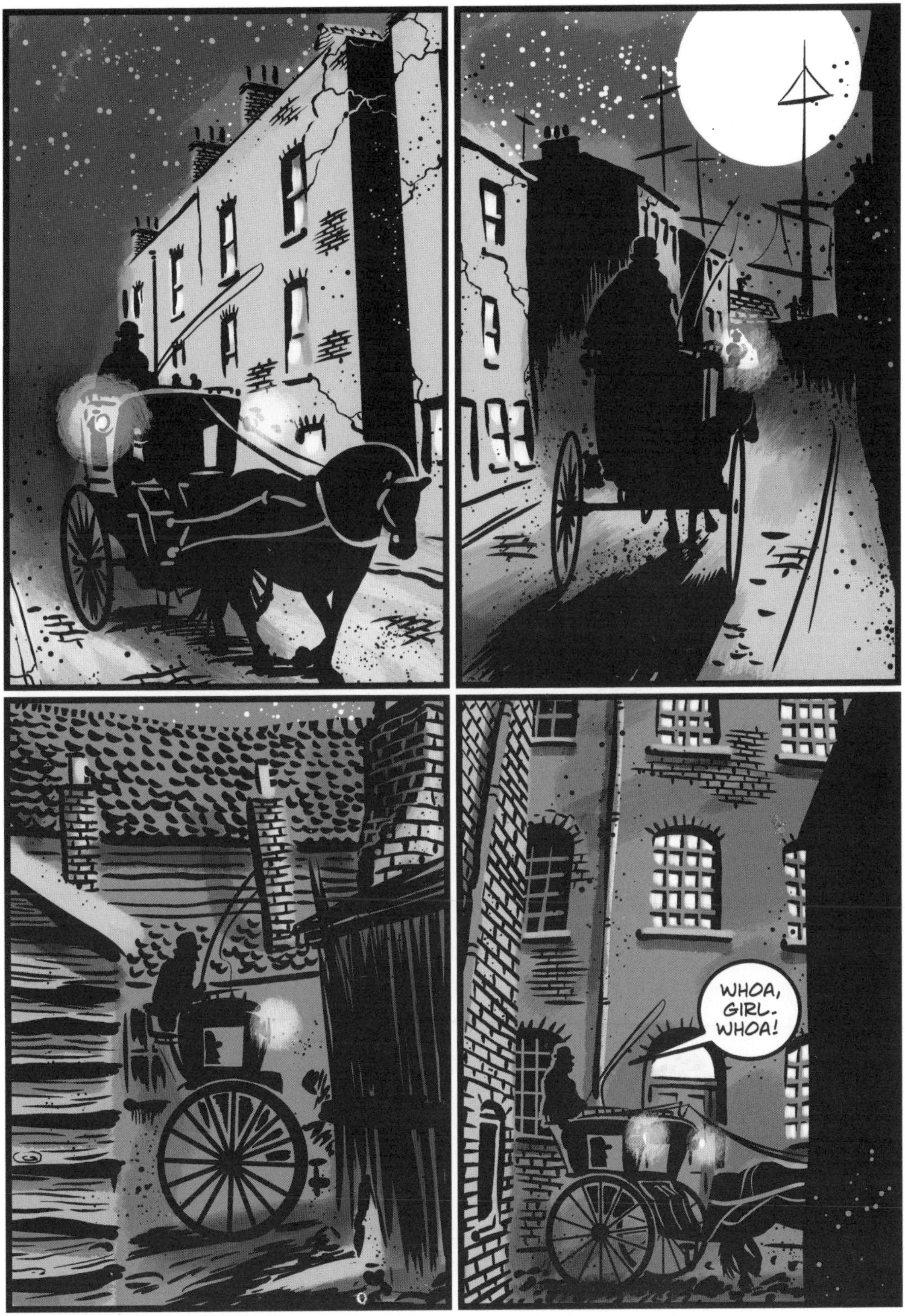
WHOA, GIRL. WHOA!

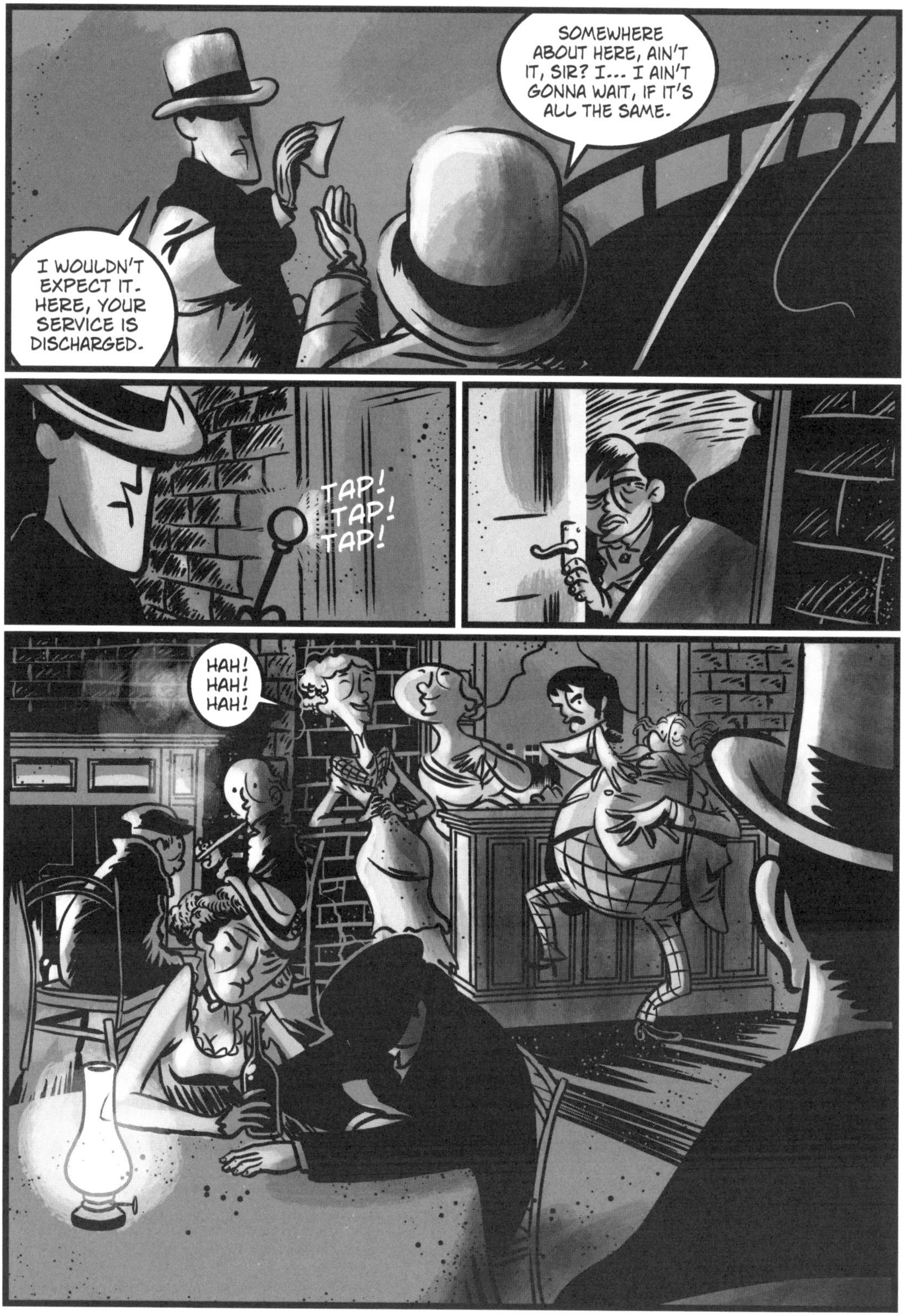
SOMEWHERE ABOUT HERE, AIN'T IT, SIR? I... I AIN'T GONNA WAIT, IF IT'S ALL THE SAME.
I WOULDN'T EXPECT IT. HERE, YOUR SERVICE IS DISCHARGED.
TAP! TAP! TAP!
HAH! HAH! HAH!

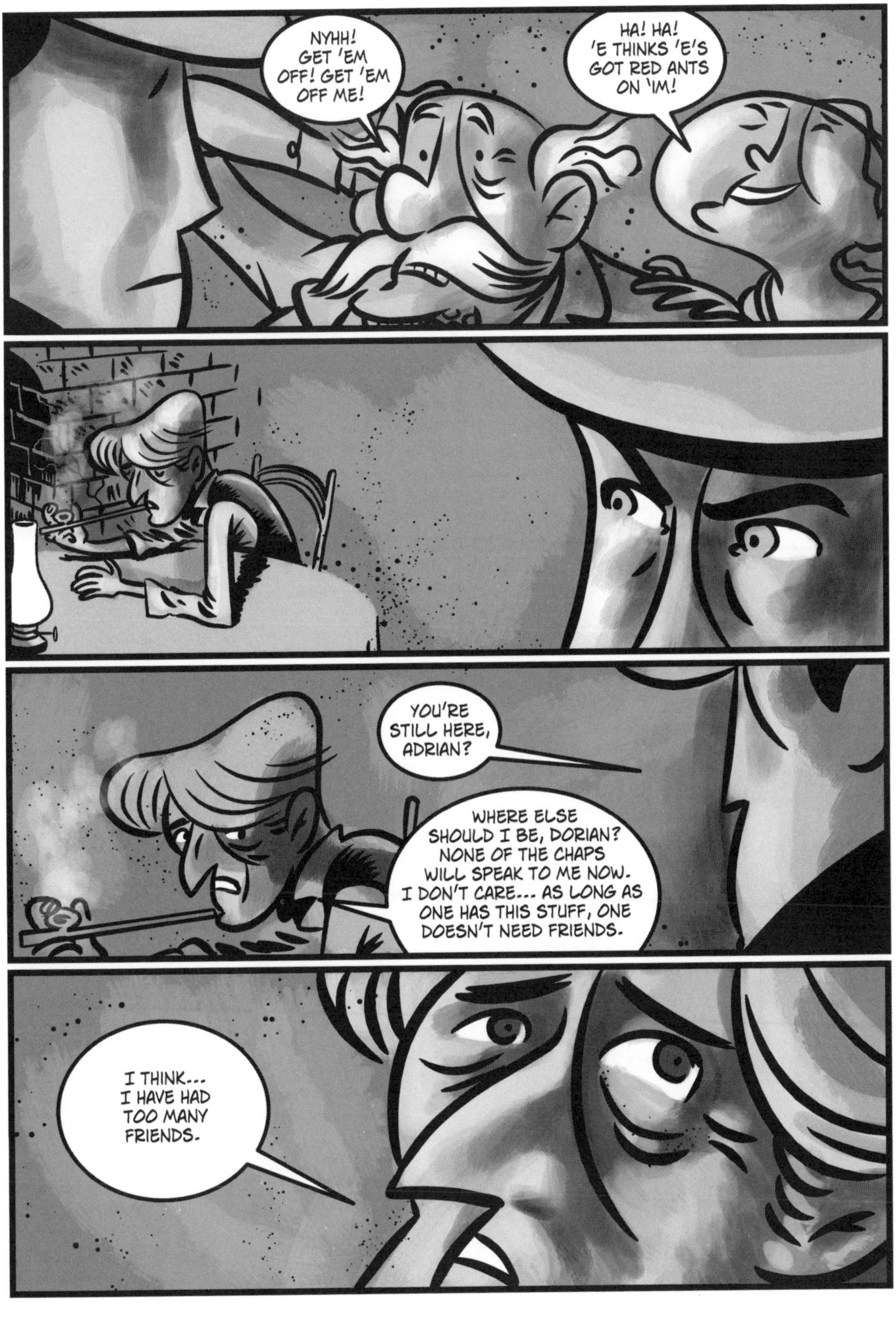
NYHH! GET 'EM OFF! GET 'EM OFF ME!
HA! HA! 'E THINKS 'E'S GOT RED ANTS ON 'IM!
YOU'RE STILL HERE, ADRIAN?
WHERE ELSE SHOULD I BE, DORIAN? NONE OF THE CHAPS WILL SPEAK TO ME NOW. I DON'T CARE... AS LONG AS ONE HAS THIS STUFF, ONE DOESN'T NEED FRIENDS.
I THINK... I HAVE HAD TOO MANY FRIENDS.

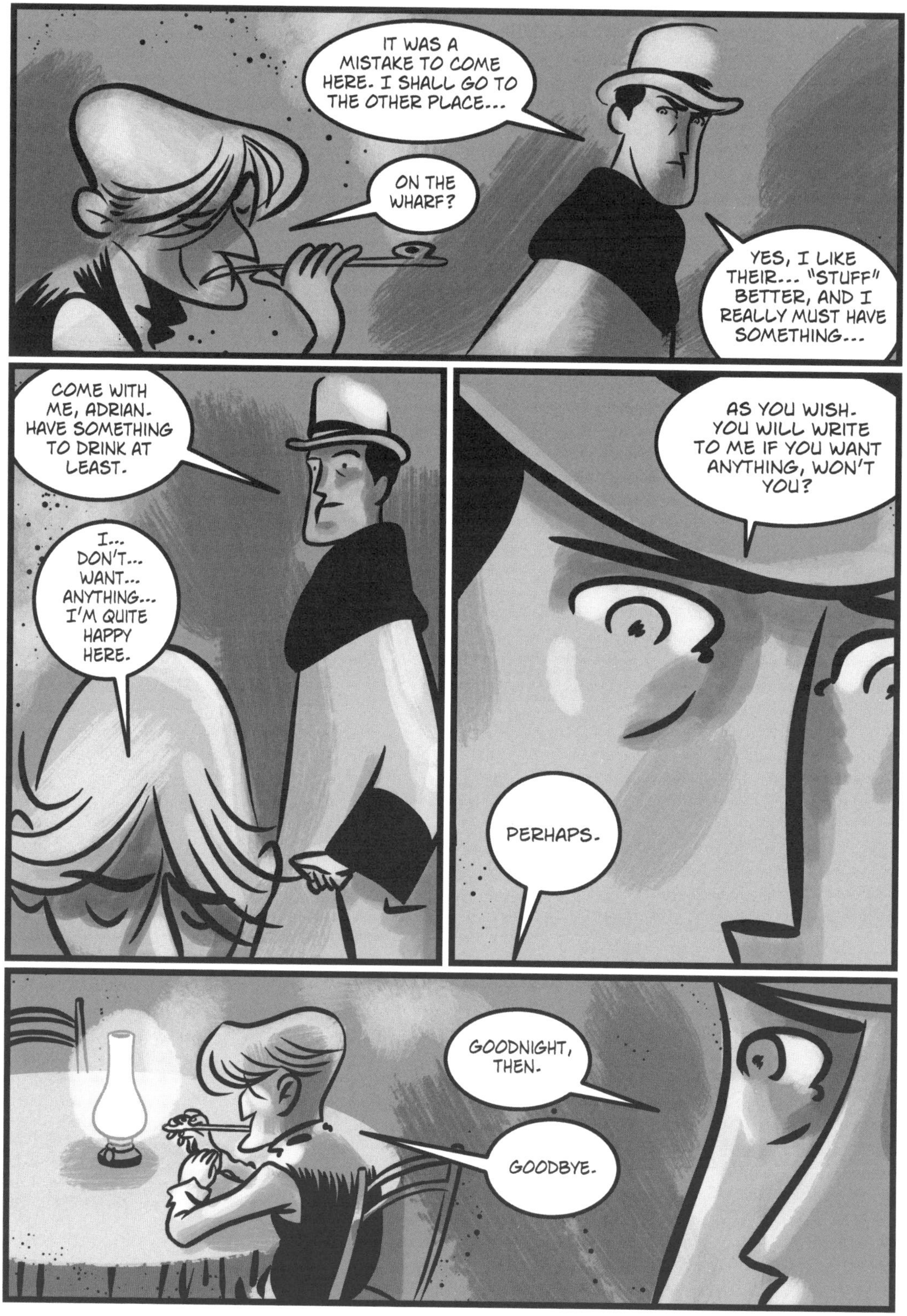
IT WAS A MISTAKE TO COME HERE. I SHALL GO TO THE OTHER PLACE...
ON THE WHARF?
YES, I LIKE THEIR... "STUFF" BETTER, AND I REALLY MUST HAVE SOMETHING...
COME WITH ME, ADRIAN. HAVE SOMETHING TO DRINK AT LEAST.
I... DON'T... WANT... ANYTHING... I'M QUITE HAPPY HERE.
AS YOU WISH. YOU WILL WRITE TO ME IF YOU WANT ANYTHING, WON'T YOU?
PERHAPS.
GOODNIGHT, THEN.
GOODBYE.

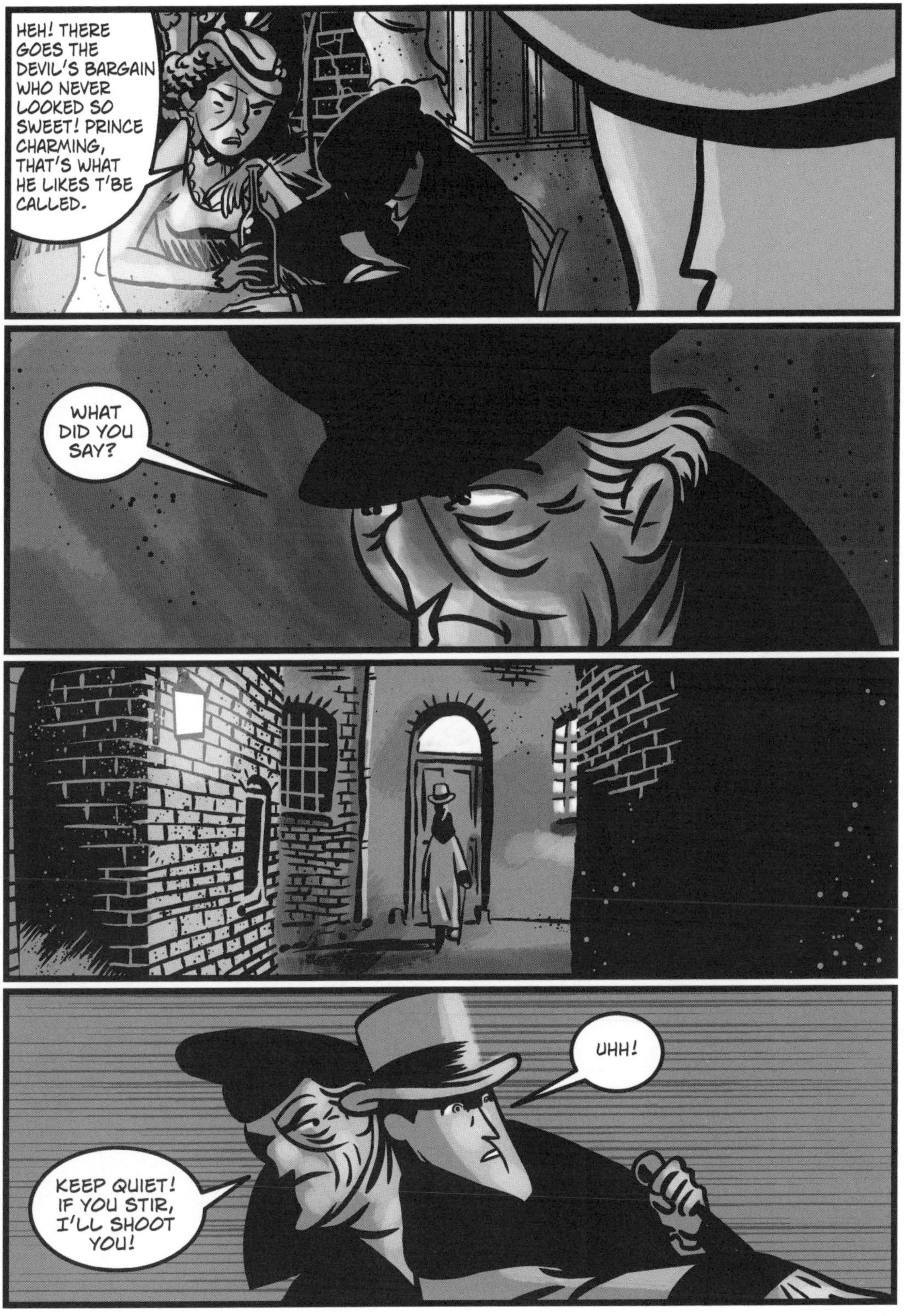
HEH! THERE GOES THE DEVIL'S BARGAIN WHO NEVER LOOKED SO SWEET! PRINCE CHARMING, THAT'S WHAT HE LIKES T'BE CALLED.
WHAT DID YOU SAY?
UHH!
KEEP QUIET! IF YOU STIR, I'LL SHOOT YOU!

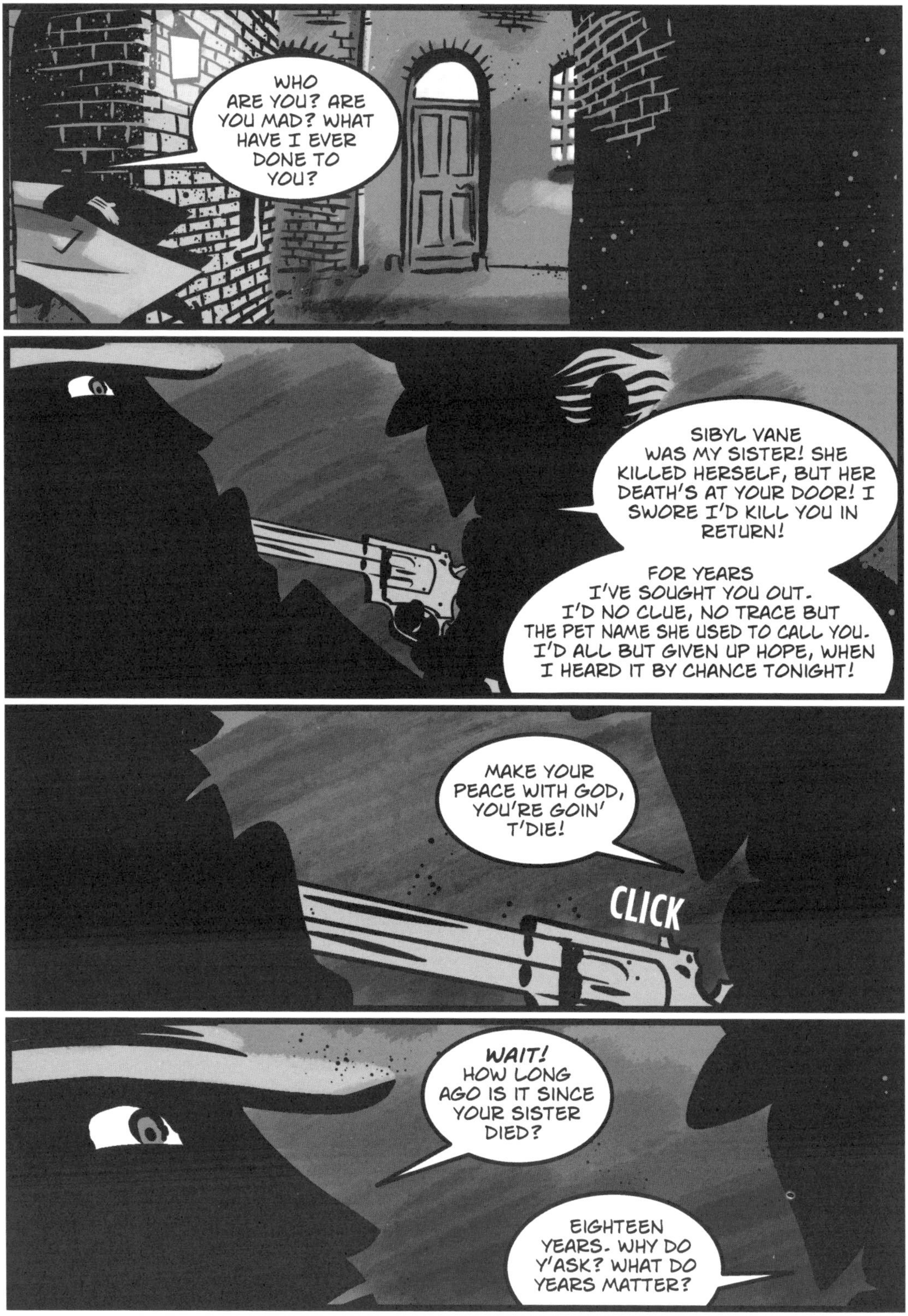
WHO ARE YOU? ARE YOU MAD? WHAT HAVE I EVER DONE TO YOU?
SIBYL VANE WAS MY SISTER! SHE KILLED HERSELF, BUT HER DEATH'S AT YOUR DOOR! I SWORE I'D KILL YOU IN RETURN!
FOR YEARS I'VE SOUGHT YOU OUT. I'D NO CLUE, NO TRACE BUT THE PET NAME SHE USED TO CALL YOU. I'D ALL BUT GIVEN UP HOPE, WHEN I HEARD IT BY CHANCE TONIGHT!
MAKE YOUR PEACE WITH GOD, YOU'RE GOIN' T'DIE!
CLICK
WAIT! HOW LONG AGO IS IT SINCE YOUR SISTER DIED?
EIGHTEEN YEARS. WHY DO Y'ASK? WHAT DO YEARS MATTER?

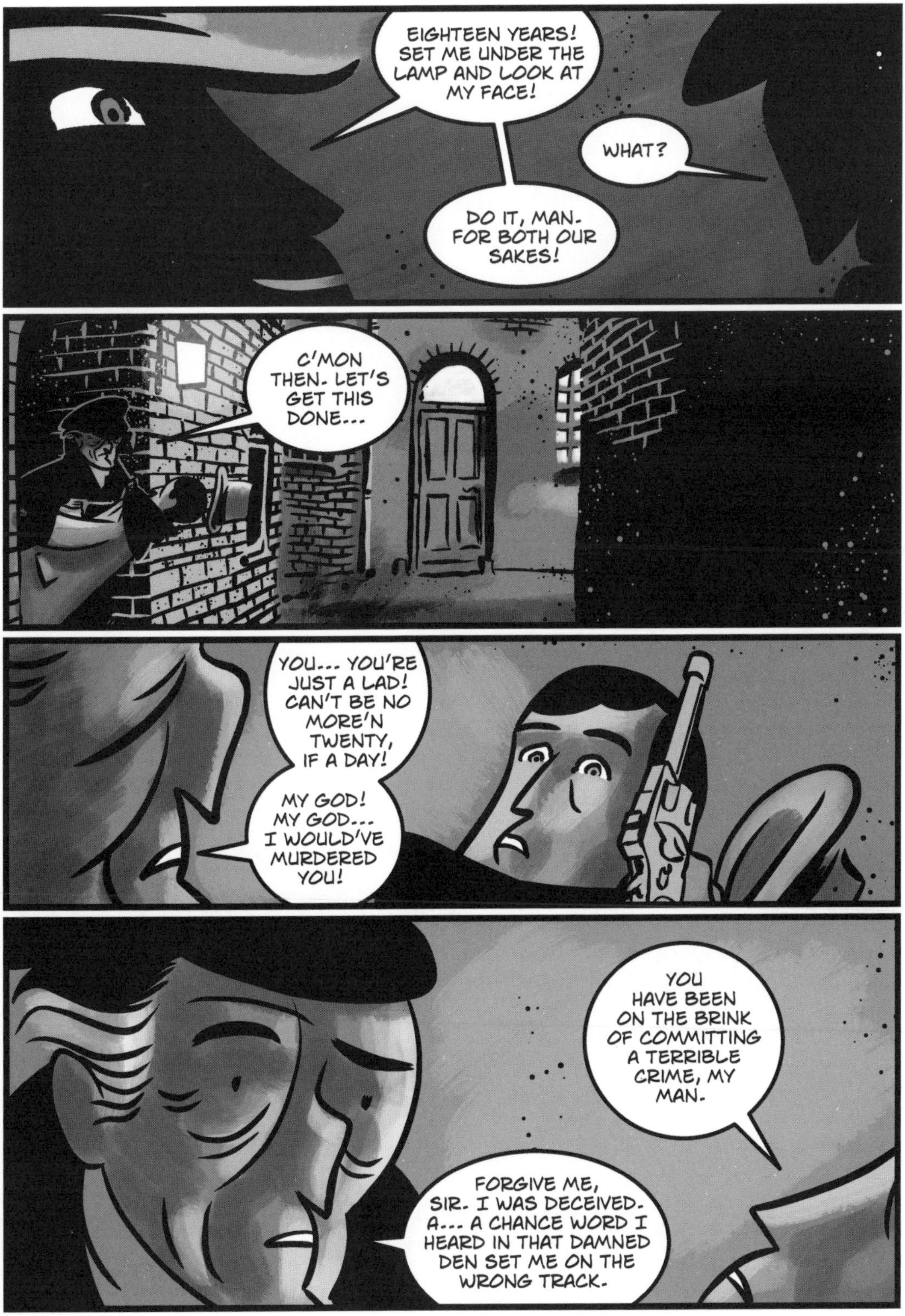
EIGHTEEN YEARS! SET ME UNDER THE LAMP AND LOOK AT MY FACE!
WHAT?
DO IT, MAN. FOR BOTH OUR SAKES!
C'MON THEN. LET'S GET THIS DONE...
YOU... YOU'RE JUST A LAD! CAN'T BE NO MORE'N TWENTY, IF A DAY!
MY GOD! MY GOD... I WOULD'VE MURDERED YOU!
YOU HAVE BEEN ON THE BRINK OF COMMITTING A TERRIBLE CRIME, MY MAN.
FORGIVE ME, SIR. I WAS DECEIVED. A... A CHANCE WORD I HEARD IN THAT DAMNED DEN SET ME ON THE WRONG TRACK.

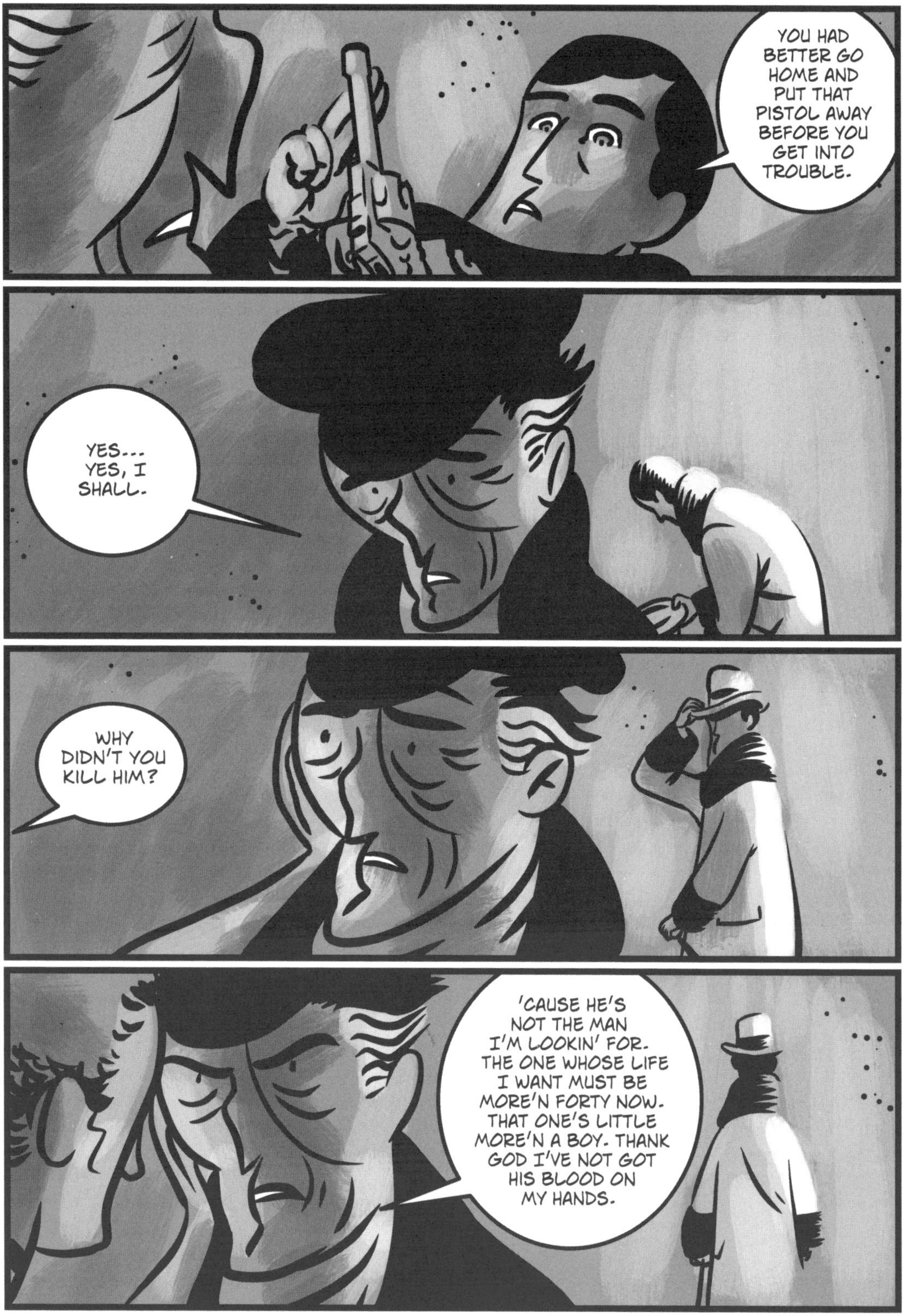
YOU HAD BETTER GO HOME AND PUT THAT PISTOL AWAY BEFORE YOU GET INTO TROUBLE.
YES... YES, I SHALL.
WHY DIDN'T YOU KILL HIM?
'CAUSE HE'S NOT THE MAN I'M LOOKIN' FOR. THE ONE WHOSE LIFE I WANT MUST BE MORE'N FORTY NOW. THAT ONE'S LITTLE MORE'N A BOY. THANK GOD I'VE NOT GOT HIS BLOOD ON MY HANDS.

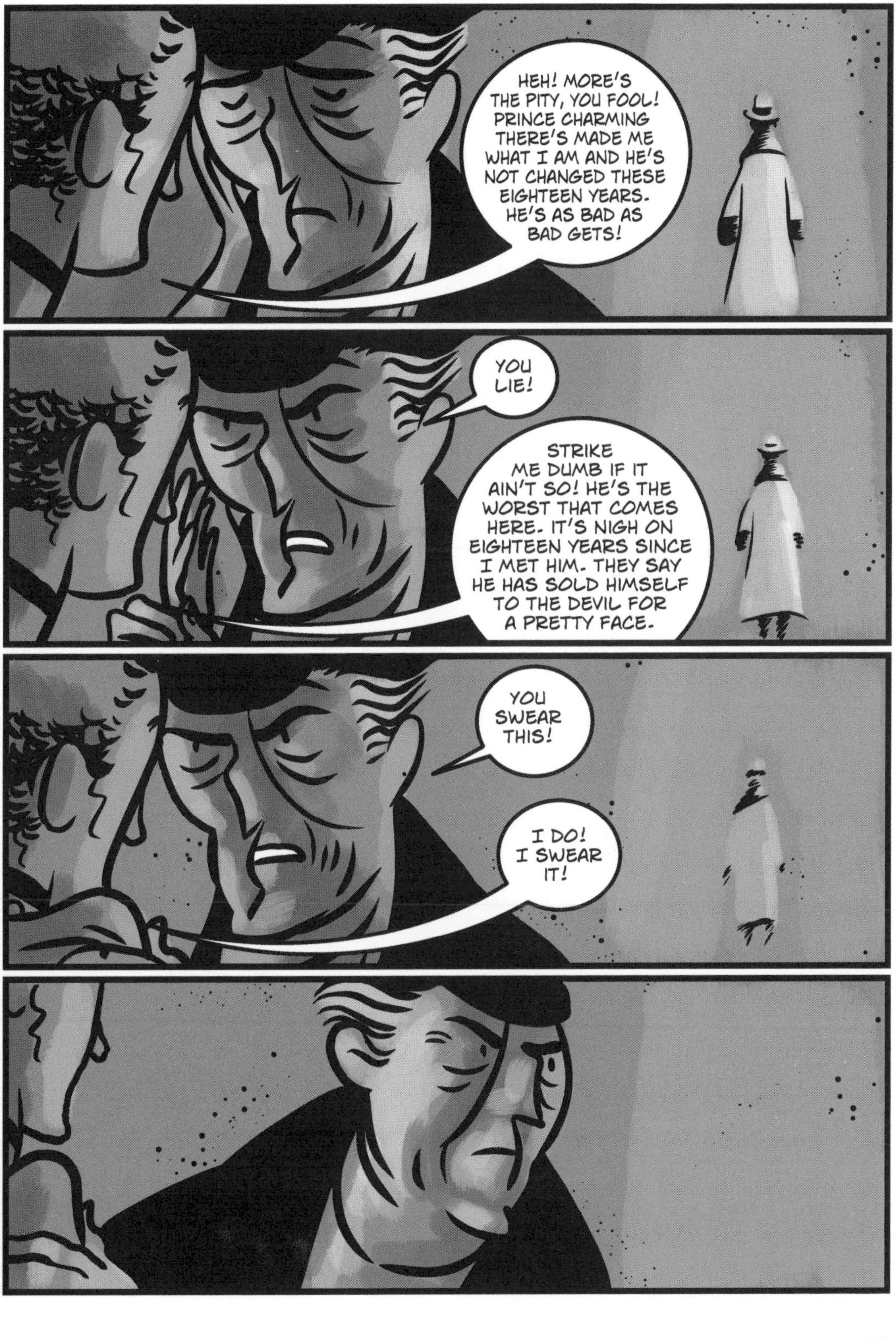
HEH! MORE'S THE PITY, YOU FOOL! PRINCE CHARMING THERE'S MADE ME WHAT I AM AND HE'S NOT CHANGED THESE EIGHTEEN YEARS. HE'S AS BAD AS BAD GETS!
YOU LIE!
STRIKE ME DUMB IF IT AIN'T SO! HE'S THE WORST THAT COMES HERE. IT'S NIGH ON EIGHTEEN YEARS SINCE I MET HIM. THEY SAY HE HAS SOLD HIMSELF TO THE DEVIL FOR A PRETTY FACE.
YOU SWEAR THIS!
I DO! I SWEAR IT!

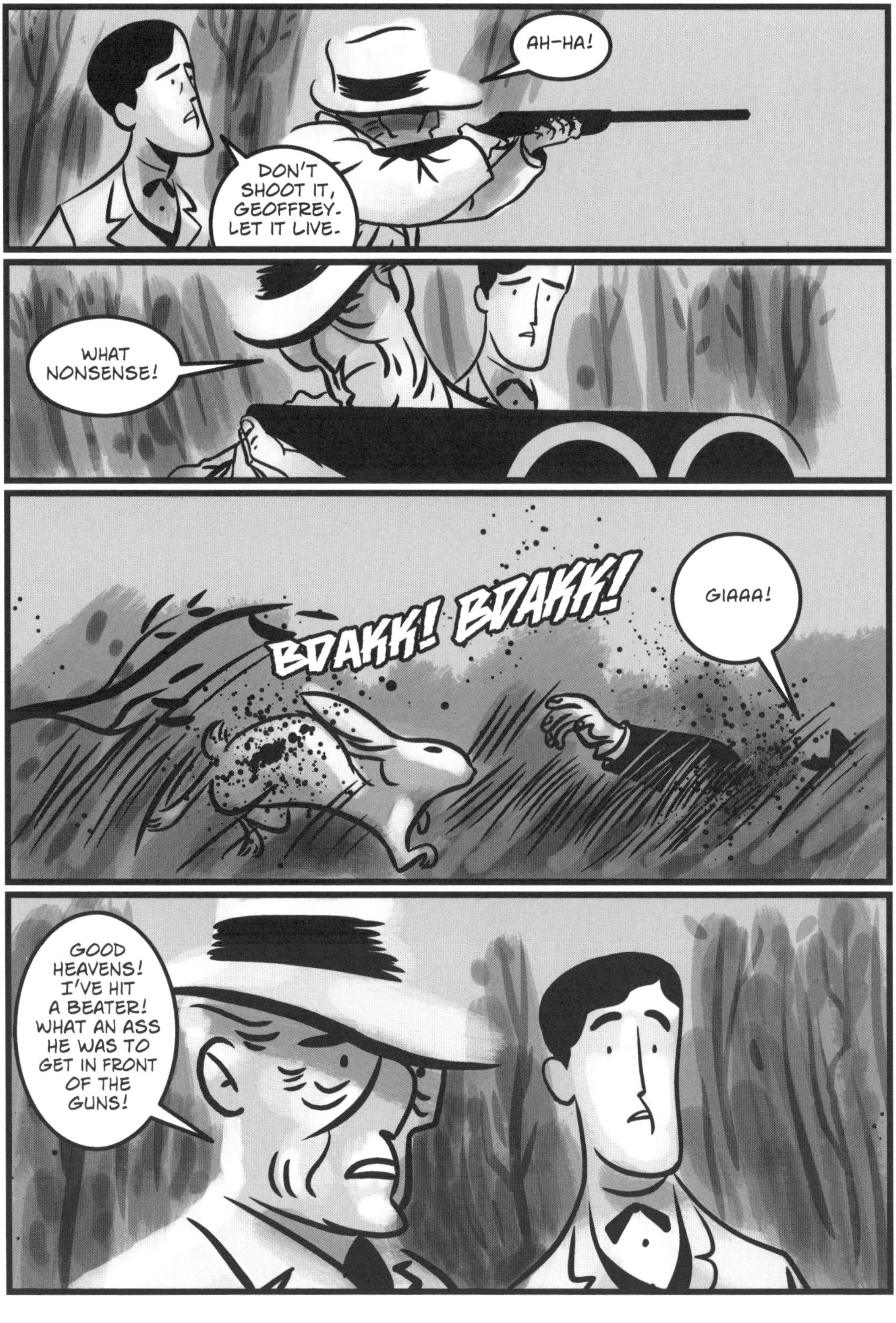
AH-HA!
DON'T SHOOT IT, GEOFFREY. LET IT LIVE.
WHAT NONSENSE!
BDAKK! BDAKK!
GIAAA!
GOOD HEAVENS! I'VE HIT A BEATER! WHAT AN ASS HE WAS TO GET IN FRONT OF THE GUNS!

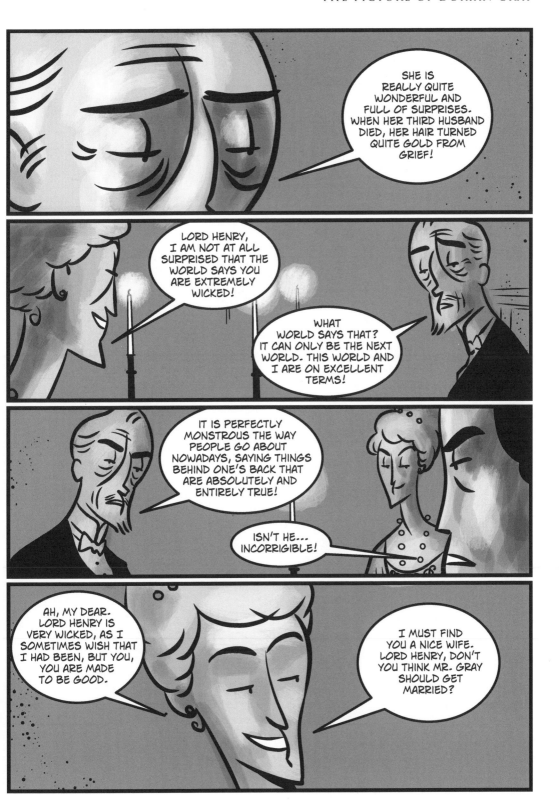

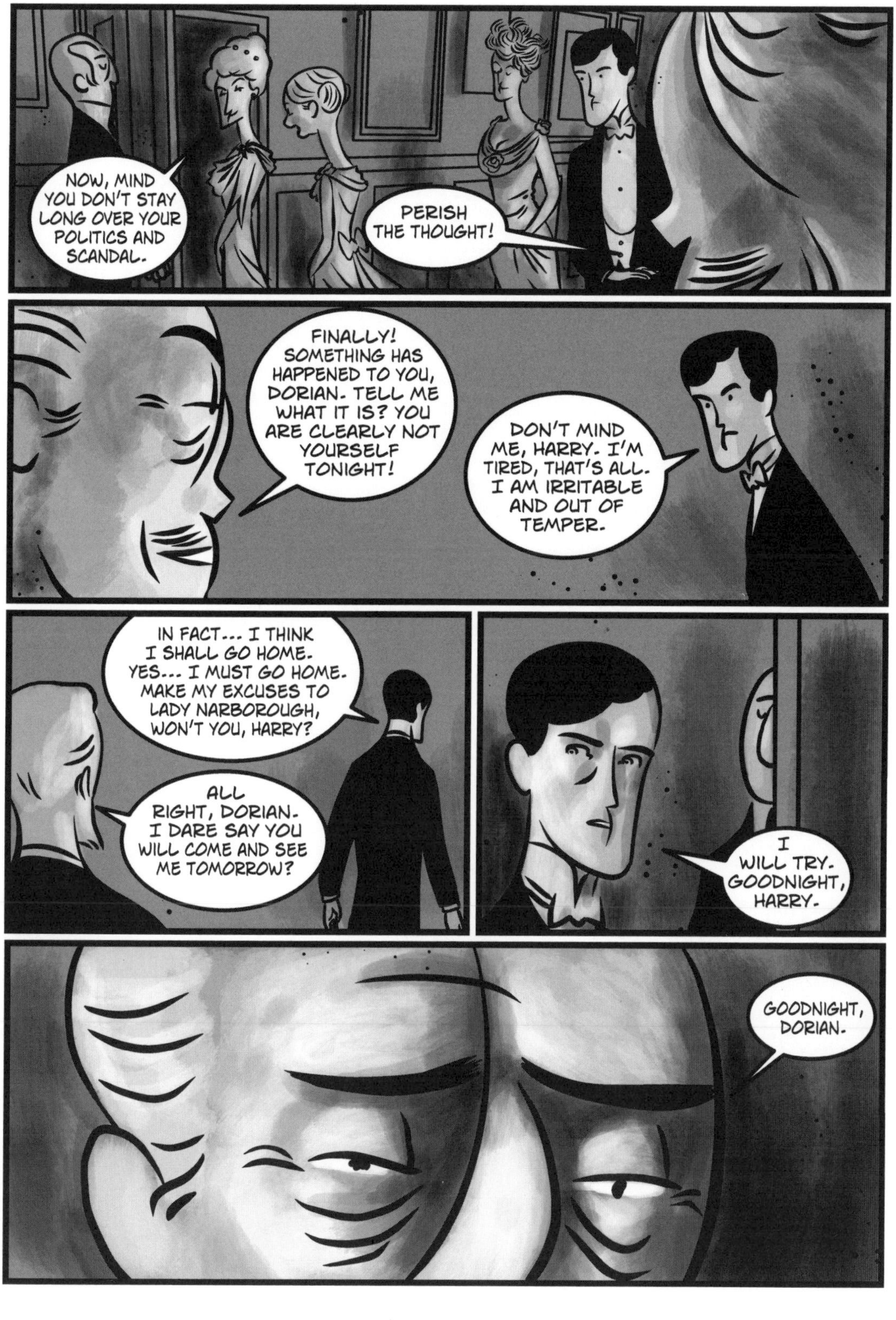
NOW, MIND YOU DON'T STAY LONG OVER YOUR POLITICS AND SCANDAL.
PERISH THE THOUGHT!
FINALLY! SOMETHING HAS HAPPENED TO YOU, DORIAN. TELL ME WHAT IT IS? YOU ARE CLEARLY NOT YOURSELF TONIGHT!
DON'T MIND ME, HARRY. I'M TIRED, THAT'S ALL. I AM IRRITABLE AND OUT OF TEMPER.
IN FACT... I THINK I SHALL GO HOME. YES... I MUST GO HOME. MAKE MY EXCUSES TO LADY NARBOROUGH, WON'T YOU, HARRY?
ALL RIGHT, DORIAN. I DARE SAY YOU WILL COME AND SEE ME TOMORROW?
I WILL TRY. GOODNIGHT, HARRY.
GOODNIGHT, DORIAN.

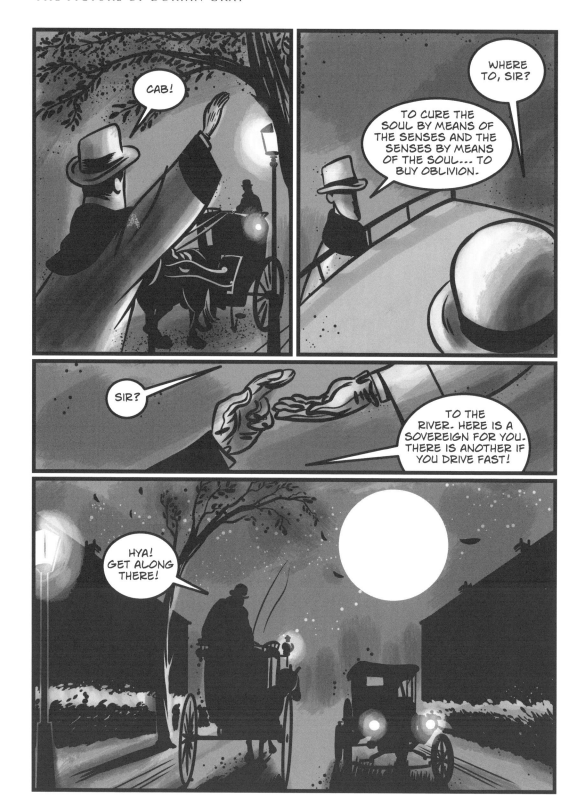

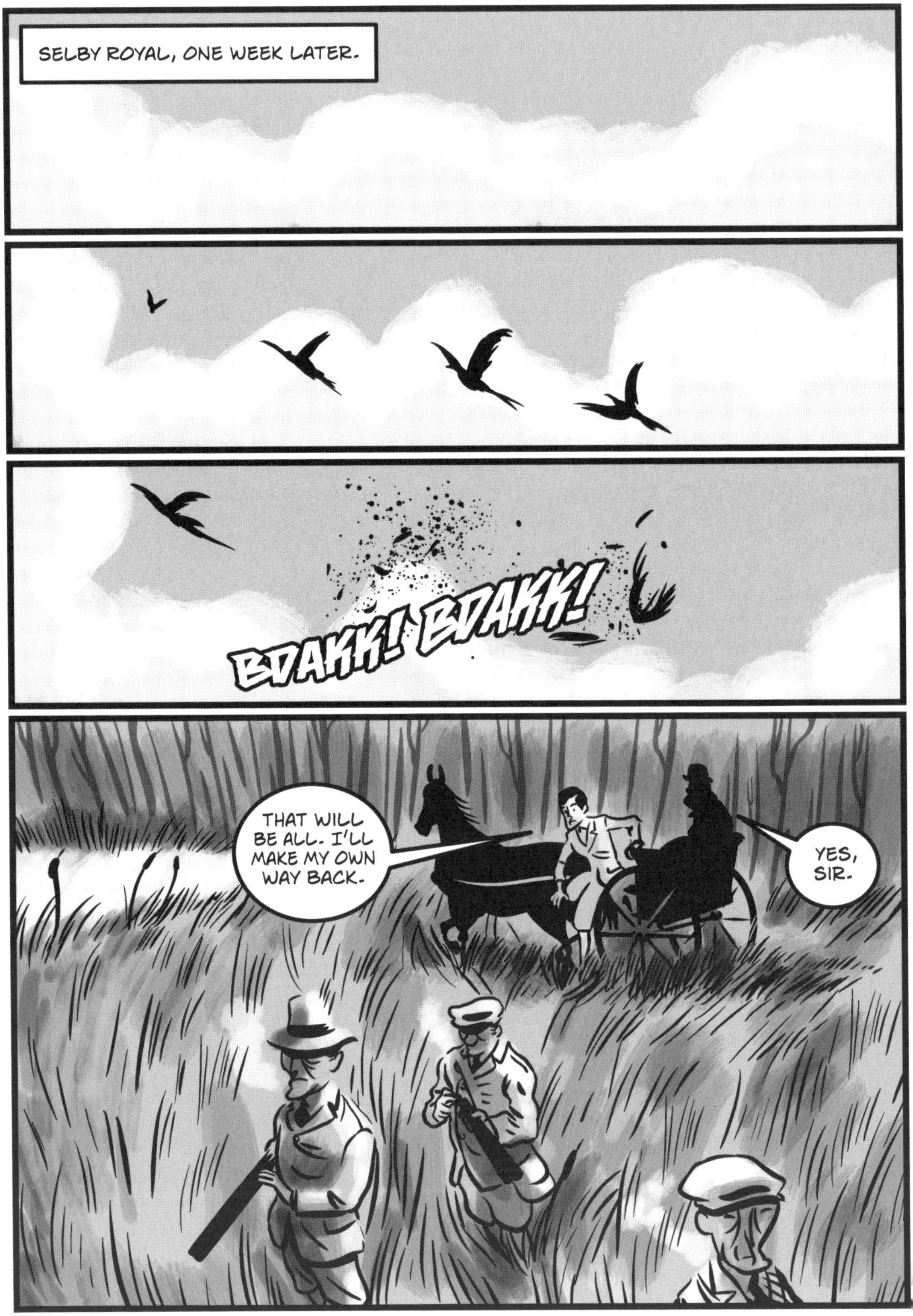
SELBY ROYAL, ONE WEEK LATER.
BDAKK! BDAKK!
THAT WILL BE ALL. I'LL MAKE MY OWN WAY BACK.
YES, SIR.

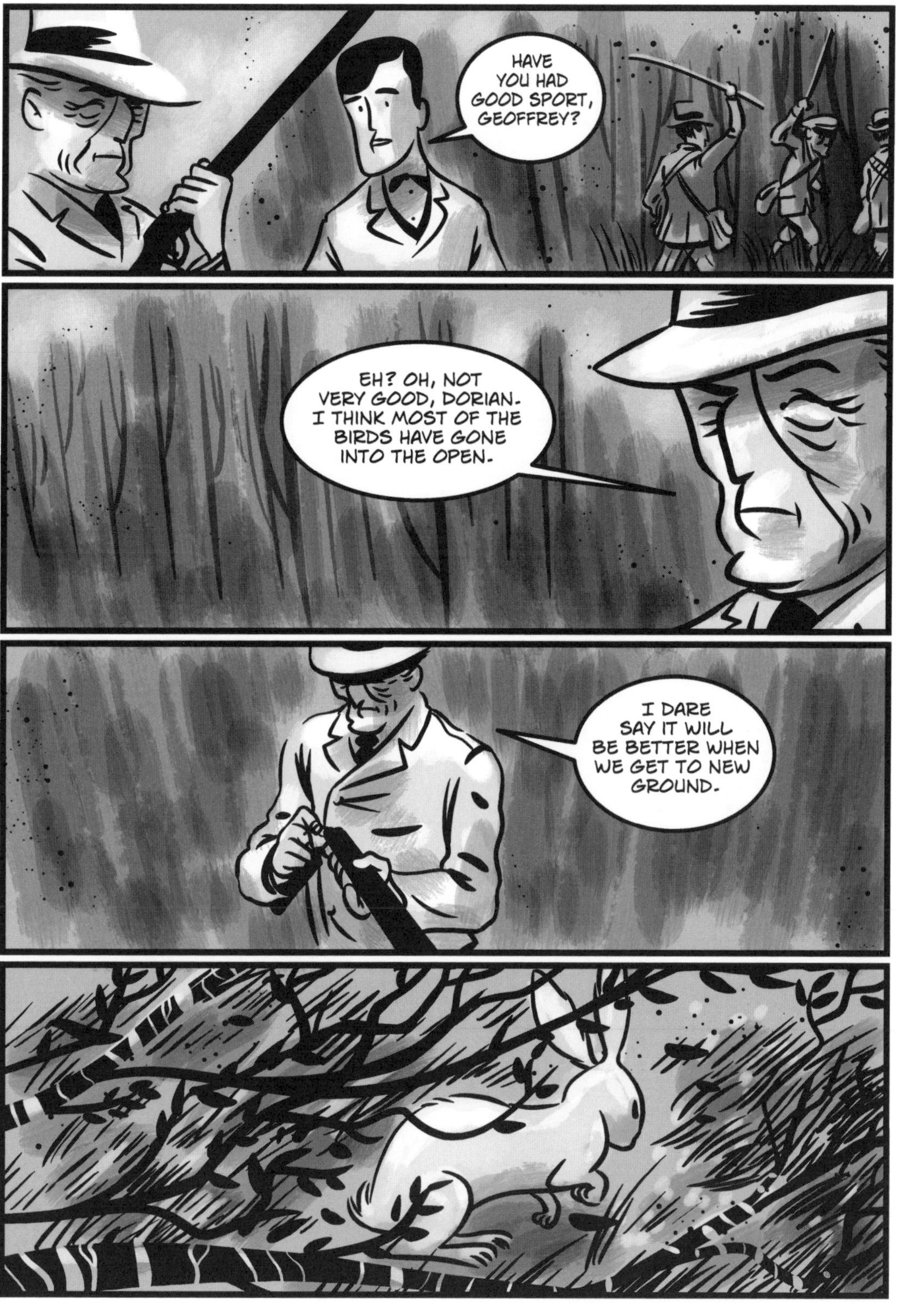
HAVE YOU HAD GOOD SPORT, GEOFFREY?
EH? OH, NOT VERY GOOD, DORIAN. I THINK MOST OF THE BIRDS HAVE GONE INTO THE OPEN.
I DARE SAY IT WILL BE BETTER WHEN WE GET TO NEW GROUND.

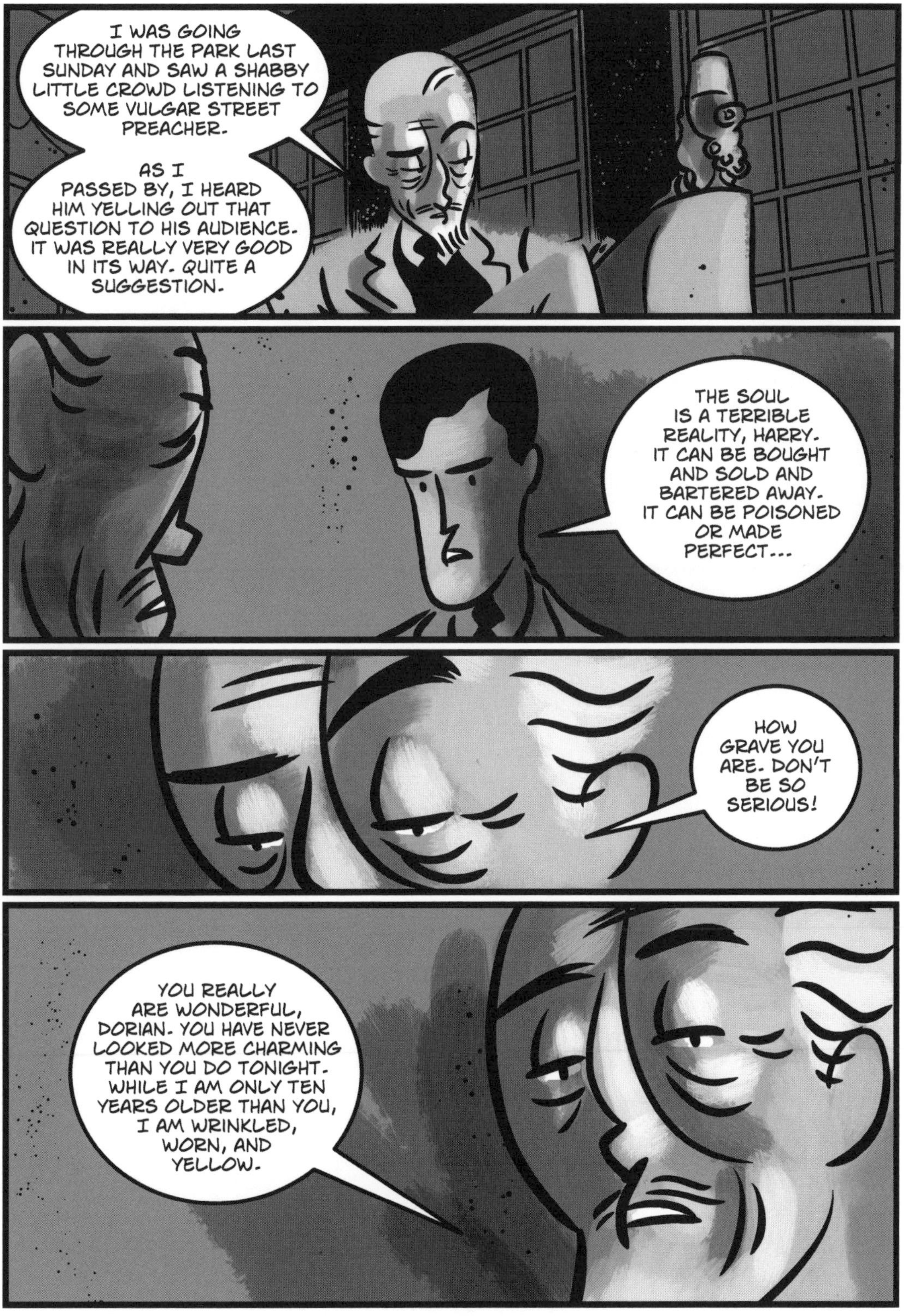
I WAS GOING THROUGH THE PARK LAST SUNDAY AND SAW A SHABBY LITTLE CROWD LISTENING TO SOME VULGAR STREET PREACHER.
AS I PASSED BY, I HEARD HIM YELLING OUT THAT QUESTION TO HIS AUDIENCE. IT WAS REALLY VERY GOOD IN ITS WAY. QUITE A SUGGESTION.
THE SOUL IS A TERRIBLE REALITY, HARRY. IT CAN BE BOUGHT AND SOLD AND BARTERED AWAY. IT CAN BE POISONED OR MADE PERFECT...
HOW GRAVE YOU ARE. DON'T BE SO SERIOUS!
YOU REALLY ARE WONDERFUL, DORIAN. YOU HAVE NEVER LOOKED MORE CHARMING THAN YOU DO TONIGHT. WHILE I AM ONLY TEN YEARS OLDER THAN YOU, I AM WRINKLED, WORN, AND YELLOW.

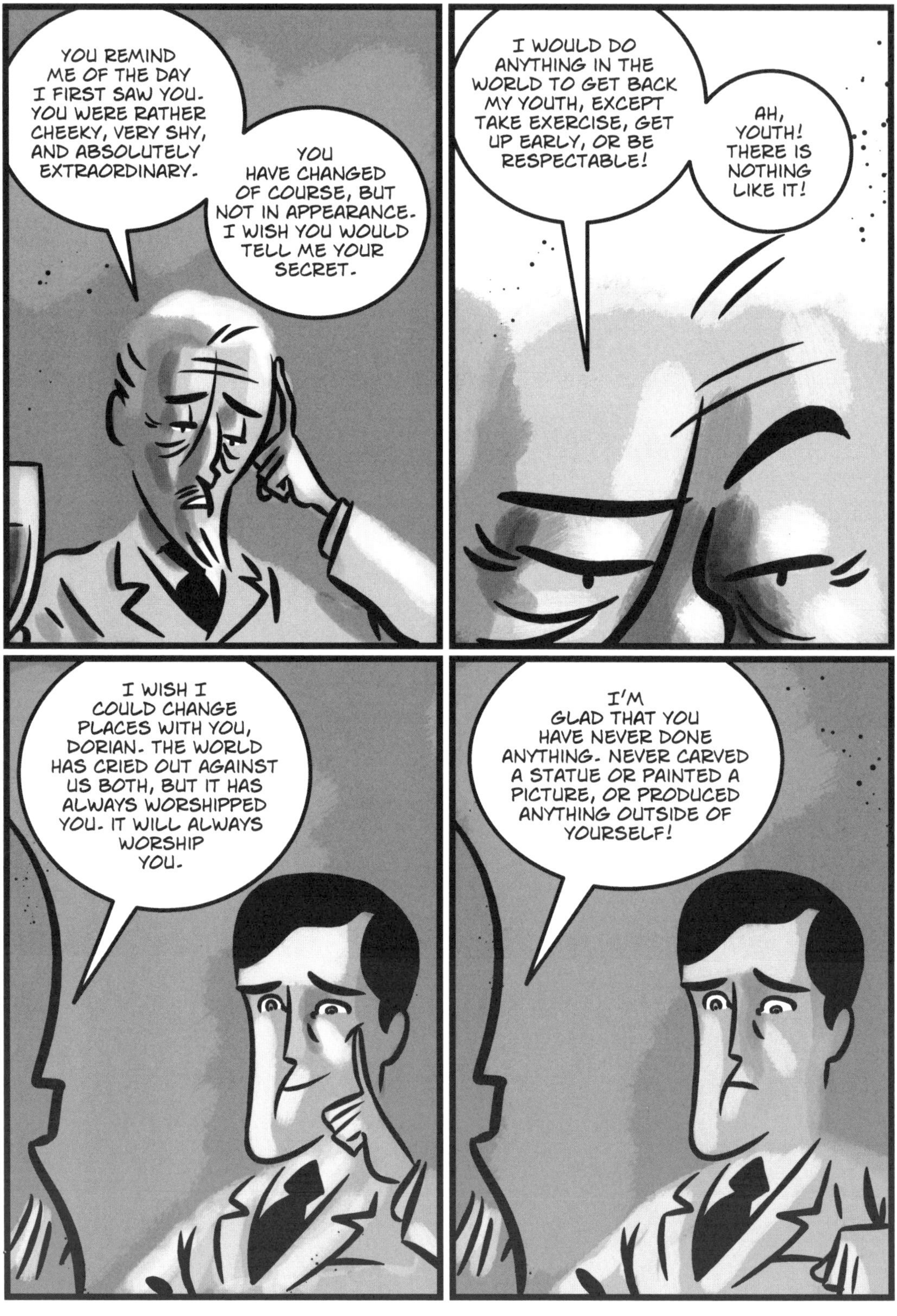
YOU REMIND ME OF THE DAY I FIRST SAW YOU. YOU WERE RATHER CHEEKY, VERY SHY, AND ABSOLUTELY EXTRAORDINARY.
YOU HAVE CHANGED OF COURSE, BUT NOT IN APPEARANCE. I WISH YOU WOULD TELL ME YOUR SECRET.
I WOULD DO ANYTHING IN THE WORLD TO GET BACK MY YOUTH, EXCEPT TAKE EXERCISE, GET UP EARLY, OR BE RESPECTABLE!
AH, YOUTH! THERE IS NOTHING LIKE IT!
I WISH I COULD CHANGE PLACES WITH YOU, DORIAN. THE WORLD HAS CRIED OUT AGAINST US BOTH, BUT IT HAS ALWAYS WORSHIPPED YOU. IT WILL ALWAYS WORSHIP YOU.
I'M GLAD THAT YOU HAVE NEVER DONE ANYTHING. NEVER CARVED A STATUE OR PAINTED A PICTURE, OR PRODUCED ANYTHING OUTSIDE OF YOURSELF!

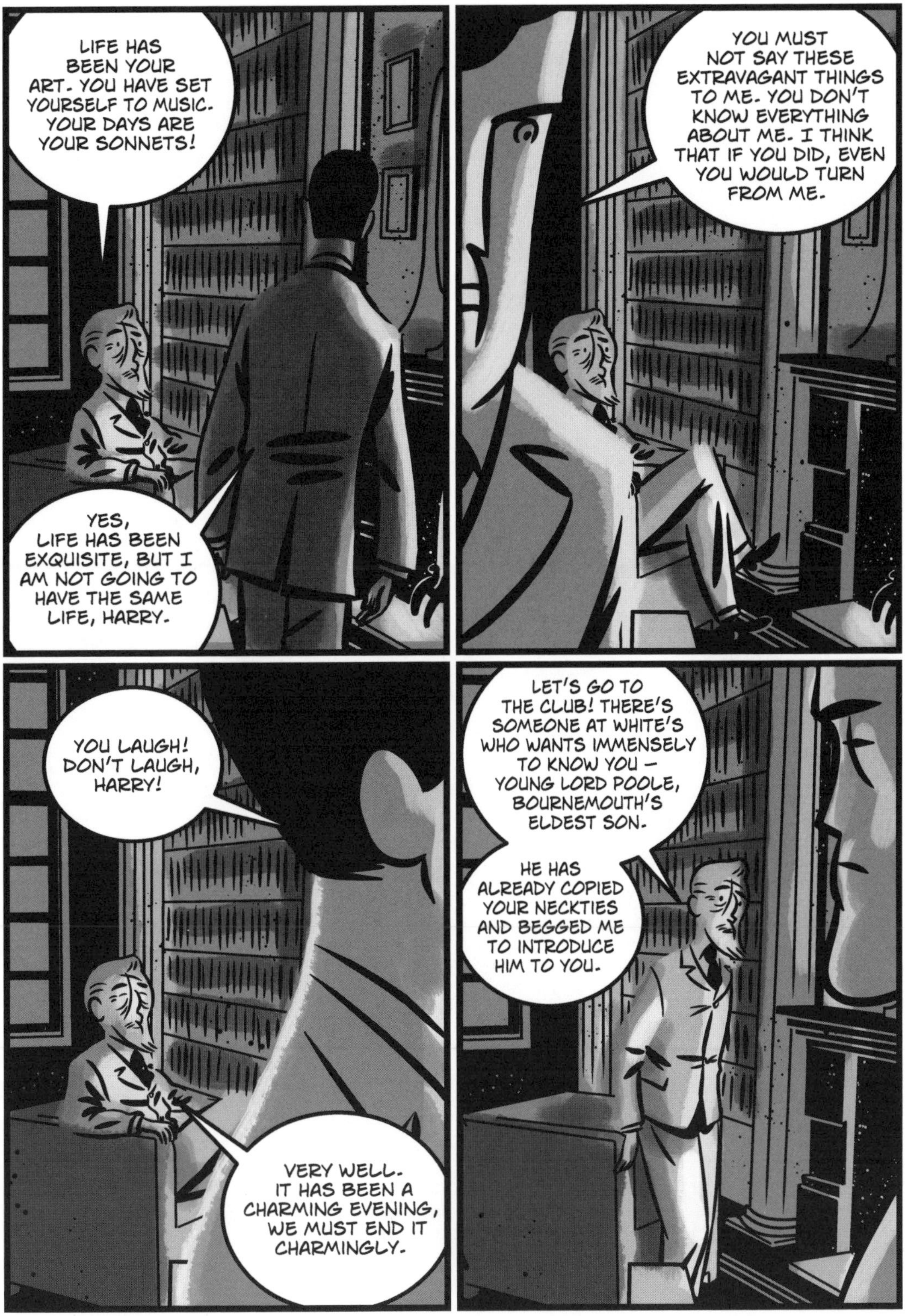
LIFE HAS BEEN YOUR ART. YOU HAVE SET YOURSELF TO MUSIC. YOUR DAYS ARE YOUR SONNETS!
YES, LIFE HAS BEEN EXQUISITE, BUT I AM NOT GOING TO HAVE THE SAME LIFE, HARRY.
YOU MUST NOT SAY THESE EXTRAVAGANT THINGS TO ME. YOU DON'T KNOW EVERYTHING ABOUT ME. I THINK THAT IF YOU DID, EVEN YOU WOULD TURN FROM ME.
YOU LAUGH! DON'T LAUGH, HARRY!
VERY WELL. IT HAS BEEN A CHARMING EVENING, WE MUST END IT CHARMINGLY.
LET'S GO TO THE CLUB! THERE'S SOMEONE AT WHITE'S WHO WANTS IMMENSELY TO KNOW YOU – YOUNG LORD POOLE, BOURNEMOUTH'S ELDEST SON.
HE HAS ALREADY COPIED YOUR NECKTIES AND BEGGED ME TO INTRODUCE HIM TO YOU.

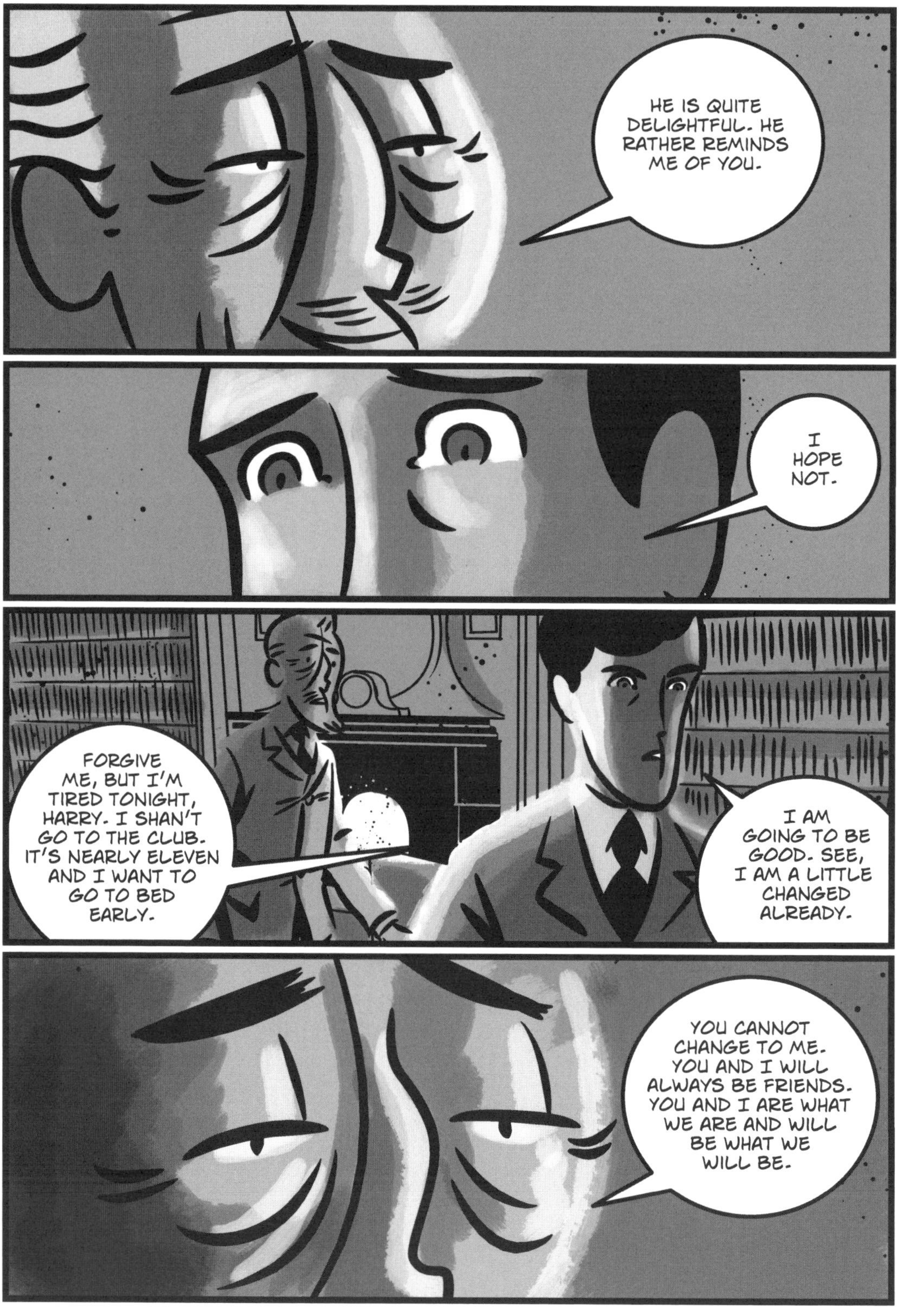
HE IS QUITE DELIGHTFUL. HE RATHER REMINDS ME OF YOU.
I HOPE NOT.
FORGIVE ME, BUT I'M TIRED TONIGHT, HARRY. I SHAN'T GO TO THE CLUB. IT'S NEARLY ELEVEN AND I WANT TO GO TO BED EARLY.
I AM GOING TO BE GOOD. SEE, I AM A LITTLE CHANGED ALREADY.
YOU CANNOT CHANGE TO ME. YOU AND I WILL ALWAYS BE FRIENDS. YOU AND I ARE WHAT WE ARE AND WILL BE WHAT WE WILL BE.

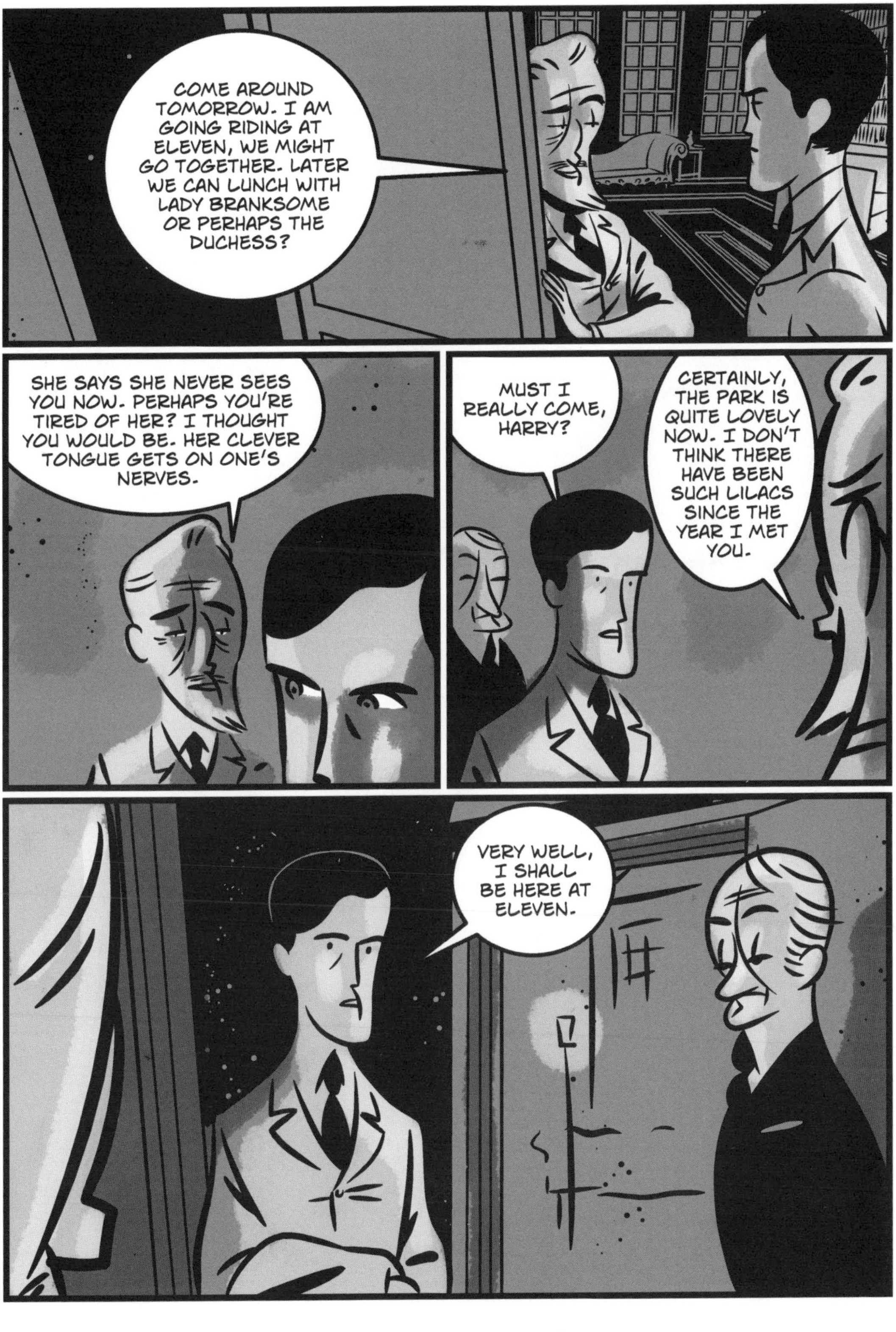
COME AROUND TOMORROW. I AM GOING RIDING AT ELEVEN, WE MIGHT GO TOGETHER. LATER WE CAN LUNCH WITH LADY BRANKSOME OR PERHAPS THE DUCHESS?
SHE SAYS SHE NEVER SEES YOU NOW. PERHAPS YOU'RE TIRED OF HER? I THOUGHT YOU WOULD BE. HER CLEVER TONGUE GETS ON ONE'S NERVES.
MUST I REALLY COME, HARRY?
CERTAINLY, THE PARK IS QUITE LOVELY NOW. I DON'T THINK THERE HAVE BEEN SUCH LILACS SINCE THE YEAR I MET YOU.
VERY WELL, I SHALL BE HERE AT ELEVEN.

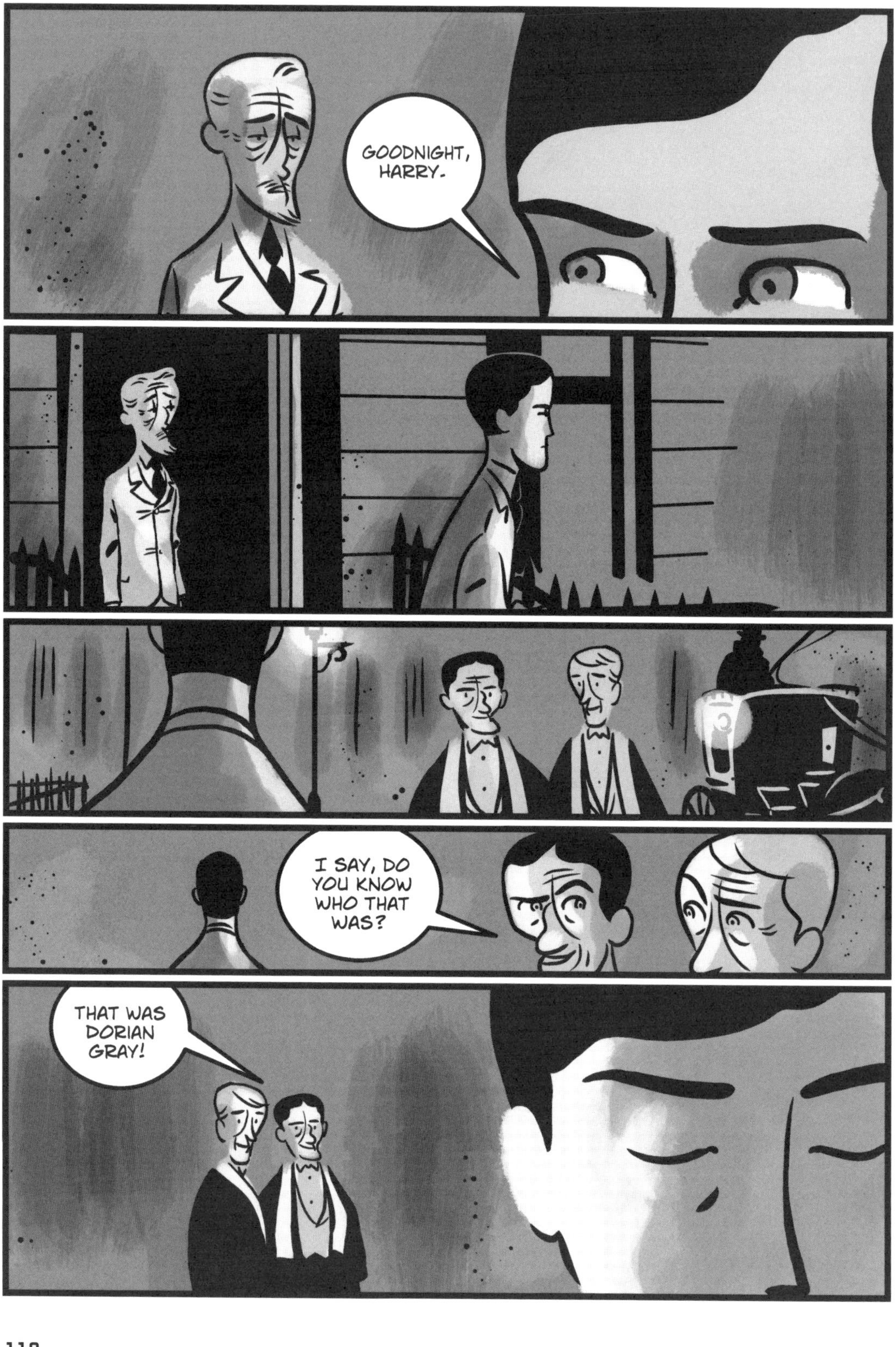
GOODNIGHT, HARRY.
I SAY, DO YOU KNOW WHO THAT WAS?
THAT WAS DORIAN GRAY!

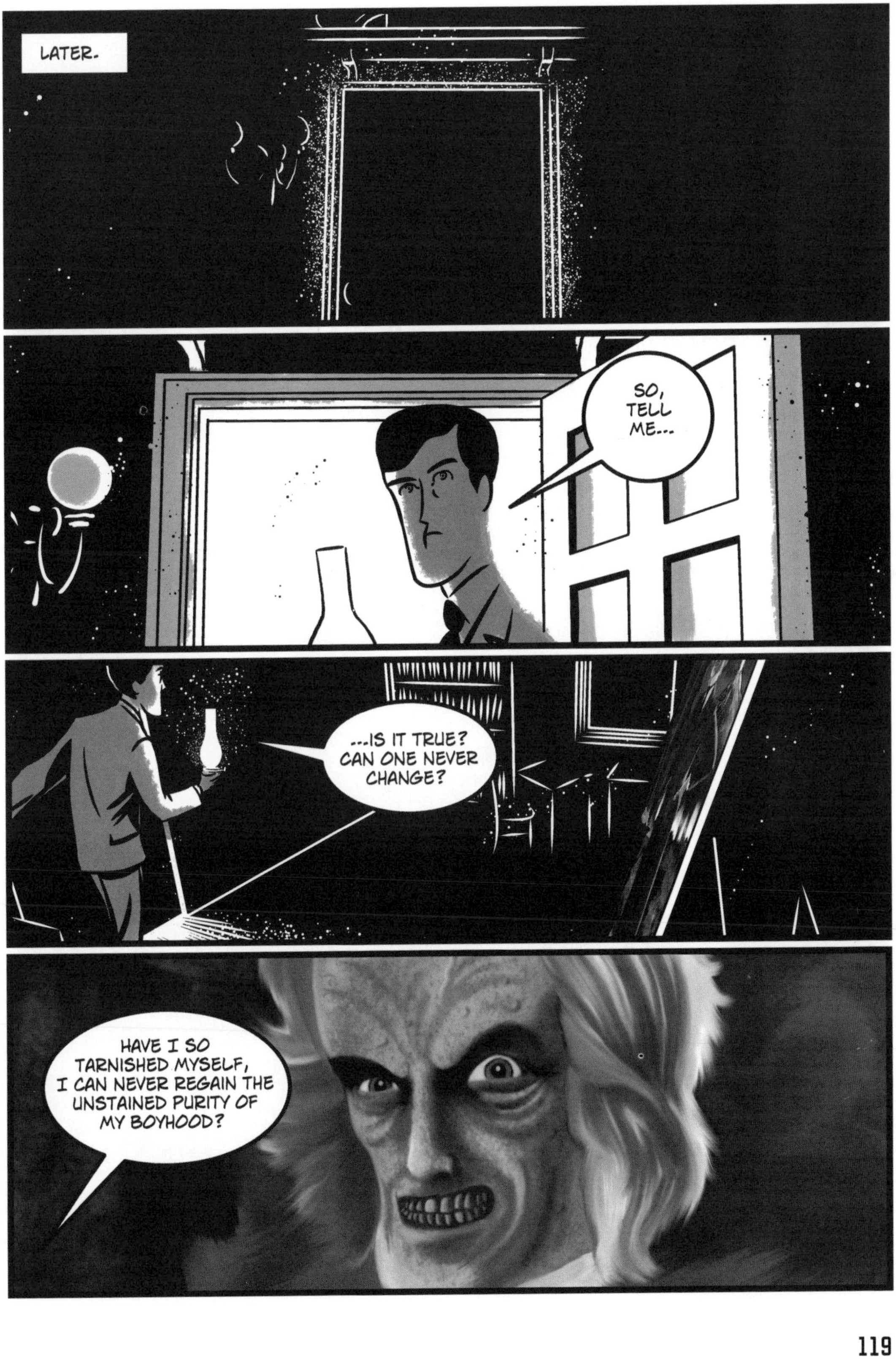
LATER.
SO, TELL ME...
...IS IT TRUE? CAN ONE NEVER CHANGE?
HAVE I SO TARNISHED MYSELF, I CAN NEVER REGAIN THE UNSTAINED PURITY OF MY BOYHOOD?

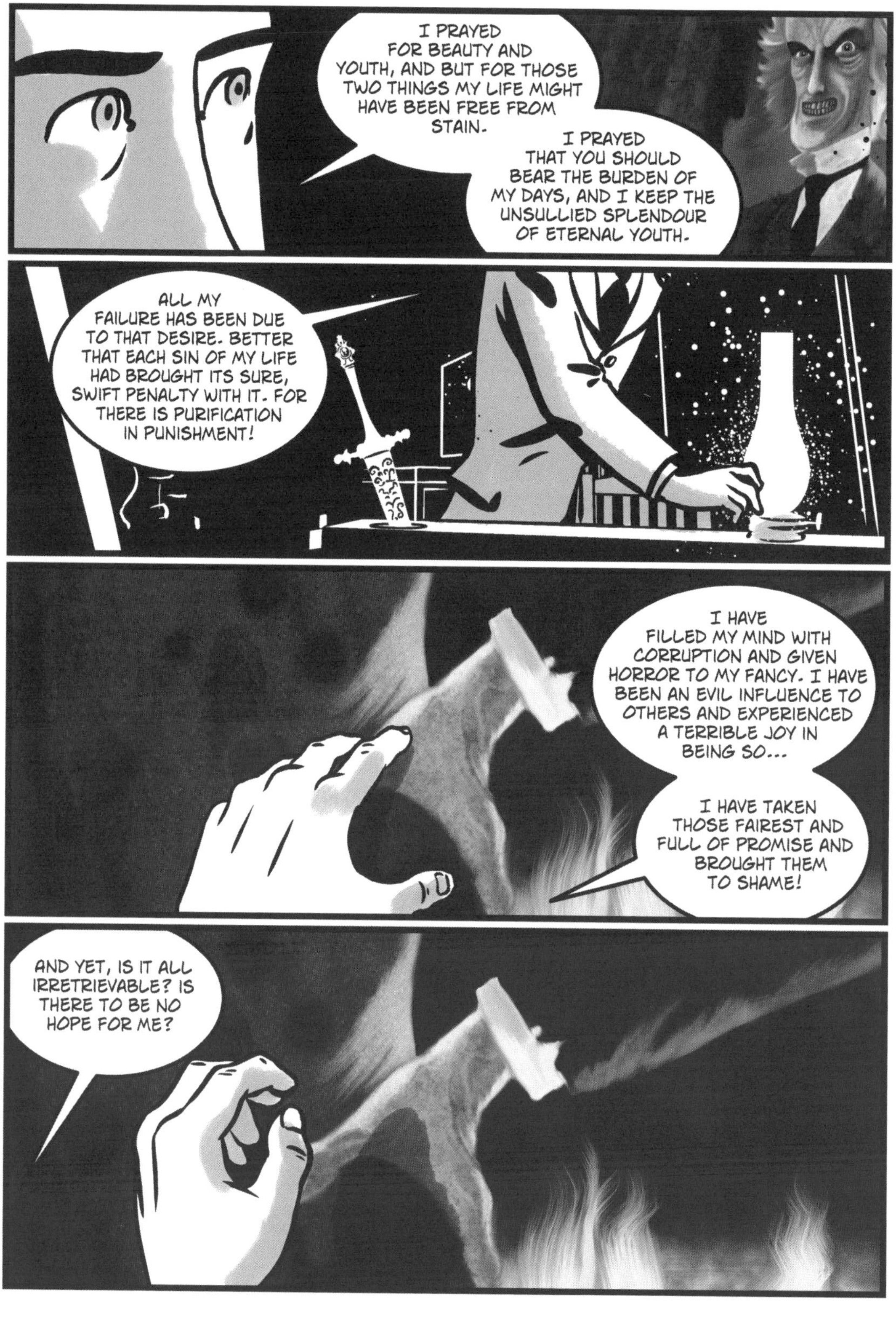
I PRAYED FOR BEAUTY AND YOUTH, AND BUT FOR THOSE TWO THINGS MY LIFE MIGHT HAVE BEEN FREE FROM STAIN.
I PRAYED THAT YOU SHOULD BEAR THE BURDEN OF MY DAYS, AND I KEEP THE UNSULLIED SPLENDOUR OF ETERNAL YOUTH.
ALL MY FAILURE HAS BEEN DUE TO THAT DESIRE. BETTER THAT EACH SIN OF MY LIFE HAD BROUGHT ITS SURE, SWIFT PENALTY WITH IT. FOR THERE IS PURIFICATION IN PUNISHMENT!
I HAVE FILLED MY MIND WITH CORRUPTION AND GIVEN HORROR TO MY FANCY. I HAVE BEEN AN EVIL INFLUENCE TO OTHERS AND EXPERIENCED A TERRIBLE JOY IN BEING SO...
I HAVE TAKEN THOSE FAIREST AND FULL OF PROMISE AND BROUGHT THEM TO SHAME!
AND YET, IS IT ALL IRRETRIEVABLE? IS THERE TO BE NO HOPE FOR ME?

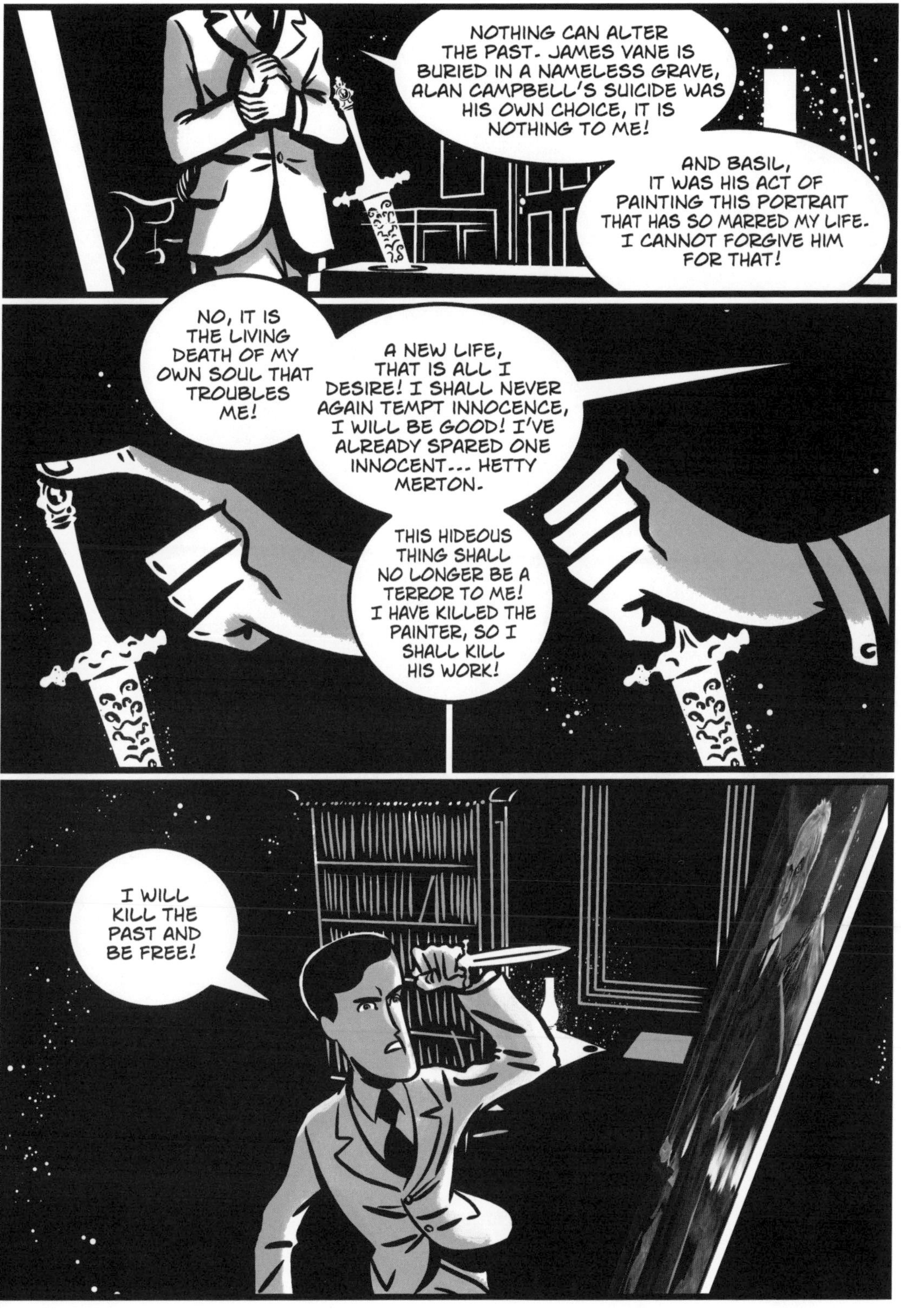
NOTHING CAN ALTER THE PAST. JAMES VANE IS BURIED IN A NAMELESS GRAVE, ALAN CAMPBELL'S SUICIDE WAS HIS OWN CHOICE, IT IS NOTHING TO ME!
AND BASIL, IT WAS HIS ACT OF PAINTING THIS PORTRAIT THAT HAS SO MARRED MY LIFE. I CANNOT FORGIVE HIM FOR THAT!
NO, IT IS THE LIVING DEATH OF MY OWN SOUL THAT TROUBLES ME!
A NEW LIFE, THAT IS ALL I DESIRE! I SHALL NEVER AGAIN TEMPT INNOCENCE, I WILL BE GOOD! I'VE ALREADY SPARED ONE INNOCENT... HETTY MERTON.
THIS HIDEOUS THING SHALL NO LONGER BE A TERROR TO ME! I HAVE KILLED THE PAINTER, SO I SHALL KILL HIS WORK!
I WILL KILL THE PAST AND BE FREE!

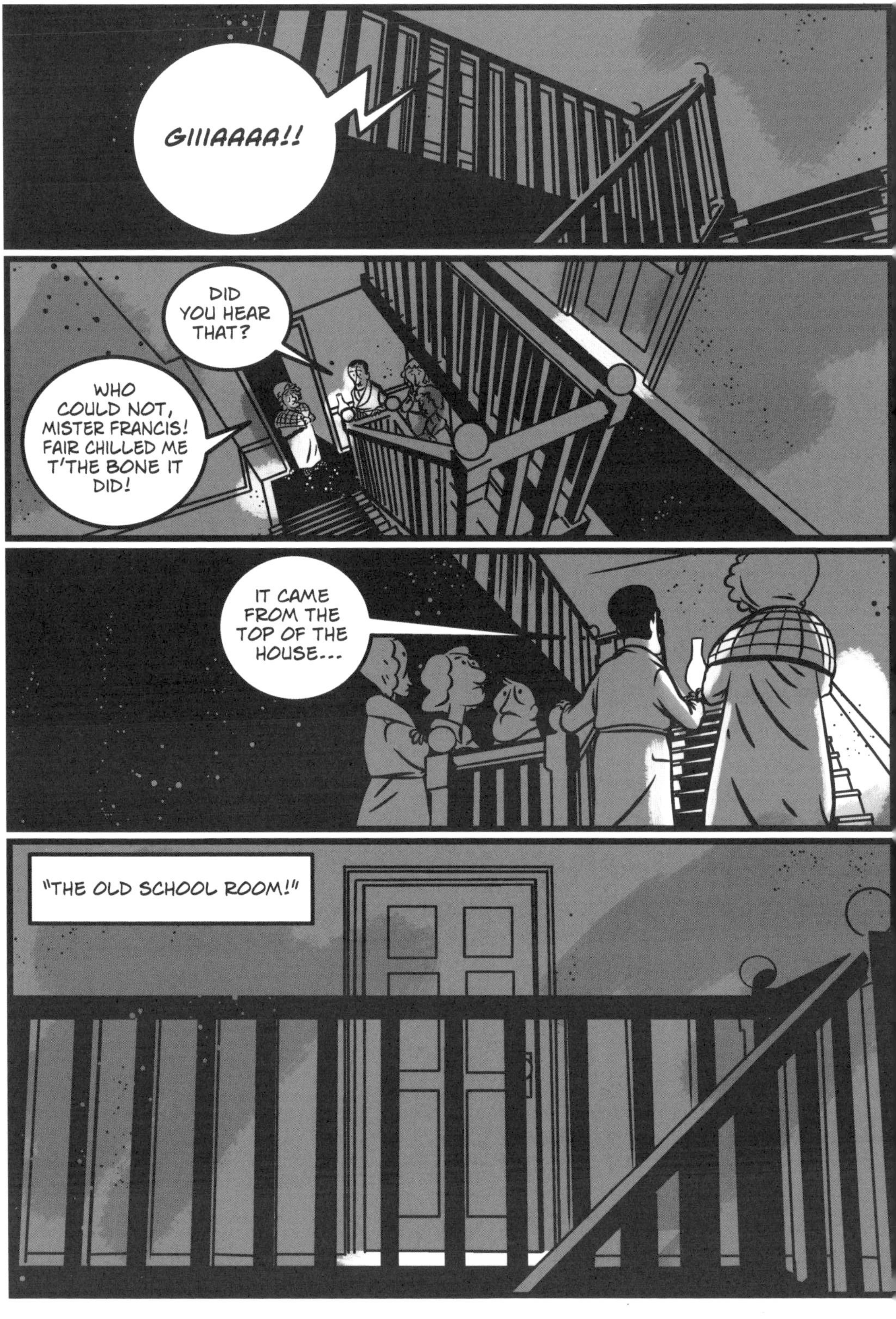
GIIIAAAAA!!
DID YOU HEAR THAT?
WHO COULD NOT, MISTER FRANCIS! FAIR CHILLED ME T'THE BONE IT DID!
IT CAME FROM THE TOP OF THE HOUSE...
"THE OLD SCHOOL ROOM!"

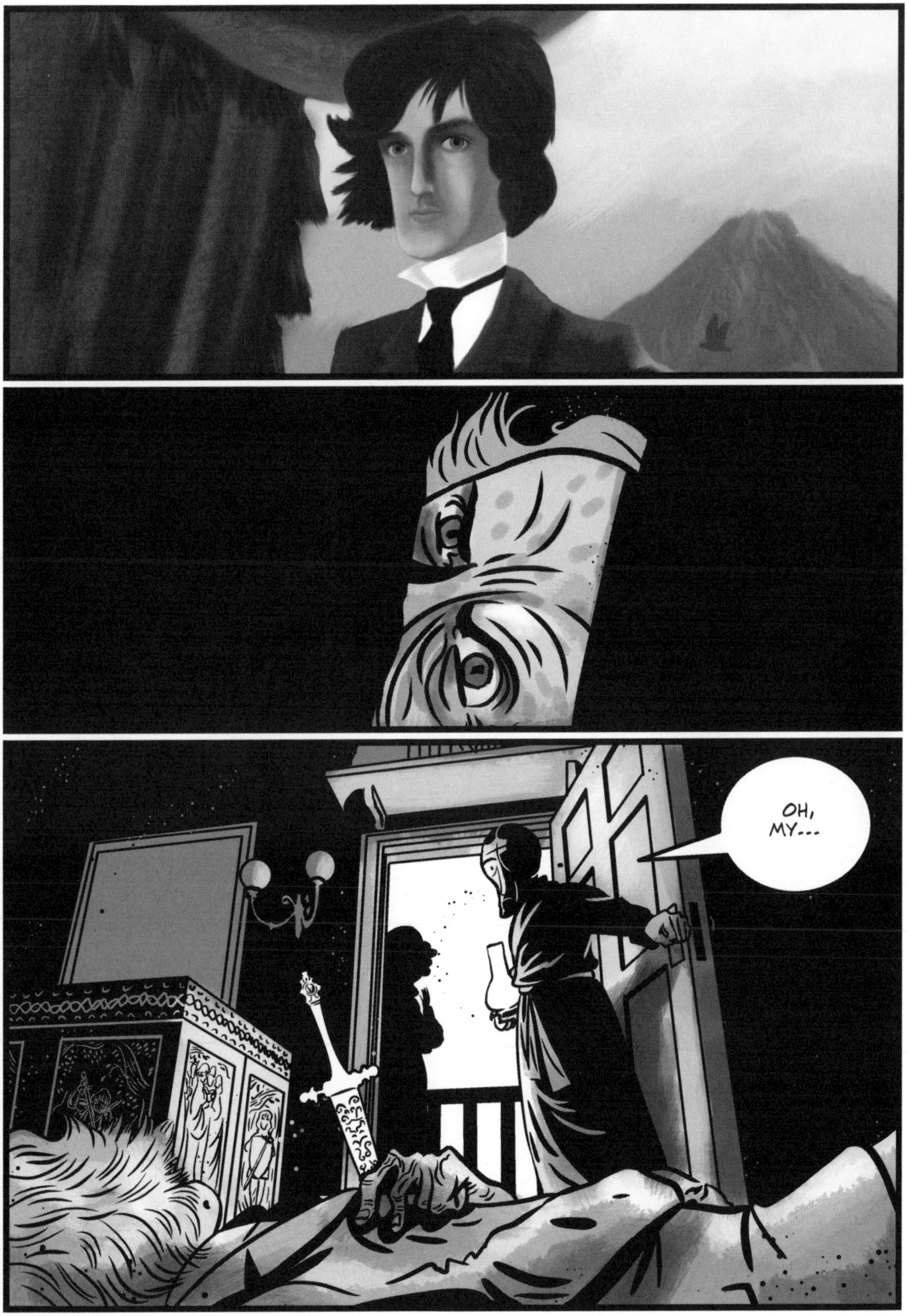
OH,
MY...

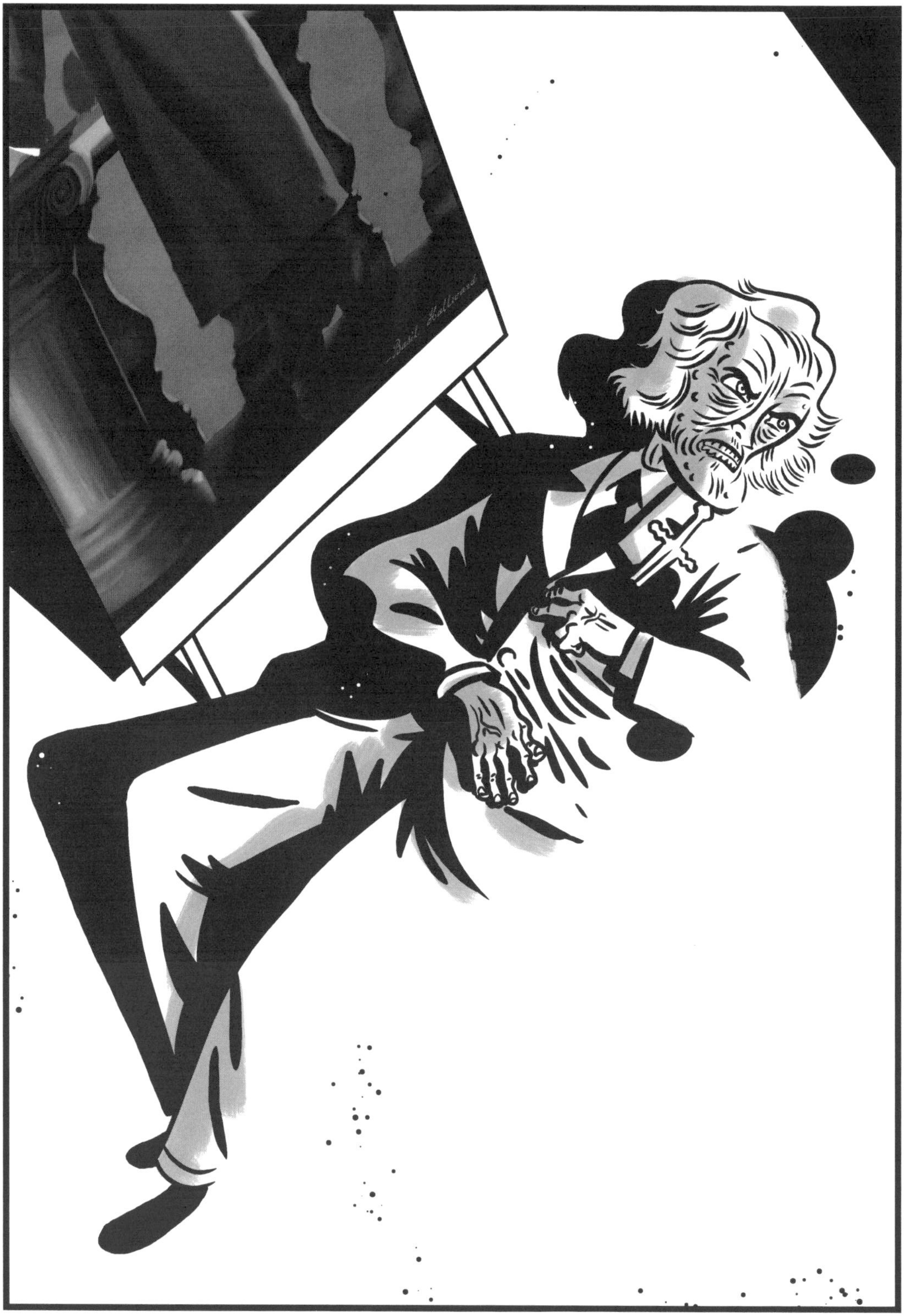
Basil Hallward

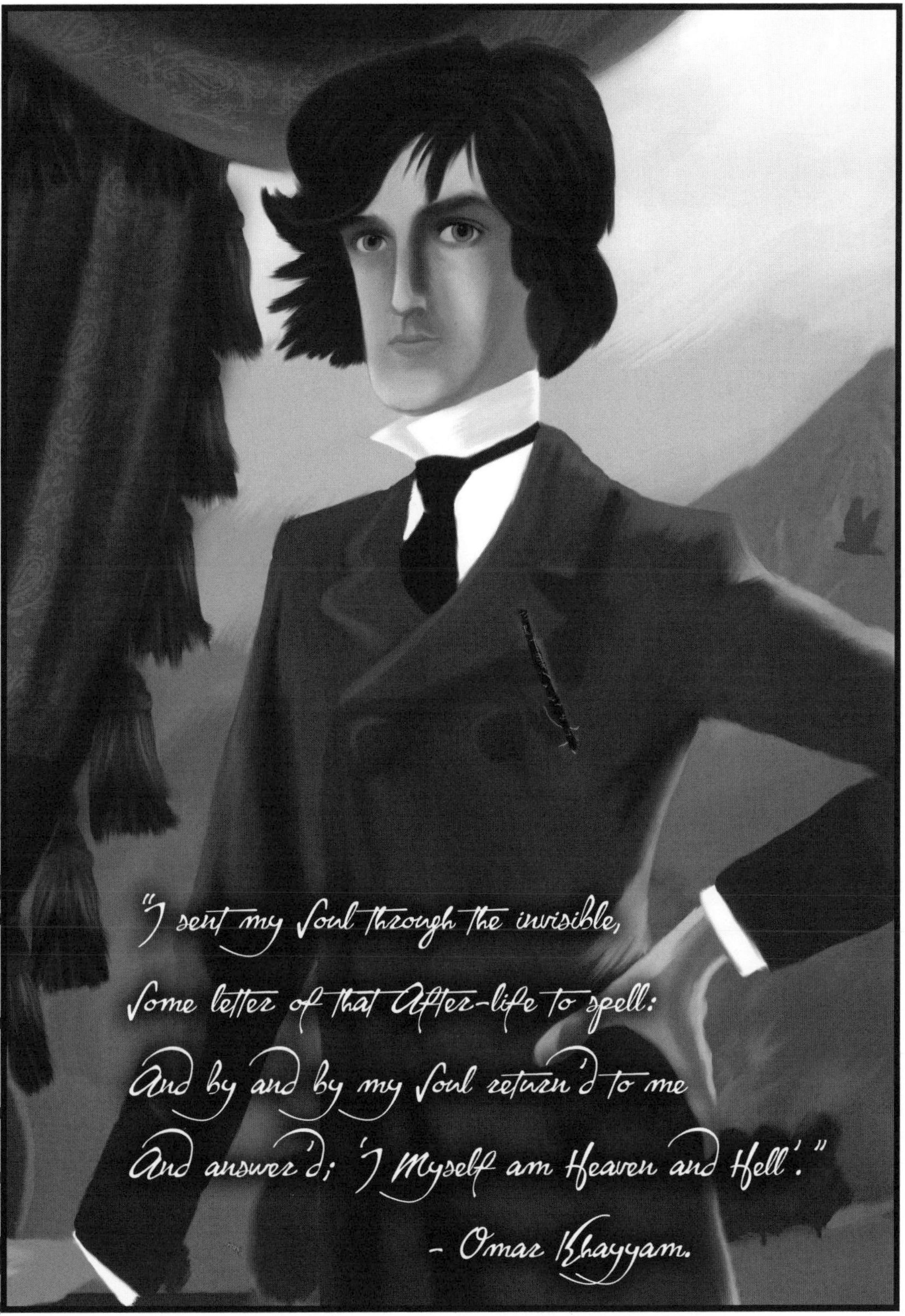
"I sent my Soul through the invisible,
Some letter of that After-life to spell:
And by and by my Soul return'd to me
And answer'd; 'I Myself am Heaven and Hell'."
- Omar Khayyam.

OSCAR WILDE is renowned for both his scathing wit and his beautifully observed social commentary. Born in Dublin in 1854, Wilde was a skilful classicist and won a scholarship to Magdalen College, Oxford from Trinity College, Dublin. He soon moved from academia to the literary world, becoming a highly visible member of the Aesthetic movement in London. After a successful tour of America, bankrolled by the operetta producer D'Oyly Carte, Wilde made a name for himself as a writer with three volumes of short fiction and a novel, *The Picture of Dorian Gray*. His reputation was confirmed by his hugely popular social plays: *The Importance of Being Earnest*, *An Ideal Husband*, *A Woman of No Importance*, and *Lady Windermere's Fan*.

The Picture of Dorian Gray was Wilde's only published novel and remains one of his best-known works. Now regarded as a classic of Gothic horror, its plot revolves around the Faustian conceit of a man who sells his soul for eternal youth and beauty. The innocent Dorian Gray, swayed by his friends' lavish flattery, makes a desperate wish that a recently painted portrait of himself might grow old in his place, leaving him young forever. When his wish is granted, Dorian begins to grow corrupt and indulgent. But even though he feels no guilt over his escalating crimes – which include murdering a friend and driving an innocent girl to suicide – the decaying portrait hidden in his house tells another tale.

The story of Dorian's transition from naive narcissism to moral bankruptcy was heavily criticized upon its initial publication in 1890. The press accused the work of being decadent and contaminating – themes raised in the novel itself – leading Wilde to make several significant revisions to the text. The resulting edition expands upon Dorian's ancestry and character, adding extra power to his eventual fall from grace, and introduces the character of James Vane, who acts as a counterpoint to Dorian's hedonistic impulses while foreshadowing the most brutal of his sins. Wilde also toned down some of the novel's homoerotic elements and added a preface, in which he attempted to answer his critics by describing his views on the nature of art and beauty.

The Picture of Dorian Gray is a fascinating examination of one man's struggle between aesthetics and morals. As a moral tale, the novel demands a terrible price of its protagonist for his crimes, both spoken and unspoken – a fact that seems to have been overlooked when the book was originally published. Perhaps the parallels between Wilde's life and his fiction were too blatant for readers in the late 1890s. Wilde once described his relationship with his characters as follows: "Basil Hallward is what I think I am; Lord Henry what the world thinks me; Dorian what I would like to be – in other ages, perhaps." It's tempting to read the novel as a somewhat veiled exploration of Wilde's own sexuality: many of the criticisms levied at the book were also directed at its author during his infamous trials.

Wilde was eventually sentenced to two years of hard labour for 'gross indecency', a period which inspired his poem, *The Ballad of Reading Gaol*. Upon his release in 1897, he fled to continental Europe, penniless and in poor health. He died three years later in Paris.